Music After Deleuze

DELEUZE ENCOUNTERS

Series Editor: Ian Buchanan, director of the Institute for Social Transformation Research, University of Wollongong, Australia

The *Deleuze Encounters* series provides students in philosophy and related subjects with concise and accessible introductions to the application of Deleuze's work in key areas of study. Each book demonstrates how Deleuze's ideas and concepts can enhance present work in a particular field.

TITLES AVAILABLE IN THE SERIES:

Cinema After Deleuze, Richard Rushton
Philosophy After Deleuze, Joe Hughes
Political Theory After Deleuze, Nathan Widder
Theology After Deleuze, Kristien Justaert
Space After Deleuze, Arun Saldanha

Music After Deleuze

EDWARD CAMPBELL

BLOOMSBURY
LONDON · NEW DELHI · NEW YORK · SYDNEY

Bloomsbury Academic
An imprint of Bloomsbury Publishing Plc

50 Bedford Square	1385 Broadway
London	New York
WC1B 3DP	NY 10018
UK	USA

www.bloomsbury.com

Bloomsbury is a registered trade mark of Bloomsbury Publishing Plc

First published 2013

© Edward Campbell, 2013

Edward Campbell has asserted his right under the Copyright, Designs and Patents Act, 1988, to be identified as Author of this work.

All rights reserved. No part of this publication may be reproduced or transmitted in any form or by any means, electronic or mechanical, including photocopying, recording or any information storage or retrieval system, without prior permission in writing from the publishers.

No responsibility for loss caused to any individual or organization acting on or refraining from action as a result of the material in this publication can be accepted by Bloomsbury Academic or the author.

British Library Cataloguing-in-Publication Data
A catalogue record for this book is available from the British Library.

ISBN: HB: 978-1-4411-0181-5
PB: 978-1-4411-5702-7
ePDF: 978-1-4411-7348-5
ePub: 978-1-4411-3759-3

Library of Congress Cataloging-in-Publication Data
Campbell, Edward, 1958–
Music after Deleuze / Edward Campbell.
pages cm. – (Deleuze encounters)
Includes bibliographical references and index.
ISBN 978-1-4411-5702-7 (pbk. : alk. paper) – ISBN 978-1-4411-0181-5 (hardcover : alk. paper) – ISBN 978-1-4411-3759-3 (ebook (epub) – ISBN 978-1-4411-7348-5 (ebook (pdf) 1. Music–Philosophy and aesthetics. 2. Deleuze, Gilles, 1925–1995–Aesthetics. I. Title.
ML3800.C166 2013
780.1–dc23
2013016929

Typeset by Deanta Global Publishing Services, Chennai, India

For Gill and Michael

Contents

Acknowledgements viii

Introduction 1
1 Music, difference and repetition 3
2 Producing new music: Rhizomes, assemblages and refrains 35
3 Rethinking musical pitch: The smooth and the striated 67
4 Thinking musical time 99
5 A Deleuzian semiotics of music 133
Conclusion 163

Notes 169
Bibliography 175
Index 187

Acknowledgements

Many thanks to Ian Buchanan for asking me to write this book and for his editorial support and to Rachel Eisenhauer and Subitha Nair from Bloomsbury Publishing for facilitating the smooth running of the project and for answering my queries. Thanks to Nick Nesbitt and Arnfinn Bø-Rygg, who read the proposal and responded with great generosity. Thanks to Cambridge University Press for allowing me to cite material that I have published previously. I am grateful to the School of Education at the University of Aberdeen for granting me 6 invaluable months of research leave. Thanks, finally, to Björn Heile, Suk-Jun Kim, Ian Russell, Pete Stollery and Chris Fynsk for helpful consultations on small but significant points of detail. Published English translations of texts have been used where available, unless otherwise noted. All other translations are by the author, unless otherwise noted. As is customary, I take responsibility for any unnoticed errors within the text.

Introduction

The philosopher Gilles Deleuze was not at all a musician and certainly not a music theorist. This fact notwithstanding, this book is predicated on the notion that many of his concepts and ideas can be of great value in rethinking music today. Composer Pascale Criton, who participated in Deleuze's seminar for several years, and who advised him on musical matters, states that despite not producing a book on music as he had done on cinema, painting and literature, 'it nevertheless occupies a privileged place in [his] thought' (Criton 2005). Many of his writings contain significant references to composers, compositions and musical ideas in ways that go well beyond the anecdotal or the incidental, and music is for Deleuze absolutely implicated with thought and, at its best, is indicative of new directions for thought that are arguably uncapturable in any other medium.

For Deleuze, philosophy concerns above all the creation of concepts, concepts that enable us to think differently. Despite the rich implication of music and thought in his writings, this book is concerned less with what he wrote about music and more with how his philosophical concepts may be productive for rethinking music. The book has five chapters, each of which is focused on a discrete Deleuzian concept or pair/group of concepts. Each chapter has a similar format in which the specific topic is introduced in a musical context, followed by a summary of related philosophical material from Deleuze's solo writings or his collaborations with Félix Guattari. This in turn leads to a series of discussions of how the philosophical concept[s] in question may relate to music.

In Chapter 1, we consider how Deleuzian concepts offer interesting ways of thinking about difference, repetition and variation in a range of musics including Western art music from Beethoven to Boulez, jazz improvisation and aspects of popular and sacred music.

In Chapter 2, it is argued that the Deleuze-Guattarian concepts of the 'rhizome, the 'assemblage' and the 'refrain' provide productive ways of thinking the specificity of any new musical work as the meeting of productive forces, of what Deleuze calls 'lines of flight', and as part of a dynamic account of musical change. The work of Deleuze and Guattari on space and time can be helpful in considering a range of musics in terms of the parameters of pitch and timbre, on the one hand and of tempo, rhythm and duration, on the other – the topics for discussion in Chapters 3 and 4. Chapter 5 looks to those parts of Deleuzian and Deleuze-Guattarian philosophy that rethink the nature of musical signs, offering valuable insights for a musical semiotics (the theory of signs) capable of working with all kinds of new music. In the course of doing all of this, the work of a number of contemporary composers and music theorists/aestheticians, for whom Deleuzian philosophy is an important reference, will also be explored.

The discussions within this book move across a variety of repertoires. Deleuze was notably modernist in his aesthetic and musical preferences and, while this is largely reflected here in discussions of music from Schoenberg to Lachenmann, including contemporary opera and music theatre, many other repertoires and genres are also explored. This includes the music of Beethoven, Brahms, Wagner, sacred psalm singing from the Scottish Western Isles, Indonesian gamelan, the music of ancient India, twentieth-century micro-tonality, aspects of jazz improvisation and experimental pop music. Within contemporary art music, there is also discussion of the music and ideas of Georges Aperghis, Pascale Criton, Pascal Dusapin, Heiner Goebbels, Gérard Grisey, Helmut Lachenmann, Bernhard Lang and Michaël Levinas. Ultimately, as Marianne Kielian-Gilbert notes

> The question is how a Deleuze-Guattari philosophy of becoming can be transformative of particular musical problems (and vice versa) and open up new ways of listening, hearing, and thinking about music. Music and music experience express modes of becoming in ways specific to their expressive language and suggestive for ways of experiencing and thinking about the world (Kielian-Gilbert 2010, pp. 200–1).

1

Music, difference and repetition

Music and identity-thinking

Perhaps above all else, the philosophy of Gilles Deleuze is one of 'difference', in which difference is favoured over identity. There are many ways in which we can conceive of music in terms of sameness or identity. Many listeners have a favourite recording of a given piece of music, whether it be a movement from a symphony, any kind of contemporary work or a pop song. It could be Carlos Kleiber's celebrated recording of Beethoven's Fifth Symphony, Glenn Gould's iconic recordings of Bach's *Goldberg Variations* or Bob Dylan's perhaps rather idiosyncratic renderings of his own songs. As we listen to our favoured recordings, we may do so in anticipation of the confirmation of what we know will happen right on cue, our expectations confirmed every time. With alternative recordings or performances, it may be that the arrangement, instrumentation, tempo, key or any number of aspects of style are different in some way from what we have become accustomed to. A sense of disappointment is not uncommon when listeners are confronted with a live performance, alternative recording, different version or new interpretation of a piece, when those features or qualities that were most admired in the first-heard performance are not present in other performances? In this situation, the favoured model serves to brand the work with a fixed identity against which all deviations are regarded as in some way deficient.

While Scott Burnham may be correct when he states that the notion that each listening experience reveals something new about a piece is 'creaky' (Burnham 1995, p. 164), he perhaps also endorses a form of identity-thinking at the heart of the listening experience when he writes:

> Why *do* we keep listening to our favourite musics?. . . . Do we really return to experience the music we value in the hope and expectation of hearing something new each time? On the contrary, I believe we return because we hear nearly the same thing each time, because the music becomes for us a magical presence we are eager to experience again. That we are enabled to enjoy an experience repeatedly because it remains basically the same may seem a paradoxical argument, and anti-intellectual in the extreme. But the musical experience is no ordinary experience; I would go so far to suggest that it is closer to the sense of uncanny presence felt by Hoffmann than it is to the tracking of a coherent process, however compelling that process may be (Ibid., p. 164).

While Burnham is not advocating the listening experience as one which entails following the same structural trajectory through each repeated audition but rather listening as a pleasurable realm where we experience music's 'uncanny presence', it is, nevertheless, always 'the same place' and 'the same uncanny presence' (Ibid., p. 165).

A tendency towards musical identity is also found in the intention of certain composers, a significant exemplar being Hungarian composer György Kurtág, who, it would seem, wishes to fix a great number of aspects of his pieces. Virtuoso performers who have worked with Kurtág tell of the almost impossibility of performing the music to the composer's satisfaction. He has a very strong idea of what the music is, how it should be played and how it should sound, and all performers have to match up. He takes great care over the notation of his scores and works with performers in a quite insistent way, trying to get them to perform pieces the way he hears them himself. Consequently, he is often frustrated when the results are not what he imagines and desires, and he laments either his inability to make his compositions consonant with his musical imaginings or the inability of performers to respond to his imaginings. In the piece *Stele*, for example, there is a passage of which he says

> I have told the musicians and indeed also the author of the program notes . . . they should think of the scene in Tolstoy's *War and Peace* where Prince Andrei is wounded at Austerlitz for the first time: all of a sudden, he no longer hears the battle but discovers the blue sky above him. That is what the music conjures up. I keep telling the story and no one responds . . . . No one can hear it. No one sees the blue sky. There's nothing to be done (Varga 2009, pp. 76–7).

The fact of a composition cannot be equated with the score any more than it can be reduced to the composer's idea, an individual performance, recording or act of listening. In an article published in 1928, the musical phenomenologist Boris de Schloezer, drawing explicitly on Paul Valéry, stated that 'a musical (or poetic) work does not exist outside of its performance', and that 'its text is only a virtuality' (Schloezer 1928, pp. 221, 223). This was modified slightly in 1947 when Schloezer posited that a musical work has 'no objective reality' and, this time drawing on the philosopher Maurice de Gandillac,[1] he went on to repeat that 'its text is only a "virtuality"' (Schloezer 1947, p. 19). Gandillac's text is inflected to say that the realization of a work 'always signifies for us the putting in actual form of a virtual preexisting reality' (Ibid., pp. 290–1), and Schloezer compares the work to a plant which 'grows from a germ and, strictly speaking, it is this germ which is a virtuality, the potential thing' (Ibid., p. 302). In all of this, Schloezer anticipates, in a musical context, aspects of what will be discussed in this chapter as Deleuzian difference with its opposition of virtuality and actuality.

A third manifestation of identity-thinking in music takes certain enunciations of musical ideas as privileged objects. This approach favours, for example, the first enunciation of a theme, motif or subject within a sonata-form movement, the initial exposition of a fugue subject, the initial presentation of a theme for a set of variations or of an operatic leitmotif over all subsequent enunciations. While themes, motifs and all other initial ideas are often transformed in the course of a piece of music, it is frequently the case in the common-practice era that one enunciation, often the first, is privileged and becomes the marker against which all further soundings are heard as variations or deviations.

As with the concept of the theme, it is often presumed that musical forms should primarily value unity, integration and identity over the seemingly secondary values of contrast, diversity and difference. Classical forms, such as that of sonata or rondo form, are all too easily caricatured as fixed identities, moulds or templates into which composers pour music or in accordance with which compositional ideas are forced to conform. With this kind of identity-thinking, sonata movements from the common-practice era are reduced to the formulaic succession of exposition, development and recapitulation. In practice, as Arnold Whittall makes clear, the relationship between 'form' and the musical work is a much more fluid and variable one to the extent that, as A. B. Marx acknowledges, 'there are as many forms as works of art' (Whittall 2007–13). Consequently, no composer of worth produces a stereotype or clone of some notional model of sonata form, and the great works in the genre, from those of Haydn, Mozart and Beethoven onwards, amaze us with their innovation in terms of form, treatment of thematicism, harmony and overall tonal construction, to name only some key qualities.

The existence of musical analyses that set out from a notional model, relating the specificity of an individual work or movement to a formal prototype, suggests strongly that an identitarian philosophy is at work as the analyst focuses on how each unique exemplar either confirms or evades the expectations set out by the notional model. In a similar way, it may be said that everything from folk song melodies to late-Romantic symphonies are often viewed, at a number of levels, through the prism of a principle of identity, which favours privileged enunciations and forms and highlights the confirmation of expectations and of deviations from those expectations. Of course, it would be foolish to deny that, in many cases, this is exactly how certain repertoires are intended to be listened to, analysed and interpreted.

Deleuzian difference, repetition, the virtual and the actual[2]

Having set out some examples of identity-thinking within a musical context, we must now look to Deleuze's critique of identity-based thought and the philosophy of difference which he proposes in its place. It is no exaggeration to state that the entire Deleuzian philosophical project centres around what he calls a new 'abstract image of thought', by which we are to understand, not merely a way of thinking, but rather that which is most often presupposed in thinking, and which tacitly and implicitly conditions thought (Deleuze 1994, p. xvi). In contrast with the traditional representational and identity-based thought, which, according to Deleuze, accounts for most previous Western thinking, this new image is to be based upon a concept of difference, which no longer reduces all differences to identities.

The image of thought which is developed in the books he co-authored with Guattari arises out of a philosophy of difference which Deleuze had already worked on in his independent studies, and most fully in *Difference and Repetition* (1968) and *The Logic of Sense* (1969). While his earlier essays explored the work of a series of anti-rationalist philosophers including Lucretius, Spinoza, Hume, Nietzsche and Bergson, the last two named are of particular importance in the development of the philosophy of difference. Bergson's philosophy, which Deleuze first drew upon in the mid-1950s, values 'internal difference', in contrast to the Platonic 'dialectic of alterity' or Hegelian contradiction (Deleuze 2004, pp. 38–40), which operate on the basis of two antithetical options, apparently oblivious to the diversity of intermediate positions made possible by a philosophy of difference.

This philosophy of difference found further support in the early 1960s in Nietzsche's critique of Enlightenment reason, which pinpoints Kant's failure to include the realm of values in his critical analysis, where he simply assumes the value of the True, the Good and the Beautiful. Nietzsche, in contrast, places a critique of values at the centre of his genealogical philosophy, as he attempts to trace their development to their origins. It is at this point that he discovers difference and two alternative approaches to the generation of difference, namely, affirmation and negation (Deleuze 1983, pp. 89–91; 1994, p. 137).

The history of thought in Deleuze's Bergsonian-Nietzschean analysis is variably exemplified in the philosophies of Plato, Aristotle, Leibniz and Hegel as favouring identity over difference, a situation he sets out to reverse with the positing of a new image of thought. Drawing upon certain Nietzschean currents, Deleuze identifies Platonism as the origin of this dominant tradition, this representational thought, which suppresses or excludes difference in favour of 'identity, resemblance and similitude' (Patton 1994, p. 145). Most philosophers 'had subordinated difference to identity or to the Same, to the Similar, to the Opposed or to the Analogous: they had introduced difference into the identity of the concept, they had put difference in the concept itself, thereby reaching a conceptual difference, but not a concept of difference' (Deleuze 1994, pp. xv, 32).

For Plato, the authenticity of something is determined by the degree of identity it shares as a copy with its original, hence the inadequacy of simulacra which are judged to be merely imperfect copies of the only true realities, the Platonic Forms. Deleuze, in contrast, rejects the philosophy of identity within the theory of Forms and seeks to overturn it through a philosophy of difference, which cannot be explained in terms of representation and identity. Accordingly, he denies 'the primacy of original over copy, of model over image', elevates simulacra and, thereby, places difference above sameness. For Deleuze, everything is a simulacrum since there are no absolute foundations or identities (Deleuze 1994, pp. 66, 128).

It is important to understand that difference, in the Deleuzian sense, is not difference '*from* or *within* something' (Foucault 1977, pp. 181–3). Where traditional thought has tended to view difference from the standpoint of sameness and unity, Deleuzian difference conceives 'difference differentially'. Within the framework of traditional identity-based thinking, 'global resemblances' are found within phenomena, which are then viewed in terms of 'differences and partial identities'. At the end of this thought process, we are left with a range of likenesses and resemblances which can be classified in terms of their degree of identity or difference from the initial idea. While dialectics recaptures every difference in a future *Aufhebung* ('overcoming'), Deleuze desires to free difference, a liberation which can only be achieved 'through the invention of an acategorical thought' (Foucault 1977, p. 186). Such a mode of thought would no longer provide primordial unities within which differences and multiplicities can be categorized, and it is this acategorical thought or univocal being which prevents the categorization of phenomena, and which enables difference to escape 'the domination of identity' (Foucault 1977, p. 192).

In aesthetic modernity, especially modernist art, literature and music, Deleuze finds a world which is defined in terms of difference and simulacra (Deleuze 1990, p. 265). He writes of the 'permutating series' and 'circular structures' of modern art, which direct philosophy away from representation, since with representation, every unique viewpoint must have a corresponding 'autonomous work with its own self-sufficient sense'. He looks instead to works such as Mallarmé's *Livre* or Joyce's *Finnegans Wake*, which challenge and invert the notion of a model or pre-eminent position, as 'the identity of the object read really dissolves into divergent series defined by esoteric words, just as the identity of the reading subject is dissolved into the decentred circles of possible multiple readings' (Deleuze 1994, pp. 56, 68–9).

Deleuze relates the concept of difference to that of repetition, which he also believes to have been subject to thinking in terms of 'the identical, the similar, the equal or the opposed' (Deleuze 1994, p. xv). He posits a repetition, no longer subject to identity and sameness, but rather to difference and variation, and which, he suggests, is best exemplified in Nietzsche's notion of the eternal return. This is not the return of the same, in the sense of history repeating itself, the same thing occurring again and again in the same way, nor is it to be understood in its moral sense as an affirmation of life. It is a return of the same which is ever different (Ibid., pp. 13, 40–1, 115, 126), and in which each return is a unique manifestation of a virtual, which is inexhaustible in its possibility, and which has no primary term (Ibid., p. 17).

The concepts of the virtual and the actual were taken up by Deleuze from his reading of Bergson, who had introduced the opposition in *Time and Free Will* (1889), developing it in *Matter and Memory* (1896), where he theorizes that memory starts out:

> from a 'virtual state' which we lead onwards, step by step, through a series of different *planes of consciousness*, up to the goal where

it is materialized in an actual perception; that is to say, up to the point where it becomes a present, active state; in fine, up to that extreme plane of our consciousness against which our body stands out. In this virtual state pure memory consists (Bergson 2004, p. 319).

Again, Bergson reflects that 'the localizing of a recollection' does not 'consist in inserting it mechanically among other memories, but in describing, by an increasing expansion of the memory as a whole, a circle large enough to include this detail from the past. These planes, moreover, are not given as ready-made things superposed the one on the other. Rather they exist virtually' (Ibid., p. 322). For Deleuze, Bergsonian virtuality involves the 'possible coexistence' of all of the degrees or nuances within something (Deleuze 2004, pp. 28, 44), and in *Difference and Repetition*, where the virtual and the actual are discussed more comprehensively, he makes clear that the virtual is not opposed to the real, that it is fully real and 'completely determined', and that it must not be confused with the possible (Deleuze 1994, pp. 209–11). Indeed, the real includes the virtual, the actual and their 'reciprocal determination' (Williams 2003, p. 164).

It is from this principle of the virtual that the eternal return operates, designating return, 'not of being and the same, but of becoming and difference', and the flux and multiplicity which it engenders result in the production of innumerable permutations of forces (Bogue 1989, pp. 28–9). Recognizing the aesthetic valency of the concept, Deleuze writes of artworks as 'immersed in a virtuality', a phrase which he exculpates from all vagueness in defining it as 'the completely determined structure formed by its [the work's] genetic differential elements, its "virtual" or "embryonic" elements'. Furthermore, these 'elements, varieties of relations and singular points coexist in the work or the object, in the virtual part of the work or object, without it being possible to designate a point of view privileged over others, a centre which would unify the other centres' (Deleuze 1994, p. 209).

Deleuze's reading of Bergson and Nietzsche, gives philosophic expression to something which, in its own way, is found in a range of modernist contexts, informing the literary production of Mallarmé, Proust, Joyce and Artaud, as well as the geometry of Klee, and which, as I have argued elsewhere, is taken up, to some extent, in the music of Boulez and others. It would certainly seem that this is the view taken by Deleuze and later shared by Guattari.

It will be argued in the remainder of this chapter that Deleuzian difference, which offers clear gains in discussion of Boulez's musical modernism, has much greater explanatory potential for a wider range of musical practices. Recapping how Deleuzian difference provides a striking parallel for discussion of what Boulez calls the 'virtual theme', we will work through some key moments in the treatment of the theme through Webern, Schoenberg and Brahms to the thematic practice of middle- and late-period Beethoven and the practice of jazz improvisation. We will also consider Boulez's rethinking of musical form, once again in ways that are consonant with Deleuzian difference, as both open form and as what he called accumulative development or kaleidoscopic form. The chapter will also investigate Deleuze's theorizing of difference in relation to lines, a phenomenon that once again parallels the heterophony that is found in Boulez as well as in several ethnic musics from around the world, and we will look in some detail at the heterophonic psalm singing of congregations in the Western Highlands of Scotland.

Identity, difference and repetition: Boulez, Webern and Schoenberg

According to Boulez, a composer who had direct contact with Deleuze and who is cited in a number of places by the philosopher, most musicians including most contemporary composers, are greatly interested, directly or indirectly, in questions of repetition and difference (Boulez 2005b, p. 156).[3] A considerable amount of space within Boulez's Collège de France lectures is spent in discussion of questions of difference and repetition in the context of twentieth-century thematicism and athematicism. While he considers thematicism in the music of Debussy, Bartók, Varèse and others, of most interest to the current discussion are his reflections on what Schoenberg, Berg, Webern and Stravinsky did with the notion of the theme, a line of thought that leads to a rather idiosyncratic account of his own compositional development.[4]

The importance attributed by Boulez to questions of difference and repetition in post-war music is rooted primarily in the theoretical and practical innovations of the Second Viennese School. Multiple manifestations of the principles of variation and non-repetition are identified within their work, in avoiding 'doubling the components within an object, non-repetition of objects, no literal return of ideas, no literal reprise of formal elements'. Nevertheless, beyond the aesthetic diversity and complexity of their individual approaches, he finds 'a single principle', namely, that of variation or non-repetition (Boulez 2005b, pp. 356–7).

In 'New Music: My Music' (c.1930), Schoenberg explains that he repeats 'little or nothing' and that repetition is almost completely replaced by variation. Something already given is altered to produce something new, with 'an apparently low degree of resemblance to its prototype, so that one finds difficulty in identifying the prototypes within the variation' (Schoenberg 1975, pp. 102–3). Whatever the complexities of his evolving relationship with repetition, many commentators agree that the truly revolutionary step taken by Schoenberg was 'the renunciation of thematic form', first accomplished with the early monodrama *Erwartung* in 1909 (Rosen 1976, p. 47). The decisive nature of this move stemmed from the fact that hitherto, the repetition of themes and the intelligible treatment of motifs had provided the clearest means of articulating musical form. Boulez, likewise, pinpoints *Erwartung*, with its almost complete 'absence of themes based on the determining *return* of privileged figures', as 'the extreme point of thematic atomisation' within Schoenberg's development (Boulez 2005b, pp. 210–11). Consequently, 'the tendency to variation, to non-literal repetition, to the evolution of forms towards a state of constant mobility' is identified as perhaps the most significant elements within Schoenberg's development (Ibid., p. 298).

With the advent of the 12-tone system and the traditional forms, which Schoenberg duly adopted in order to make larger structures once again possible, thematic repetition of a sort reappeared with the restatement of the series, and Boulez takes issue with the 'confusion between theme and series', the 'ultra-thematicisation', which he believes to be an inherent flaw in his system and its inevitable consequence (Boulez 1991, p. 212). In the third of the

Op. 23 piano pieces, for example, transpositions and inversions of a five-note segment are used to produce all of the harmonic and melodic material, while the fifth piece uses a 12-note row in such a way that the order of the pitches almost never changes throughout (Ibid., p. 290).

According to Rosen, of the three main Second Viennese composers, only Webern 'made a profound exploration of athematic forms' (Rosen 1976, p. 112), and Boulez describes how, within Webern's early works, thematicism is intimately related to the privileging of particular intervals. This process led to a consequent weakening, if not the outright annihilation, of all distinctions between what had formerly been perceived as 'principal figures' and 'secondary figures' (Boulez 2005b, pp. 218–19, 224). In the Op. 9 *Bagatelles* (1911–13), we are faced with the paradox of a thematicism which, from one point of view, is no longer apparent in any accepted sense of the term while, from a different perspective, it is equally capable of being perceived as thematically all-pervasive. Boulez considers it to be Webern's 'most radical work in terms of non-repetition' since, for example, in the fifth bagatelle, Webern imposes non-repetition strictly and allows nothing to return in exactly the same way. For Boulez, at this point of Webern's development, 'maximum coherence equals maximum perceptual insecurity'.

In his two lecture series, *The Path to Twelve-Note Composition* (1932) and *The Path to the New Music* (1933), Webern recalls that his works of the free atonal period were informed by the conviction that repetition should be avoided and that music should constantly present something new. He tells of how he came to reject this view, becoming convinced that continual novelty and the avoidance of repetition destroyed comprehensibility and problematized the possibility of extending musical form (Webern 1963, p. 55). With the advent of the 12-tone system, he returned to the principle of repetition as the 'easiest way to ensure comprehensibility' through the constant return of the given sequence of 12 notes (Ibid., p. 22).

Webern, in the early 1930s, defines a musical motive, along with Schoenberg, as 'the smallest independent particle in a musical idea', and such motives are said to be recognizable simply through their repetition (Ibid., pp. 25–6). At this stage of his career, he views Western music as the development of repetition with 'ever-increasing freedom', so that variation is to be seen as a kind of freer form of repetition (Ibid., p. 31). He believes that the 12-tone system, with its practice of not repeating any note until all 12 have sounded, provides a new thematic technique with the advantage of even greater freedom. As he says, 'unity is completely ensured by the underlying series. It's always the same; only its manifestations are different' (Ibid., p. 40). Webern bases this fundamental conviction upon Goethe's image of the 'primeval plant; the root is in fact no different from the stalk, the stalk no different from the leaf, and the leaf no different from the flower: variations of the same idea' (Ibid., p. 53). For Webern, Goethe's idea is applicable to everything, including music; hence his assessment that variation form is somehow 'the primeval form, which is at the bottom of everything. Something that seems quite different is really the same'.

In this return to repetition, Webern does not, however, use literal repetition, but rather seeks to deduce all of his material from 'a single Idea', which exists at the precompositional level (Boulez 2005b, pp. 223–5). Boulez notes the paradoxical, and possibly contradictory, nature of this aspect of Webern's aesthetic, whereby he aspires to present absolute unity and constant variation simultaneously within his material, but it is Webern's attempt to integrate these seemingly mutually exclusive ideas which results in what Boulez estimates to be Webern's greatest achievement.

For Boulez, 'Webern's principal contribution remains . . . in having overturned the notion of the theme from the real to the virtual' (Boulez 2005b, p. 225). In his Op. 27 *Variations for Piano*, for example, we no longer find a set of variations beginning in the traditional way from a recognizable theme, such as Schoenberg provides in his Op. 31 *Variations for Orchestra*, but instead variations based on what Boulez terms a virtual theme. In the first movement of the Op. 27 *Variations*, the 'images' which Webern engenders from his materials are not linked uniformly to a primordial idea, as with traditional variations. They are, rather, diverse occurrences of an idea which never itself becomes perceptible and which is only ever perceived in its multifarious manifestations (Ibid., pp. 385–6). The idea is therefore said to be virtual, meaning that it preexists all themes and acts as the condition for 'the definition of real images and their developments' (Ibid., p. 150).

Webern's athematicism or virtual theme implied for Boulez and his generation a renewed variation principle in which thematic elements are separated, given autonomy and recombined in variation. According to this new principle, no particular version of a thematic idea, such as the initial aggregate or the first-heard phrase, is favoured over any other. Even so, certain elements may have a 'primordial' but not 'definitive' place, as the musical language no longer begins with standard recognizable objects, but rather with basic elements which continually recombine to create objects related through their similarity and difference (Ibid., p. 298).

Athematicism: The virtual theme

In a retrospective reading of his own creative development, Boulez, in his 1980s Collège de France lectures, applies this Webernian concept of athematicism to his own early works beginning from the *Sonatine* for flute and piano (1946), which was also his first serial composition. He locates the athematicism of the work:

> in rejecting an *absolute* form of a theme, in order to end up with a notion of a virtual theme, (1) where the elements are not fixed at the beginning in a totally defined form, (2) where priority is not given above all to the intervals as the source of musical development, but where the other elements, duration in particular, can play a more important role to which the pitches are subordinated (Boulez 2005b, p. 223).

Athematicism is an important element in the *Sonatine* where the material, which is referred to as athematic, is deduced from 'an abstract network of possibilities which defines the circumstances of this or that appearance' (Ibid., p. 150). Despite this, the *Sonatine* does not in fact mark a definitive break with thematicism since it contrasts 'general thematicism, the theme reduced to a single cell, athematicism based on the neutrality of the constituent elements and on the force of the envelope, and precompositional athematicism' (Ibid., p. 296).

The theme is said to no longer exist within itself, but rather as a developmental function in the articulation of form (Ibid., p. 242).

Consequently, it can be explicit, amorphous or anywhere between the two (Ibid., pp. 291–6). Like its formal model, Schoenberg's first Chamber Symphony, Boulez's *Sonatine* contains, within a continuous composition, four distinct movements, each of which has its own 'principal theme', deduced from the 'initial theme' which is enunciated in the first movement. In this sense, each of the four movements is defined by the particularity of its thematic material. Athematicism, on the other hand, is used as a means of transition, linking the four movements within the continuous thread of the piece. These transitions are of '"vague" character', 'do not have a precise thematic profile' and produce the formal opposition of athematic transitions and thematic movements. The boundary separating thematicism and athematicism is breached when the threshold of perceptibility has been crossed. Boulez tells us that he produces athematicism in the *Sonatine* through 'privileging' one of the parameters in relation to the others and through employing 'sufficiently neutral' material. In the transitions, he makes rhythm the single organizational factor and repeats a single rhythmic cell which has been abstracted from the 'principal theme'. Removed from its context, it assumes a 'totally neutral character'. Secondly, he neutralizes the pitch material, leaving the 'choice of pitches to the application of a rhythmic grid', which is used in a totally 'undifferentiated' way. Coherence in the longest transitions is provided by their distinctive envelopes of density and register.

While we are focusing here on Boulez's trajectory, the impression must not be given that he was alone in his treatment of repetition at this time. His great contemporary Karlheinz Stockhausen also produced an atomized pointillistic music which, like Boulez's progression towards the idea of the virtual theme, had its roots in Webern's reduction of musical themes and motifs. In 1952/53, Stockhausen writes:

> no repetition, no development, no contrast. Those devices all assume the existence of *Gestalten* – themes, motives, objects - that are repeated, varied, developed, contrasted; dissected, elaborated, expanded, contracted, modulated, transposed, inverted or turned back to front. All that has been given up since the first purely pointillistic works. . . . One never hears the same thing twice (Cited in Maconie 1976, p. 35).

The open work: Virtual form

In the mid-1950s, interest in difference over identity, manifest at the level of the virtual theme from the *Sonatine* for flute and piano onwards, was extended by Boulez to musical form itself. He addressed the topical question of chance within music in his 1957 article 'Alea', opposing the total indeterminacy favoured by John Cage, which entailed the throwing of dice, tossing of coins, use of radio tuners and multidirectional score-reading. For Boulez, chance is unacceptable since it excludes choice, and he posited instead what he called 'controlled chance'. Controlled chance found expression in what became known as open form, which aimed to create a 'sort of multi-circuited labyrinth', offering, not the infinite chance possibilities preferred by Cage, but rather, multiple choices of equal weight and value for the performer, within a composed framework (Boulez 2005b, p. 320).

While open form is most often seen as a reaction to Cage's ideas on total chance, Mallarmé's influence is also most apparent, and there is no doubt that the poet's great poem 'Un Coup de dés' and his *Livre*, an unfinished mobile book, were decisive influences on Boulez. Published only in 1957, the *Livre* was to allow mobility at every level of the text, from that of individual words and phrases to complete pages, and would read in more than one direction. For Boulez, its multiple routes, reversibility and variability were a revelation which, he says, 'corroborated' his own ideas (Ibid., p. 167) and suggested the possibility of finding musical equivalents (Boulez 1986, p. 147).

An interest in open form at this time was common to composers Karlheinz Stockhausen, Henri Pousseur, Luciano Berio and others. Stockhausen's *Klavierstück XI* (1956), for example, involves a certain degree of indeterminacy through its 19 mobile structures, from which the performer chooses randomly, but with the help of fixed performing instructions. This, like Boulez's Third Sonata for piano, results in a work with many possible versions. In 'Alea', Boulez described his intention as a search for 'an evolving form which rebels against its own repetition; in short, a relative formal virtuality', a conception of form which simply extends the tendency within contemporary music in the mid-1950s towards variable concepts (Boulez 1991, p. 35).

Open form, as Boulez conceived it, is based upon multiple relationships which, in an effort to break with traditional 'unidirectional form', require the performer to make certain choices involving several possible routes through a score, comprising both fixed and a certain number of mobile elements (Boulez 2005b, p. 199). In this way, Boulez accepts responsibility for composing out the various possibilities within an idea, but then leaves the task of choosing from among these possibilities to the performer. In the face of several musically interesting alternatives, he was reluctant to restrict himself to only one when he could retain multiple options. Consequently, he contrasts the possibility of 'a real, completed text', which sets out from 'fixed and privileged thematic givens', with that of 'a potential virtual text' which is in a constant state of renewal and of evolution (Ibid., p. 325).

With a virtual or open form, no one version or performance will be theoretically any more valid than any other, since each possible version of the work, which exercises certain options while bypassing others, becomes simply a 'virtual variation' of the virtual form (Ibid., p. 407). Works by Boulez which include elements of open form are the 1962 version of *Don* from *Pli selon pli*, *Structures II*, *Éclat*, *Domaines* and *Rituel*, but it is most clearly used in the Third Sonata for piano whose multiple possibilities defy, at least in theory, any definitive ordering and, therefore, performative repetition. In the Third Sonata, Boulez, like Mallarmé, attempted to provide an open form in which the performer has a certain degree of choice over the material which is used and the order in which it is played. To date, only two of the five formants (movements) have been completed, which enables them to be combined in a total of four ways, which will be increased to eight on completion of all five formants. Ivanka Stoïanova, the first scholar to write about Boulez's music and ideas in terms of Deleuzian difference, discusses the relationship between the composer's Third Sonata and Mallarmé's mobile poetry, suggesting that the sonata realizes within music a similar 'profound identity' and play of repetition as difference (Stoïanova 1974; 1978).

Difference as 'accumulative development'

While Boulez's interest in the possibilities of the open form work cooled over time, elements of mobility continued to feature in his music, and he remained as committed as ever to ideas of difference and multiplicity. At the level of form, his pieces begin to resemble Stravinsky's sectional forms, and he commends the originality of Stravinsky's discourse, which bases musical form on the permutation and return of recognizable sections. He notes, in particular, how Stravinsky succeeded, in *Les Noces* and the *Symphonies of Wind Instruments*, in transforming the ancient forms of the litany and the verse response couplet into an entirely new concept, in which formal development is paradoxically produced through formal return, in a thematicism which is based upon modified repetition (Boulez 2005b, pp. 232, 276). Indeed, 'Stravinsky's conception of melodic development is based on psalmody and litany where deviation is minute in relation to the original model, but where the intervening extensions, contractions, displacement of accents . . . finds its profound force in accumulation' (Ibid., p. 235).

Stravinsky's sectional forms operate through the alternation of blocks of familiar material whose varied re-occurrence constitutes the formal development (Boulez 2005b, pp. 235–6). Van den Toorn writes of *Les Noces* as possessing 'a form or architecture constructed with relatively heterogeneous blocks of material, which exhibit, upon successive (near) repeats, an unusual degree of distinction and insulation in instrumental, dynamic, rhythmic-metric, and referential character' (Van den Toorn 1983, p. 177). On the *Symphonies of Wind Instruments*, he writes again of 'a highly incisive form of abrupt block juxtaposition' and '(near) repeats' (Ibid., p. 339), while Taruskin highlights 'its fascinating mosaic structure, in which discrete sections ("blocks") in varying but strictly coordinated tempi are juxtaposed without conventional transitions' (Taruskin 1996, p. 1486).

Perhaps thinking more of his own forms, Boulez prefers to describe Stravinsky's sectional forms as constituting 'accumulative development', thus avoiding any sense of repetition and, perhaps also, Stravinsky's identity-based aesthetic (Boulez 2005b, p. 236). He speaks of 'a kaleidoscopic form where the alternation of accumulative thematic developments creates the form'. Again, he professes his growing attraction for a formal conception which gives equal status to 'return and variation' (Ibid., pp. 318–19).

Perhaps the simplest form of accumulative development is the verse-response form of a piece such as *Rituel*, which is made up of 15 sections, in which the even-numbered are verses and the odd-numbered are responses. In *Originel* from . . . *explosante-fixe* . . . , Boulez simply alternates two kinds of music, this time a series of six poetic, improvisatory sections, each time punctuated with a cadence. *Transitoire VII* from . . . *explosante-fixe* . . . is clearly sectional in form, but in a much more elaborate way, and its ten distinct ideas, which occur variously from one to six times in the course of the movement, interlock in a kind of musical chain.

Heterophony: The virtual line

The final manifestation of difference to be considered in Boulez's work is that of heterophony, which consists in the production of virtual melodic lines, analogous to his virtual themes, virtual forms and accumulative developments. While the original meaning of the term is now uncertain, it is commonly used today, particularly by ethnomusicologists, to describe the 'simultaneous variation, accidental or deliberate, of what is identified as the same melody' (Cooke 1980, p. 537; Malm 1977, p. 194). It is fundamental to many non-European musical traditions, including the gamelan music of Southeast Asia, the instrumental music for the Japanese Gagaku, Chinese folk music, the chanting of Bornean head-hunters, Tuareg love songs, Mongolian folk singing and the Hebridean tradition of congregational psalm singing (Malm 1977, pp. 33, 59–60, 143).

Boulez defined heterophony as part of his creative wherewithal in *Boulez on Music Today* (Boulez 1971, pp. 117–29), where he wrote of the need to broaden and generalize its use. He tells us that it can be defined

> as the superposition on a primary structure of a modified *aspect* of the same structure; . . . . In heterophony, several aspects of a fundamental formulation coincide (examples are found above all

in the music of the Far East, where a very ornate instrumental melody is heterophonous with a much more basic vocal line); its density will consist of various strata, rather as if several sheets of glass were to be superposed, each one bearing a variation of the same pattern (Ibid., pp. 117–18).

For Boulez, heterophony 'is a way of affirming the identity of the group while acknowledging variants, even individual "deviances"' (Boulez 2005a, p. 601). Examples can be found in many of Boulez's compositions, including *Le Visage nuptial*, *Don* from *Pli selon pli*, *Figures – Doubles – Prismes*, *cummings ist der dichter* and *Rituel*. Nevertheless, it becomes a more prominent feature within certain compositions from the 1970s onwards, and he has acknowledged the connection linking the development of his own heterophonous lines with the visual experiments, drawings and paintings of Paul Klee.

For Boulez, the important principle to be learnt from Klee is the simple notion of an original line being surrounded by a number of secondary lines, and the geometric organization of such secondary lines relative to the original line (Boulez 1989, p. 53). Klee envisages a curved line, first of all on its own, secondly, decorated by complementary lines and thirdly, 'circumscribing itself'. In the final stage of this reflection, he has 'two secondary lines moving around an imaginary main line' (Klee 1953, pp. 16–17; 1961, pp. 105–7), and he illustrates the point humorously with the image of a walking man whose dog is also walking freely at his side.

Linda Doeser, describing how Klee uses 'secondary lines to enhance, complement and counterbalance a primary line', highlights what would seem to be the essential issue when she writes that Klee's primary line 'was not, in fact, drawn and existed as only a concept' (Doeser 1995, p. 44). In other words, if Klee has a primary line, it does not appear in the frame of the picture since it is a virtual line. Likewise, Boulez's heterophonies, in which simultaneous manifestations of a melodic line appear in superposition, are equally different manifestations of a virtual melodic line. This virtual line cannot be simplistically reduced to any one favoured version of the line and will certainly not be found in the score, since all of the drawn melodic lines are particular manifestations of the virtual line.

That Boulez should choose to discuss heterophony in terms of multilinear logic is striking and brings to mind Deleuze's *The Fold: Leibniz and the Baroque* (1988) where the philosopher developed his philosophy of difference further, in elucidating the concept of the fold, with illustrations from Klee and Boulez. For Deleuze, the co-existence of Klee's multiple lines are examples of what Leibniz called incompossibility, that is, the possible co-existence of ideas or notions which are mutually contradictory, and which cannot co-exist within the same world, within a traditional worldview. Deleuze and Boulez seem to be in agreement, however, in suggesting that for many modern philosophers and artists, 'divergences, incompossibilities, discords [and] dissonances' coexist 'in the same world' (Deleuze 1993, pp. 81–2). Deleuze draws a further parallel between the passage from the closed world of compossibles to the open world of divergent incompossibles and the progressive development of musical harmony. The latter is traced through the emancipation of dissonance, the development of harmony, its eventual dissolution, to polytonality and to the incompossibility of Boulez's polyphony of polyphonies, or heterophonies. Modernist creators such as Mallarmé, Klee and Boulez turn away from the unilinearity of compossibles in favour of incompossibles, which affirm divergences and no longer suggest the traditional world of the familiar (Ibid., p. 82).

Of course, Boulez is not the only composer working after 1945 to utilize the possibilities of heterophony within his works, and Messiaen uses it to great effect in, for example, the Epode from *Chronochromie* (1960) with its birdsongs played on 18 solo strings. Heterophony is also a significant part of Birtwistle's compositional technique with Michael Hall stating that all of Birtwistle's music is 'a single line filled out by other lines moving in parallel motion with it, or by heterophony' (Hall 1984, p. 8).

Deleuzian difference beyond modernism

Deleuze's appeal to Leibnizian incompossibility shows that while he finds difference and the virtual primarily in the context of aesthetic modernism, this is not exclusively the case, and it in no way exhausts the provenance of the concept. While Deleuze's invocation of Leibniz may amount to the rediscovery of a road most often not taken, it also invites us to revisit older musical repertoires with Deleuzian difference in mind as an active principle, capable of contributing significantly to our understanding of the past as well as the present. Ultimately, the justification for doing so is dependent upon the capacity of Deleuze's concepts to articulate aspects of the music and to offer a more truthful or productive account of its working. Just as Deleuze does not hesitate in going against the philosophy of identity in its Platonic and Hegelian formulations, the current study seeks to offer alternative ways of viewing repertoire which is more often discussed in terms of more traditional epistemological paradigms.

It is not immediately apparent where exactly Deleuzian difference lies in relation to more traditional musical concepts, and while we could rely on a certain degree of terminological similarity and overlap in the work of Deleuze, Boulez and their fellow moderns, we cannot hope to find this in the music which will be discussed here, as we consider thematic working in Beethoven, developing variation in Brahms and Schoenberg, aspects of jazz improvisation and heterophonic psalm singing from the West Highlands of Scotland.

Gaelic psalm singing as heterophonic difference

The difference which was identified in Boulez's heterophony is also encountered in the much more ancient heterophonies of more traditional cultures throughout the world. Gaelic psalm singing, as it is practised in the Free Churches in the West Highlands of Scotland, for example, forms a distinctive tradition of heterophonic singing, that is found nowhere else in Western Europe.[5] The psalms, as they are sung in this tradition, are unaccompanied, unharmonized and are highly ornamented in performance. With the exception of the first line, which is read by the prayer leader, a precentor intones each line of the psalm text and is joined by the entire congregation. The performance of Gaelic psalms is generally slow and congregational singing is unconducted, the precentor's job being to initiate the singing by setting the pitch and communicating the text and melody of each line to the worshippers. The psalm melody, as it is sung by congregations on the Isle of Lewis, for example, is usually extremely ornamented by each individual singer in such a way that the result is heterophonic in terms of both melody and rhythm. No real trace is left of either the metrical rhythm of the translated text or of the borrowed psalm tune which, it may be said, remains as a virtual melody around which each member of the congregation weaves one of its innumerable actualizations. As Lachlan MacBean notes 'the music has been lengthened out and elaborated until its whole spirit and character is changed and we have in effect new tunes' (MacBean 1887, p. 2).

While the original metrical psalm tune 'Martyrs', first published in Scotland in 1615, is very simple, it is not possible to make an accurate transcription of a given performance by a West Highland Gaelic congregation, in which each singer's rendition will be different in terms of pitch and rhythm as well as out of phase in terms of tempo. As John Purser notes, the heterophonic effect is manifest with even a small number of singers (Purser 1992, p. 146). In a similar way, the simple and four-square metrical psalm tune 'Coleshill', when performed by a West Highland congregation, is woven into what Purser describes as 'a wonderful Celtic knot, embellishing and intertwining, transforming it into something rich and strange in which each verse takes over two minutes to perform, so that the words are stretched out and become living, singing things' (Ibid., p. 145). As Purser notes, 'the freedom to decorate the melody so that each member of the congregation makes an individual act of worship out of his or her own singing fulfills the highest ideals of the Reformation by processes the reformers probably never envisaged' (Ibid., p. 147).

Composition, improvisation, variation and Deleuzian difference

Deleuzian difference pertains to that continuum of possibilities that links composition and improvisation, the seemingly fixed and the fluid. This spectrum of creative possibilities lies between the recreation of an already completed, most often notated, piece of music, on the one hand, and the production of something completely original, on the other, an apparently spontaneous act of performance. In the eighteenth century, the musical work became autonomous and capable of generating all kinds of musical ideas, as planned by a composer and then interpreted by performers and listeners. Improvisation, in contrast, has existed as a concept in Western art music since the late fifteenth century, variably determinable by what constitutes a 'fixed' musical work at any given moment in time. It can mean making changes to a notated musical text or completing a musical idea which is only partially notated and which gives the performer choices with regard to melodic variation, ornamentation, harmonic scheme, tempo and so on. This process can be taken to the point where the identity of the original material is almost completely obscured but, even here, secondary factors may persist, thus ensuring recognition and continuity. It would be a mistake to simply equate composition with identity and improvisation with difference, and these twin poles are, in fact, never mutually exclusive, since every composition has variable elements and every improvisation depends upon the establishment of conventions and rules regarding the desirability of factors such as an agreed starting point, repetition, variation, sequence, style, forms of ornamentation, techniques and strategies for dealing positively with the unexpected and with mistakes.

Where Western culture has generally regarded improvised music as inferior to composed music, for West Asian societies, improvisation is often an ideal that is associated with ideas of freedom, self-determination and exemption from restriction. In performances of Javanese gamelan, for example, those performers who depart most significantly from the model are esteemed very highly (Nettl 2007–13). Improvisation is often the result of variation of some kind of starting material, a phenomenon which can proceed in a great many different ways. In North India, for example, instrumentalists first perform a short composition called a 'gat' in its integral form before it then becomes the basis for improvisation, in which the demands of a given rhythmic cycle ('tala') are observed (Ibid.). In the West, the concept of a set of variations on a well-known melody or a bass line became established in the sixteenth century, with the possibility of varying both the melody and/or the harmonic scheme (Horsley 2007–13).

Much Western jazz begins with the enunciation of a 'standard' tune, something, for example, from the Broadway song repertoire, which is performed first with its original melody and chord changes, both of which then become the basis for improvisation by each of the musicians in turn.[6] Jazz solos are most often based on the harmonies and/or the melody of a theme, while the form is made up of a mixture of prearranged and improvised components. Complete spontaneity and innovation within free improvisation are relatively rare in jazz, as elsewhere, as musicians usually need to work on the basis of at least some shared conventions to enable them to perform together. For Paul Berliner, 'the very attempt to distinguish between improvisation and composition ends up in insurmountable aporia and tautologies' (cited in Nesbitt 2010, p. 160).

Despite the availability of a range of improvisation techniques, including 'paraphrase', 'formulaic' and 'motivic' variation, not all jazz is improvisational. While Philip Auslander has written of the 'fundamentally unrepeatable' quality of jazz, stating that 'non-improvisational jazz is arguably an oxymoron', Björn Heile suggests that statements such as this run the risk of mythologizing jazz as 'a spontaneous expression of instinctual musicality' (Heile 2011, p. 89; 2013).[7] On the basis of recorded concerts featuring the Duke Ellington Band from their European tours in 1969 and 1971, Heile, focusing on the Billy Strayhorn classic *Take the A Train*, notes that not only the Big Band arrangement but also the trumpet solo is retained note-for-note in every recorded performance. While Louis Armstrong was in the habit of retaining the general outline and a number of significant details of a solo that had been particularly successful, Charlie Parker, the greatest exponent of formulaic improvisation, never repeated a solo literally, instead making all kinds of significant changes. Thomas Owens has identified about 100 motifs or fragments, which Parker, reworked skilfully time and again throughout approximately 250 of his many solos (Kernfield 2007–13). Nick Nesbitt has written of Deleuzian difference with regard to the improvisations of the great jazz saxophonist John Coltrane and others, arguing convincingly that even the simple three-chord structure that is central to blues music, far from being an impoverishment, serves 'as the basis for framing an infinite potential of expressive possibilities', capable of giving rise to invention of the calibre of Coltrane's solo for 'Blue Train'. For Nesbitt,

Coltrane's solo, as with all great improvised jazz, actualizes something virtual, something which consists essentially of *'unformed matters and nonformal functions'* (cited in Nesbitt 2010, p. 173).

In more general terms, the concept of 'variation' was first applied systematically in Western art music in the sixteenth century, when sets of variations began to be composed, but, as one of music's richest concepts, it predates this moment as a tendency in a range of musics. Variation is dependent on the repetition of a given unit such as a motif, theme, melody, chord sequence, bass line or rhythmic figure that is modified and transformed in a number of ways, and Elaine Sisman has produced a taxonomy of variation types, all of which preserve certain aspects of the theme while changing others, including ostinato, constant-melody or cantus firmus, constant-harmony, melodic-outline, formal-outline, characteristic, fantasy and serial variations (Sisman 2007–13). It is interesting to note, from the point of view of Deleuzian difference, that the very first enunciation or couplet in many variation sets from the sixteenth and seventeenth centuries, is itself a variation, with the integral, privileged version of the theme only appearing in the seventh couplet (Ibid.).

Beethoven and thematicism

While Beethoven's compositional processes and forms have often, from the writings of E. T. A. Hoffmann onwards, been thought in conjunction with Hegel's dialectical philosophy,[8] there are grounds to suggest that Deleuzian difference may offer an alternative way of considering certain aspects of Beethoven's practice, aspects that have already been commented upon by Adorno, Dahlhaus and others, albeit within a dialectical framework.[9] While Dahlhaus's account is very much his own, it nevertheless builds in significant ways on the prior work of Schoenberg and Adorno. For reasons of economy, the account that is presented here draws primarily from Dahlhaus with some support from Adorno.

Despite acknowledging the pre-eminence of the notion of 'unity in diversity, or diversity in unity' in the age of Beethoven (Dahlhaus 1991, p. 122), Dahlhaus is dismissive of exaggerated emphasis on motivic and thematic coherence, where the analyst strives to show

how everything within a movement is derived from one motivic or intervallic cell (Ibid., p. 91). This, he suggests, leads to the impossible situation where so many 'transformational possibilities' are apparent that 'virtually everything can be derived from everything else'. Unsurprisingly, he also rejects the organic model of formal development which underlies this approach, and according to which, musical cells contain within themselves all of their possibilities in latent form, needing only to be allowed to develop in the course of a piece (Ibid., p. 92). Consequently, he rejects the positing of any one definitive starting point for the development of a musical form, while also acknowledging the practical difficulty of marking out motives or themes which quite often are rather ambiguous in nature (Ibid., pp. 92–3, 109).

The notion of the 'underlying idea', which for a long time was attributed directly to Beethoven, is identified by Dahlhaus as having a 'complex relationship' with that of the 'theme', with which it is not synonymous (Ibid., p. 143). He distinguishes between the 'theme', defined as the 'generative idea', 'principal idea' 'or first subject' within a piece and the 'underlying idea', which is 'an overall conception of a movement that is not yet "the image in its entire extent"' (Ibid., pp. 143–4). In keeping with his earlier analysis of the variable aspects of a 'theme', the 'underlying idea' is defined as 'the manner in which a specific association is made between the development of the thematic material, the design of the tonal ground plan, the disposition of the formal functions, and the succession of the aesthetic characters' (Ibid., p. 145). Discussing the first movement of Beethoven's D major sonata, Op. 10 No. 3, he states that

> The 'idea' does not consist in a tangible circumstance from which everything else could then be derived, but in a nexus of relations in which the "foundation circumstances" – the hierarchy of what came first and what came later – are uncertain. It is in no way necessary to conclude that all the premises and implications which come to light out of the "given" form during the reconstruction of the "form in the process of becoming", were constantly present in the composer's mind while he was writing the piece. From the hermeneutical point of view, however – and independently of psychological considerations – the total

configuration of the form-determining elements has to be regarded as the starting point of the work's conception (Ibid., pp. 146–7).

Of Beethoven's C minor Piano Variations, WoO 80, Dahlhaus notes that the theme is comprised of four elements, an ostinato, a harmonic scheme, a 'melodic framework' and an 'actual melody', any of which is capable of becoming the material of particular variations, either alone or together with other components. With such flexibility, Beethoven's thematic material is capable of generating an almost unlimited range of variations which do not need to be related to an essential melodic or harmonic scheme, identified at the outset, while nevertheless continuing to maintain a sense of thematic identity (Ibid., pp. 157–8).

While the traditional concept of the theme is that of a gestalt, a musical idea not only with consequences but a reference point which is returned to in the course of a movement, Beethoven was working around 1802, according to Dahlhaus and Adorno, on the problem of creating musical forms which are:

> simultaneously thematic and non-thematic: thematic to the extent that a thematic substance is the prerequisite of a formal process; non-thematic in so far as the composer avoids setting down a fixed, pregnantly delineated formulation at the beginning of the work to provide the "text" for a commentary. In brief, the "thematic material" is no longer a "theme" (Ibid., p. 167).

In the first movement of the D minor Sonata, Op. 31 No. 2, for example, Dahlhaus finds that

> Nowhere, in fact, is there a "real" statement of the first subject. But because Beethoven avoids "presenting" the themes, and goes straight from a protoform to developmental elaboration, the form *is* process. Nowhere is the thematic material "given", in the sense of a text on which a development section comments; rather, it is involved in developmental process from first to last-either as anticipation of thematic working to come, or as consequence of thematic working already past. It exists exclusively in transformations . . . it has no existence as a substantive structure,

or a source-shape to which the thematic-motivic working refers back' (Ibid., pp. 170–1).

Consequently, the underlying material for the movement is more a 'thematic configuration' than a theme, understood as a grouping of components which is either 'pre-thematic' or 'post-thematic' without ever being properly thematic (Ibid., p. 171). Similar judgements are made regarding the variations in the 'Eroica' Variations, Op. 35, and the first movement of the 'Eroica' Symphony where, in the latter case, Beethoven again seems to move straight from 'protoform' to 'derivation' bypassing any expounding of a theme properly speaking (Ibid., p. 174).

Dahlhaus takes this line of thought even further, coining the term 'subthematicism' to describe how, for example, Beethoven's String Quartet in A minor, Op. 132, derives essentially from four pitch classes (G#-A-F-E) which constitute, in a latent way, 'the true fundamental idea of the movement, the element which unites all its parts', pervading the motivic material, but in a subthematic way (Ibid., p. 204). This 'fundamental idea', however, is not limited to this work but is found also in varied forms in the Quartet in C# minor, Op. 131, the Quartet in Bb major, Op. 130, as well as the *Grosse Fuge*, Op. 133 (Ibid., p. 204). Thematic process differs in these works in that their fundamental principle of coherence retires from the musical surface to a 'subthematic' level, which Dahlhaus describes as 'abstract', 'latent' and as a 'network'. Of the A minor Quartet, Dahlhaus states that its 'fundamental idea' is

> less a 'theme' or a 'motive' – that is, a 'concrete' melodic-rhythmic construct, generated from an assembly of intervals, a configuration of durations, and an ordered system of accents – and more an intervallic structure, independent of rhythm and metre and with variable durations and accents, which permeates the music and links its parts together from within. Even the expression "intervallic structure" . . . is still not abstract enough (Ibid., p. 205).

For Dahlhaus, this level of operation pertains to qualities as fundamental as the arrangement of 'two rising or falling semitone steps with a variable interval between them', qualities which provide the 'substratum' for the 'subthematic' (Ibid., p. 205), and he notes that no 'fundamental form' of the 'four-note figure' which is shared by the Opp. 132, 130, 133 and 131 Quartets exists anywhere within the works, appearing always and only in its multifarious variant forms (Ibid., pp. 227–8).

Whatever the views of Dahlhaus's critics, Adorno, whose terminology does not concur exactly with that of Dahlhaus, is equally forceful in stating that Beethoven's ascetic approach to material ensures that nothing whatsoever is 'reified' or 'repeated' and that everything 'ready-made' and pre-existent is dissolved into such elementary terms that it barely qualifies as material, a point which is as true of form as it is of thematicism (Adorno 1998, pp. 39, 66). While all of this work on Beethoven has been accomplished in the context of the Hegelian dialectic, most of the foregoing seems to be capable of operating outside of a dialectical understanding, and it raises the question of the extent to which we can speak with justification of Beethoven's 'generative idea', 'underlying idea', 'thematic configuration' and 'subthematicism' as various manifestations of the Deleuzian 'virtual'. What the Frankfurt philosophers refer to as 'reification' and the fluidity that is its opposite becomes, for Deleuze, the opposition of the molar and the molecular. Finally, bearing in mind the fluidity of Deleuze's own concepts, both in his solo writings and in those with Guattari, that virtuality and actuality take different forms at different moments in Beethoven's output is in no way problematic for a Deleuzian understanding.

Schoenberg, Brahms and developing variation

It is possible to develop this line of thought beyond Dahlhaus's work on Beethoven to Schoenberg's contested identification of 'developing variation' in music from 1750 right down to his own music, but most particularly in the work of Brahms. While Schoenberg employs the term 'developing variation' for the music of Bach, Beethoven, Brahms and his own music, it is used more sparingly by other writers. Despite the existence of several definitions in Schoenberg's writings from 1917 onwards, with concomitant changes in 'emphasis and nuance',[10] developing variation can be defined as a form of variation technique where:

> variation of the features of a basic unit produces all the thematic formulations which provide for fluency, contrasts, variety, logic and unity on the one hand, and character, mood, expression, and every needed differentiation, on the other hand – thus elaborating the *idea* of the piece (Schoenberg 1975, p. 397).

For Schoenberg, a piece of music is constituted by 'nothing but the endless reshaping of a basic shape' so that 'there is nothing . . . but what comes from the theme, springs from it, and can be traced back to it; to put it still more severely, nothing but the theme itself. Or, all the shapes appearing in a piece of music are *foreseen* in the "theme"' (Ibid., p. 290). Synthesizing Schoenberg's various attempts at definition, Walter Frisch, who devotes an entire monograph to 'developing variation' in Brahms, describes it as 'the construction of a theme by the continuous modification of one or more features (intervals, rhythms) of a basic idea, according to certain recognized procedures, such as inversion, fragmentation, extension, and displacement' (Frisch 1982, p. 220; 1984, p. 9). Brahms is cited by Schoenberg on the grounds that he 'develops or varies his motives almost at once', and developing variation is found in Brahms's songs and chamber music works from 1864–79 as well as in the Second, Third and Fourth symphonies, in thematic working, development sections and entire works, as his motivic development grows in intensity and pervasiveness, permeating all aspects of the musical texture including phrase structure and 'metrical framework' (Frisch 1984, p. 17). Where Haydn and Beethoven used the technique 'primarily, if not exclusively, for purposes of development, Brahms used it as an underlying principle governing all the sections of entire movements' (Dahlhaus 1989, p. 256). In the first ten bars of Brahms's Quartet in G-minor, Op. 25 (1861), Dahlhaus finds an extreme example of developing variation in which everything is formed from one 'initially inconspicuous four-note idea', the interval of a falling second which appears in various formulations including imitation, inversion and sequence (Ibid., pp. 256–7).

Within his own compositional practice, Schoenberg identifies in *Die Jakobsleiter* that all the 'main themes had to be transformations of the first phrase' and that 'the basic motif was not only productive in furnishing new motif-forms through developing variations, but also in producing more remote formulations based on the unifying effect of one common factor: the repetition of tonal and intervallic relationship' (Schoenberg, cited in Haimo 1997, p. 353). In terms of his 12-tone practice, Schmalfeldt notes that developing variation operates in such a way here that 'the distinction between model and variant, theme and its development, the subjective and the objective is destroyed' (Schmalfeldt 1995, p. 50). Since the concept of developing variation has not met with anything like universal acceptance, we can simply note here that while a number of scholars believe that it is adequate for dealing with the music of Schoenberg and Brahms, others restrict its validity solely to that of Schoenberg.

Conclusion

As Nick Nesbitt has shown, the opposition of difference and identity at the heart of Deleuze's philosophy can be used profitably in the exploration of a number of musical repertoires, and he has attempted, in a much more wide-ranging narrative, to think aspects of Western music from medieval modality, through common-practice tonality and late-nineteenth-century chromaticism to musical modernism, in this way (Nesbitt 2004, pp. 54–75). Such a programme has been beyond the possibility of the current study which has opted to focus on a smaller number of case studies, which it is hoped indicate in some detail how the imperative of Deleuzian difference is that we think music in a new way, no longer focusing on it as something static, unchanging, eternal, always the same, but as dynamic, changing and always shifting. In each case, we may say that Deleuzian difference has been discovered *avant la lettre*.

The challenge for music analysis, from the perspective of Deleuzian difference, entails the articulation of responses to musical questions that are not reduced to identitarian modes of thought. With a Deleuzian perspective, tonality becomes a virtual system, giving rise to any number of actualizations, a principle that is equally the case for all musical modes, scales and series. In a similar way, musical genres, usually *post-factum* theoretical formulations, abstracted from the study of entire repertoires, can also be understood as operating as virtual forms. In this way, even compositions, recuperable under established formal rubrics such as that of sonata form, become actualities of a virtual idea whose possibilities are inexhaustible, unforeseeable and only recognized in retrospect. Ultimately, as Hulse suggests, the term 'genre' has to do with what Deleuze and Guattari would describe as 'molecular' flows of 'ideas and fragments' which are assembled uniquely as a work of art before dispersing again for the creation of an equally new work (Hulse 2010, p. 42). In formulating the point in this way, we are already moving onto the subject matter of the next chapter where we will explore in detail the formation of musical rhizomes and assemblages. Nevertheless, Hulse is correct in noting that scholars at times suppress the importance of the flows and communications which take place within genres that are always open, porous and in motion.

Even with the limit example of the exact repetition of a musical motive, phrase, theme, subject or rhythm, it is widely accepted that a second enunciation can never be identical to the first. At a structural level, the fact of its different placing within the framework of a movement and the particularity of its interpretation make it automatically unique and individual. This may well be an area where Deleuzian difference calls us to give up all laziness in our listening habits, the kind of listening which takes shortcuts and which thinks, 'no need to listen to this bit as it's just the same as what went before'. As for dismantling notions of identity, it may be difficult to go further than Harrison Birtwistle, who is reported as having claimed that he could have composed the same piece with entirely different pitches, a statement which perhaps raises the question of difference and identity more poignantly than any other. Of course, Mauricio Kagel had already done so. Having composed the piece *Morceau de concours* for the first time in 1971, he produced a second version in 1992 which is so different from the first that, as Björn Heile notes, they 'don't have a single note in common', thus posing the question of how we are to conceive of them as the same piece (Heile 2006, p. 111). Perhaps the most identitarian category in music is that of 'music' itself, that impulse which says 'this is music, but that isn't'. Again, this is an impulse which reduces all musics to good and bad copies of an ideal of what music is. The Deleuzian alternative is ultimately one in which all musics are actualities of music in its virtual state, a statement which for some will be so bland as to be meaningless.

2

Producing new music: Rhizomes, assemblages and refrains

Deleuze and Guattari and the assemblage

While the philosophy of difference, which was the subject of Chapter 1, draws primarily on Deleuze's early work *Difference and Repetition*, the concepts that are explored in Chapter 2 arise primarily out of his shared projects with Félix Guattari. Deleuze's philosophy, in both his solo writings and his work with Guattari, is not a fixed system of thought and the collaborative studies introduce the reader to a continuous stream of new concepts which not only articulate and re-articulate a difference-based, non-representational, fluid and molecular image of thought, but also embody it. In *A Thousand Plateaus*, the second of their Capitalism and Schizophrenia volumes and the companion to *Anti-Oedipus*, this new difference-based image of thought is embodied in three main concepts – as a rhizome, as a plane of immanence (or consistency) and as a Body without Organs. It is not intended that these concepts should necessarily be combinable in one perfectly coherent super-system, and the desirability of having more than one conceptual means of referring to this image of thought, and the impossibility of linking words and things in simple morphologies is integral to their philosophy.

For Deleuze and Guattari, the history of Western music is really a history of innovation with each new work of any significance constituting a response to a particular problem. Drawing upon the concepts of the rhizome and the assemblage, this chapter will present a reading of musical innovation from the point of view of rhizomatic thinking/practice and the creation of assemblages. Deleuze and Guattari employ Boulez's concept of the 'diagonal' to describe the new and distinctive contribution made by every innovative writer, scientist, philosopher, musician and so on within her or his respective area of inquiry. Every new creator takes her or his place on an already existing plane, composed of many such lines, and the originality of each contribution is thought of as the drawing of a new diagonal or transversal line which forms itself between already existing points and lines and, doing so, creates a new line in a new space. Setting aside the portraits of the Classical, Romantic and Modern eras in music sketched out by Deleuze and Guattari in *A Thousand Plateaus*, the chapter will consider a number of musical assemblages from recent Western art music, jazz and popular music. It will explore how new music is formed from all kinds of unexpected rhizomatic connections operating between concepts of music, social practice, the development of instruments and instrumental techniques, musical systems, notation, performance styles and practice, developments in technology, performance spaces, musical institutions, recording and reproduction of music, relationships with literature, visual arts and philosophy and innumerable other factors.

In 'Rhizome', the opening plateau or chapter of *A Thousand Plateaus*, Deleuze and Guattari articulate the vegetal model of the rhizome, which stands in opposition to a more traditional image of thought, defined as arborescent (Deleuze and Guattari 1988, p. 15). In contrast with the hierarchically structured branches found within tree systems, in which possibilities unfold in unambiguously structured and limited ways, the Deleuze-Guattarian rhizome has lines which allow the connection of any of its points with any other (Ibid., pp. 7–8). Where arborescent systems have 'hierarchical modes of communication and preestablished paths, the rhizome is an acentred, nonhierarchical, nonsignifying system' (Ibid., p. 21) in which 'semiotic chains' from different 'regimes of signs' can link up in any number of ways (Ibid., p. 7). While rhizomes, such as are found in the natural world, do not in fact allow such free association between their stalks and lines, with the Deleuze-Guattarian rhizome, 'communication runs from any neighbour to any other, the stems or channels do not preexist, and all individuals are interchangeable, defined only by their *state* at a given moment' (Ibid., p. 17). While the rhizome can be broken at any place, it continues to operate as old lines are capable of making new connections and new lines can form (Ibid., p. 9). Rhizomes are multiplicities that are anti-genealogical and irreducible to prior or overarching identities (Ibid., p. 8). They are processes, not structures, have no beginning or end but rather a middle, are formed from lines which vary, expand, capture and shoot off in any direction whatever (Ibid., p. 21). They do not trace an underlying plan but rather pertain 'to a map that must be produced, constructed, a map that is always detachable, connectable, reversible, modifiable, and [which] has multiple entryways and exits and its own lines of flight' (Ibid., p. 21). Consequently, they cannot be analysed in terms of underlying structures.

In addition to this, trees can transform into rhizomes (Ibid., p. 17) and 'there are knots of arborescence in rhizomes, and rhizomatic offshoots in roots' (Ibid., p. 20). Furthermore, between the arborescent and the rhizomatic lies a third possibility, a 'radicle-system', a false multiplicity in which, while the 'principle root' is no longer active, an 'indefinite multiplicity of secondary roots' have grafted onto it and flourish there. The problem with this is that a certain 'unity subsists, as past or as yet to come, as possible'. Deleuze and Guattari relate this phenomenon explicitly to modernism and William Burroughs's cut-up method is cited as an example in which, despite its foldings and cuttings, a 'supplementary dimension' is implied, suggesting that unity continues to function surreptitiously (Ibid., pp. 5–6, 16–17). Again, while Joyce's novels are multiple in terms of their freeing of word and of language, they nevertheless seem to restore unity in the domains of the 'sentence, text or knowledge' (Ibid., p. 6).

In *A Thousand Plateaus*, Deleuze and Guattari provide a sketch of how all of this pans out in musical terms. While the Western tonal system is identified as embodying an arborescent image of thought, an alternative rhizomatic image is accomplished through what they refer to as a 'generalized chromaticism', in which all of the 'sound components – durations, intensities, timbre, attacks' are placed 'in continuous variation', and through which 'music itself becomes a superlinear system, a rhizome instead of a tree' (Ibid., p. 95). While John Cage is credited with having first produced such music, Boulez's metaphor of composition as the weed-like proliferation of musical material provides sufficient justification for it also to be described as rhizomatic (Ibid., p. 519). It would seem that for Deleuze and Guattari, only music allowing continuous variation on every parametric level can aspire to the condition of generalized chromaticism, whether this be, for example, in Cage's indeterminate works, all kinds of serial and post-serial compositional approaches, graphic score works, free improvisation or electronic music.

Planes, assemblages and milieus

This new rhizomatic type of thought or creative process is further elaborated in the books *A Thousand Plateaus* (1980) and *What is Philosophy?* (1991), as the authors probe its workings and introduce the reader to a more worked-out conceptual apparatus, some of which was familiar from previous works such as *Anti-Oedipus* (1972) and *Kafka: Toward a Minor Literature* (1975), and some of which was new. They now define the two mutually dependent aspects of philosophy as the development of a perspective through the creation of concepts and the tracing of, what they call, an abstract plane of immanence or a plane of consistency. Each concept, which is alternatively referred to as a concrete assemblage, is said to be comprised of indivisible component parts (Deleuze and Guattari 1994, p. 36). It is non-representational, self-referential and defined by the unity of its parts, termed consistency, as well as by the intersections it makes with other concepts, both on its own and on neighbouring planes (Ibid., pp. 22–3). Each plane of immanence is described as 'a table, a plateau, or a slice' on which concepts form points. However, the plane itself is not to be equated with the concepts which have traced it (Ibid., p. 35). Fluid, not static, existing points meet and new points are introduced as the plane is modified, crosses other planes or is fashioned anew from scratch. Such planes of immanence are drawn by lines of flight through processes termed territorialization, deterritorialization and reterritorialization, which describe the movement of points as they form new planes or move from one plane to another (Deleuze and Guattari 1988, p. 270).

Where the plane of organization seeks to restore fixed entities and labours endlessly to block all lines of flight or deterritorialization on the plane of immanence, the plane of immanence is employed in escaping from the plane of organization, attempting to dissolve its fixed functions and to construct itself ever differently from new combinations of concepts or assemblages. For Deleuze and Guattari, there is a continual passage from one plane to the other, between the planes of immanence and organization, though this is something we might not be aware of (Deleuze and Guattari 1988, p. 270). The plane of immanence or consistency is not, however, chaotic. Consequently, they suggest that to avoid a situation where the plane of consistency becomes completely 'undifferentiated', it is 'necessary to retain a minimum of strata, a minimum of forms and functions, a minimal subject from which to extract materials, affects and assemblages' (Ibid., p. 270).

Deleuze and Guattari posit the existence of many such planes, each of which constructs immanence in its own way, and it is suggested that all great philosophers form a new image of thought by tracing their own plane of immanence (Deleuze and Guattari 1994, pp. 50–1). All creative innovation, in fact, is said to involve processes of deterritorialization in which concepts break down and are uprooted from their context only to reassemble with other heterogeneous elements to form new assemblages, perhaps on a different plane altogether (reterritorialization). The Deleuze-Guattarian project consists precisely in the study of these lines, the study of the deterritorializations and consequent reterritorializations by which the elements of an assemblage, which has broken down, come to form new assemblages. Concepts or assemblages are defined primarily by their points of deterritorialization and reterritorialization in a dynamic system which is in constant variation (Deleuze and Guattari 1988, pp. 93–4) and, for Deleuze and Guattari, we can trace the lines of deterritorialization as they fragment an assemblage only to reassemble themselves in ever-new configurations in the process of reterritorialization, thus forming new, and equally transient, assemblages.

For Deleuze and Guattari, historical developments in musical expression have likewise depended upon such deterritorializations, as lines of flight escape from musical assemblages to form new ones. Deterritorialization is defined further in terms of Boulez's concept of the diagonal, which conceptualizes the contribution of an original creator as a quasi-diagonal line which passes between previously accepted horizontal and vertical coordinates. For Deleuze and Guattari, the creative artist or philosopher takes her or his place on an already existing plane, composed of many such lines. The originality of her/his creative effort is thought of as the drawing of a new diagonal line which is not formed simply through the connection of points on already existing lines, in other words, through an eclectic amalgamation of aspects from the work of others. Instead, it forms itself between already existing points and lines and doing so creates a new line in a new space. This new line, this diagonal or transversal, marks out a philosophical or musical territory of its own, one which has never been known before. Consequently, every great musician invents a new diagonal that is irreducible to and passes between previous and current 'harmonic vertical and melodic horizontal' coordinates upon the musical plane. Each diagonal or transversal introduces new techniques and amounts to a line of deterritorialization which traces its own unique coordinates and forms a new plane of consistency (Deleuze and Guattari 1988, p. 296; 1994, p. 191).

This new image of thought is also defined as a 'Body without Organs', a concept which may be equated with the plane of immanence (Deleuze and Guattari 1988, pp. 72, 154) and which can be used of any kind of phenomenon which is viewed in a fluid state of perpetual becoming rather than as an already fully 'organized and integrated' object or thing (Grosz 1994, p. 203). It directs us to make connections with a work and what lies outside of it, since this new image of thought is not concerned with traditional forms of explanation, interpretation or analysis (Ibid., p. 198). Indeed, according to Grosz, it rejects:

> the domination of linguistic/literary/semiological models, which all seek some kind of hidden depth underneath a manifest surface. Rather, [Deleuze and Guattari] are interested precisely in connections and in interrelations that are never hidden, connections, between not a text and its meaning, but, say, a text and other objects, a text and its outside (Ibid., p. 198).

While Grosz's text pertains primarily to the status of literary texts, her description applies equally well to musical texts and practices. She continues:

> It is thus no longer appropriate to ask what a text means, what it says, what is the structure of its interiority, how to interpret or decipher it. Instead, one must ask what it does, how it connects with other things (including its reader, its author, its literary and nonliterary context) (Ibid., p. 199).

The concept of the musical transversal or diagonal, meaning the processes of musical deterritorialization and reterritorialization, is linked by Deleuze and Guattari with that of the refrain or ritornello, an explicitly musical concept, introduced most comprehensively into Deleuze-Guattarian philosophy in *A Thousand Plateaus*. The refrain is a 'territorial assemblage' (Deleuze and Guattari 1988, p. 312) and, just as birds mark out their territories with their songs, musical refrains likewise mark out territories. Deleuze and Guattari speak of refrains, in a general sense, as comprising '*any aggregate of matters of expression that draws a territory and develops into territorial motifs and landscapes*' (Ibid., p. 323). More specifically, the term refers to the sound component within an assemblage. Assemblages, in turn, are said to be composed of all 'kinds of heterogeneous elements' that are drawn from a great variety of different milieus which, for Deleuze and Guattari, are the distinctive parameters or dimensions of a phenomenon.

An ethological example, which illustrates the concepts of the milieu and the assemblage, is the description of the nesting behaviour of a particular species of male wren. This, we are told, consists of 'a dance, clicking of the beak, an exhibition of colours, a posture with neck outstretched, cries, smoothing of the feathers, bows, a refrain'. The discrete elements of this behaviour are each taken from the separate milieus of colour, smell, sound, posture and so on, which all come together to form a territorial assemblage. The originally disparate elements from the varied milieus are now held together as a territorial assemblage by precisely that quality which Deleuze and Guattari refer to as consistency or consolidation (Ibid., pp. 323, 329). As they see it, consistency does not operate by traditional tree systems of thought, but rather through the freer association of elements permitted by rhizomatic thinking (Ibid., p. 328). So it is that 'heterogeneities', which had previously co-existed independently or followed one another sequentially, are now united within the same assemblage without surrendering anything of their heterogeneity (Ibid., pp. 329–30). The only necessary condition for this is that 'the matters of expression' must be such that they make consistency possible.

Assemblages are composed from diverse milieus, and musical sound is only one component among others within a musical assemblage, since it is formed equally from literary, artistic, philosophical and many other milieus, the elements of which are assembled to form an expressive musical territory or refrain. Musical refrains, in turn, are continuously being uprooted and deterritorialized through the working of transversals (Ibid., p. 303).

Musical rhizomes and assemblages: Selective studies

In the monograph *Geste-texte-musique* (1978), published just 2 years after the appearance of the essay *Rhizome*, Ivanka Stoïanova presents a detailed account of the operation of certain works in the traditions of Western art music from the 1960s and 1970s that can unequivocally be described as rhizomatic. Stoïanova writes not of contemporary musical works but of 'musical enunciations' ['énoncé musical'], and she considers the working of graphic score works, 'impulsion texts' ['textes-impulsions'], 'scores of programmed actions' ['partitions-programmes d'action'] and gestural compositions including new music theatre. Unlike traditional works, musical enunciations reject fixed objects, historic formal schemes, architectural structures, conventional narrative and teleology in favour of process, play, experimentation, multiplicity, multi-directionality, plurivalence, discontinuity, heterogeneity, and they disregard all boundaries between genres and art forms, to the extent at times of effacing both the compositional subject and object (Stoïanova 1978, pp. 11–15).

At the beginning of the text, *Rhizome*, Deleuze and Guattari feature an extract from Sylvano Bussotti's graphic score composition *pièces de chair II – Part XIV*, the 'piano piece for David Tudor 4' (1959), chosen undoubtedly in the conviction that it, or a graphic musical score like it, conveys the concept of the rhizome as well or better than any other available visual image. While Deleuze and Guattari do not discuss the phenomenon of graphic score composition as employed in works such as Earle Brown's *Folio* (1952–4), John Cage's *Concert for Piano and Orchestra* (1957–8) or in scores by Bussotti, Haubenstock-Ramati, Kagel, Schnebel and Logothetis, to name only some of the best-known exponents, Stoïanova does so (Stoïanova 1978, pp. 82–4). Graphic scores have no precise or binding outcome in terms of sound, and every realization will be different from every other. While the composer can recognize a particular realization as in or out of line with the piece's aesthetic values, considerable latitude remains to the performer and the visual and audible dimensions assume a different relationship from that involved in the interpretation of traditionally notated Western scores. Graphic scores allow innumerable opportunities for 'deviation, ramification, decentring and pulverisation' thus evading any kind of structural limitation or blockage (Ibid., p. 189).

By 'impulsion-texts', Stoïanova means those musical works such as Stockhausen's *Aus den sieben Tagen* (1968) in which the text impels the performer to produce a particular sound or musical action in the absence of any kind of notated or graphic score. One extract from the text of Stockhausen's piece instructs the performer to 'play a sound, play it for so long until you feel that you should stop' with no indication given of what kind of sound is to be played or of how it is to be played, thus opening up a wide field of possibilities for spontaneous exploration. As with the open form work, Stoïanova notes that performances of such works often fail as performers opt for already-tried and tested realizations in preference to the dangers of the moment (Ibid., p. 86). Mauricio Kagel's *Sonant* (1960) is an example of what Stoïanova calls a 'score of programmed actions' and one of the first compositions in which the composer introduces the concept of instrumental theatre, which he was to use in many later pieces (Ibid., pp. 86–7). The music of *Sonant* is produced by the physical actions performers engage in with their instruments and 'the physicality and kinesis' of their playing is central to the sonic result

(Heile 2006, 35–6). The score for the movement 'fin II – invitation au jeu, voix' is completely 'verbal', and only the actions that are to be undertaken on the instruments are designated.

The final category considered by Stoïanova is that of contemporary music theatre, understood as a kind of 'gesture-action-music-theatre' (Stoïanova 1978, pp. 201–4) in which all boundaries between musical genres and the individual arts are annulled. The work becomes a place where divisions between music, sound, noise, word, writing, action, gestures, light, colour, painting and so on are erased, thus creating a multiplicitous and plurivalent work (Ibid., p. 202). The individual elements can be linked in 'pluri-directional' and 'non-linear' ways to produce multiple, different realizations in which the focus is often no longer on the presentation of a linear narrative. Kagel's *Staatstheater* (1970) is an excellent example of how rhizomatic a work can be. Omitting traditional score, libretto, stage characters and specified stage setting, Kagel subverts expectations of linear narrative and scenic illusion (Heile 2006, pp. 57–8). *Répertoire*, a 'theatrical concert piece', which is the first of the nine parts of *Staatstheater*, is made up of 100 actions which can be ordered freely by the performers in front of a screen. The second piece *Einspielungen* for loud-speakers can likewise be realized in multiple ways as the conductor of the ensemble of instrumentalists and/or singers makes selections from the intervals, rhythmic schemes and intensity schemes provided by the composer. A number of sequences can be performed and recorded simultaneously, and there are three possibilities for performance: a 'live' performance, the playing of a recorded version or the superposition of this 'music for loudspeakers' with other pieces from *Staatstheater* (Stoïanova 1978, p. 205). In the third piece, *Ensemble* for 16 voices, a number of sequences, in the form of parodic clichés of material from the traditional operatic repertoire, are sung successively and are superposed freely on top of one another. The final piece *Parkett* fuses together all of the innovative procedures from the previous pieces and can be realized by anything from 10 to 76 performers. It also includes within itself elements of the sixth and eighth pieces of the work *Spielplan* and/or *Freifahrt* as well as some action sequences from the fifth piece *Saison* (Ibid., pp. 207–8) and, as Stoïanova notes in summary, the entire piece is one great 'reservoir of materials' (Ibid., p. 214).

Deleuze's molecular philosophy has its roots in the work of seventeenth-century philosopher Baruch Spinoza, who theorizes the working of the world in terms of organic and inorganic, human and non-human bodies, which encounter and operate on one another in a multiplicity of ways. In this respect, Deleuze's two books on Spinoza, *Expressionism in Philosophy* (1968) and *Practical Philosophy* (1970, rev. 1981) lay the ground for the rhizomatic thought later developed in *A Thousand Plateaus*. For Amy Cimini, who picks up on the musical potential of this Deleuzian Spinozism, 'listeners, performers, instruments, spaces, musical forms, and sonorous vibration' can be thought of as bodies of equal value, capable of affecting and being affected by one another, in such a way that analysis of the musical work becomes the task of unpicking the relations of the respective bodies which have reached a unified, composite state in the art work (Cimini 2010, p. 137). Cimini is interested in the speculative possibilities inherent in Deleuzian Spinozism, which prompts questions concerning the precise nature of these bodies or 'sound particles' or of how we can think them as affecting one another with their 'micro-movements' (Ibid., pp. 138, 144).

Bruce Quaglia, following Berio's suggestion that every aspect of music is made up of a network of 'Texts', argues that a composer is less the centred subjectivity that is usually presumed to be the case and more what Deleuze and Guattari term a 'desiring machine' (Quaglia 2010, pp. 232–3). Quaglia picks up on Berio's career-long habit of taking up his own earlier works as well as folk music and the work of other composers in order to create something new from them, usually something different from and more open than the source material. A number of the pieces in his virtuosic series of *Sequenzas* for various solo instruments, for example, were transformed thus becoming new works, some of which were titled *Chemins*, with some of the *Chemins* in turn being transformed into further works. So it is that elements of *Sequenza VI* were reworked to form *Chemins II* for chamber orchestra and viola soloist, which itself was reworked to form both *Chemins II b/c* and *Chemins III* for large orchestra and soloists (Ibid., p. 242). On the basis of study of Berio's compositional sketches for *Chemins III*, Quaglia reveals that this final transformation was accomplished by affixing/taping the parts of the pencil score of *Chemins II* onto much larger pages, in such a way that the composition of *Chemins III* 'seems to have proceeded by rhizomatic growth outward from the details of the taped-up score' (Ibid., p. 242).

Challenging the view that jazz works on the basis of the spontaneous exercise of individual freedoms by intentional subjects, Nick Nesbitt posits that all musical creation and expression, not just jazz improvisation, should be thought of as the working of assemblages or of 'asubjective sounding machines' with inexhaustible creative possibilities. Drawing also on the actor-network theory of Bruno Latour, Nesbitt suggests that the kinds of assemblages that are formed in jazz are ones in which a diversity of human and non-human 'actors' are territorialized within an improvisation to form, for example, 'an instrument-club-musician-head-solo-influences-practice-time-mood assemblage' (Nesbitt 2010, p. 159).

Focusing on John Coltrane's experiments in jazz from his introduction to the Miles Davis Quintet in 1955 through his 'spiritual awakening' of 1957 to the moment of the album *Giant Steps* (1960), Nesbitt is interested in the 'systematic investigation of the forms and language of the post-bop jazz tradition' that was accomplished during this period (Ibid., pp. 175–6). Restricting ourselves to the Deleuzian elements of Nesbitt's analysis, the moment from *Giant Steps* to the album *Out of This World* (1962) is lauded as a 'breakthrough' in which fundamental musical coordinates are replotted through the formation of an absolutely new assemblage comprising the selection of pitch modes, 'McCoy Tyner's quartal harmony over perfect-fifth piano ostinatos and bass pedals, the openness of pentatonic melodic material and the churning, kinetic flow of Elvin Jones's polyrhythmic independence and erasure of overt reference to beat'. While many of these components derive from previous assemblages, including African music, blues and spirituals, these forces are reterritorialized in a completely new assemblage with its own unprecedented and idiosyncratic 'musical logic' (Ibid., pp. 178–9).

In a similar way, for Jeremy Gilbert, the improvised jazz-rock of Miles Davis or the German experimental band *Can* are examples of rhizomatic improvisation in which 'the lines between composers, producers, performers and audiences' become blurred (Gilbert 2004, p. 120). Davis's jazz fusion albums such as *Bitches Brew* and *On the Corner* are credited with forming new musical assemblages through both the introduction of electric instruments and the significant involvement of producer Ted Macero (Ibid., pp. 122–3). Macero's contribution was as essential as that of the individual band members, since he edited, tape-spliced and re-arranged parts of the recordings in such innovative and transformative ways that the resulting studio versions became the basis for the live performances given later by the band. German band *Can* operated in a similar way to Davis's fusion groups, improvising for extended periods and then editing the results in equally transformative ways (Ibid., p. 124). For Gilbert, this music with its absence of hierarchy and its 'lateral connections between sounds, genres and musicians' is rhizomatic in its avoidance of any sense of creativity as individual self-expression or of the 'spontaneous purity' of an authentically original performance. In contrast with such rhizomatic musical production, Gilbert suggests that the concept of the orchestral concert is an arborescent one with its static linearity and its hierarchical regulation of creative energy or Deleuzian 'desiring-production' (Ibid., p. 128).

Drew Hemment considers how the phonograph and recording technology form an assemblage which creates 'the material conditions for [popular] electronic music' (Hemment 2004, p. 77). The development of Western 'classical' music, according to Hemment, is dependent upon an assemblage which includes 'technologies of instrument construction and auditorium design, and a whole micropolitics of playing and listening' (Ibid., p. 79). The musical difference that was always the case prior to the age of sound recording relied upon the ephemeral nature of sound and ensured that every performance of a piece of music was different, unique and dependent upon the occasion, individual performers, instrumental forces, acoustic conditions and the placing of listeners in relation to the sound source. All of this changed irrevocably with the advent of sound recording, where the capture of 'a singular snapshot' replaced 'the aura of the artwork with the permanence of the "audio-document"'(Chanan 1995, cited in Hemment 2004, p. 79). Hemment thinks of the development of electronic music as forming 'a counter-history marked by accident, manipulation and reuse that detached itself from the *telos* of representational technologies' (Hemment 2004, p. 80) in that the sound trace produced in a recording now becomes the basis for new re-workings and transformations. Where sound recording was concerned with capturing the most impeccable reproduction of live sound, popular electronic music focused instead on exploiting the possibilities opened up by the unintended and previously undesired circumstantial noises and blemishes which occurred in the recording process (Ibid., pp. 82–3). This resulted in a shift in interest from the actuality of 'live' performance to studio processes, and from the capture of live performance to the creation of sound works formed from the creative possibilities offered up by 'previously recorded sounds, analogue signals and abstracted codes' (Ibid., p. 83).

Hemment reads the development of popular electronic music in Deleuzian terms as the production of a number of successive assemblages each with concomitant processes of deterritorialization, territorialization and reterritorialization. 'Jamaican dub' in the 1970s, for example, focused on remixing, manipulating and reshaping existing recordings, displacing the older studio model with a new molecular assemblage of 'turntables, mixer, amps, speakers, DJs, MCs and crew', that is of 'bodies, technologies and sounds'. Studio production became even more deterritorialized with the appearance of the 'bedroom producer' (Ibid., p. 84), and the migration in the 1980s of house music and techno from Chicago, New York and Detroit, to Europe and the United Kingdom in particular, while transforming European popular music, also resulted in the music's reterritorialization at the hands of the music industry machine. Things molecularized again in the early 1990s when the efforts of entrepreneurs and marketers were undermined by further developments, for example, with the appearance of jungle as a fusion of hardcore and ragga (Ibid., pp. 86–7).

Dusapin, Faust and the Rhizome

French composer Pascal Dusapin, who first read the essay *Rhizome* in 1976, has stated on a number of occasions that it was 'a foundational event' for him, since it enabled him to take leave of the arborescent model of thought which, as Deleuze and Guattari claimed, had previously dominated Western music (Dusapin 2009, pp. 23–4). In the belief that it permitted him to compose 'non-variational' music with 'deviant contours', he states that it 'supported several aspects' of his music and 'liberated [him] totally' (Stoïanova 1993, p. 191). Stoïanova corroborates Dusapin's claims noting that his works, like the Deleuze-Guattarian rhizome, are 'fundamentally anti-genealogical' (Ibid., pp. 191–2) and that his 'formal rhizomes' proliferate in ever-different multiplicities, destabilizing his works by means of 'non-repetition, non-development, de-variation [and] non-exploitation'.[1]

While Dusapin's musical language has changed in a number of ways since the 1990s, the concept of the rhizome has remained an important one for him at a number of levels, which we can consider through his fifth opera *Faustus, The Last Night* (2003–4). This opera, in one night and eleven numbers, is based on Christopher Marlowe's play from 1604 and has a libretto by the composer. Focusing exclusively on Faustus' last night and the end of his 24-year pact with the devil, Dusapin tells us that he developed a new way of working in this opera by drawing on the methods of film-maker Jean-Luc Godard. As with Godard, the text and music of the opera were composed simultaneously, the libretto being formed by the composer from 'bits and pieces of texts, bits of memories of books, miscellaneous citations, from films, newspapers, things heard here or there, in a word from everything that was at hand' (Dusapin 2009, p. 170). The libretto is constructed from ideas and quotations from Marlowe's play, as well as extracts from Dante, Saint Augustine, the Bible, William Blake, William Shakespeare, John Clarke, Gustave Flaubert, Hölderlin, Gérard de Nerval, Caligula, Al Capone, Melville's 'Bartleby', Samuel Beckett, Olivier Cadiot and many others including an unidentified quotation from George W. Bush. Dusapin acknowledges that, 'with the exception of the best-known references', excerpts from other texts are so interwoven with his own contributions that it would be very difficult to identify them. Terming them 'cut-ups', after William Burroughs, they are often simply a few words or phrases which may be 'linked by assonance, meaning or style', and they are subject to 'endless semantic shifts and drifts' (Dusapin 2006, p. 17). Of course, Deleuze and Guattari also cite the example of Burroughs's cut-up method in *Rhizome*, a text which, as has been noted, has had a significant influence on Dusapin (Deleuze and Guattari 1988, p. 6).

Stoïanova refers to Dusapin's 1982 piece *Niobé ou Le Rocher de Sipyle* (1982) as having a 'rhizomatic montage of texts' (Stoïanova

1993, p. 193), and this is equally the case with *Faustus, The Last Night*. Dusapin has drawn attention to some of the ways in which connectivity is exercised in the opera's text: a line which Marlowe gives to Faustus is redistributed by Dusapin to Mephistopheles or, in another place, Faustus repeats the words 'Or do I dream? . . . . I do not sleep: I see, I hear, I speak', originally spoken by the character Sly in Act I/ii of Shakespeare's *Taming of the Shrew* (Dusapin 2006, p. 17). There is no attempt to work through Marlowe's play, and number one in Dusapin's Faustus, for example, begins with the lines 'Adders and serpents. Let me breathe awhile' which are taken from Act V, scene 2 of Marlowe's play. Most of the rest of the text in this short opening number is taken from Marlowe Act II/iii. Number 2 in the opera has a section from Marlowe Act II/iii followed by some of Act V/ii, some lines from St Augustine on the nature of time, Marlowe Act II/iii, a line from Herman Melville's *Bartleby* and eight lines from William Blake's poem 'The Everlasting Gospel'.

In terms of musical composition, Dusapin states that he does not like theories but that he creates systems and methods, the basis for which he often forgets while he is using them (Dusapin 2009, p. 8). In composing he seeks 'points of flight', overflow points, which he imagines in terms of music that is teeming with vegetal growth, like a tropical forest with thousands of proliferating species (Ibid., p. 12). His aim is to discover endlessly 'new ways of increasing flux', and he rejects the idea of basing a work on a 'central idea', opting instead to create 'junctions' which are continuously ramified as in nature (Ibid., p. 22). He is uncompromising in stating that these 'branching models are not trees' since trees contain within themselves an element of replication, of copying, in other words, that aspect of the organic natural model which Webern admired in Goethe. Dusapin believes that he is left with something which 'seems unanalysable' but in which, at a particular level, everything is still interconnected and derived.

In response to the Deleuze-Guattarian rhizome, which Dusapin describes as a 'pretext', he uses the term 'non-development' for the 'wandering and proliferation' within his pieces which avoids any idea of centre and confounds all sense of 'place and topology' (Ibid., p. 96). In terms of means, he explains that 'each time the material arrives at its point of maximal tension' he 'immobilizes it' and then begins again. This results in very short forms that are linked using procedures which he describes as deflecting, curving, connecting, diverting and grafting (Ibid., pp. 96–7). Music, for Dusapin, is therefore 'a pure world' of Deleuzian 'becomings where everything is movement and returns to the movement that engendered it', and where 'to compose, is to never begin, to recommence, or to finish. To compose is to continue' (Ibid., p. 110).

The orchestral writing in *Faustus: The Last Night* is described by Dusapin as 'moving heavily, drawn with sombre and tenebrous musical lines' which he imagines as retracting and expanding in an animalesque kind of way (Ibid., p. 171). He professes to setting out on his compositions without any kind of global plan or vision and that he usually begins 'with the first note of bar 1 without knowing what will happen with bar 2' (Stoïanova 1993, p. 188). In this way, he composes second by second and with only the next two or three bars in mind, a practice he relates again to Deleuzian virtuality (Ibid., p. 193). Beginning, for example, with two pitch classes of the same duration (for example C and D), he plays with the possibilities which the two notes present in terms of repetition as well as rhythmic, accentual and timbral variation (Dusapin 2009, pp. 12–13, 36–7, 121–2). His concern is not with respecting the constraints with which he began but rather with 'the mechanisms which deviate unceasingly from the initial decision' (Ibid., pp. 14–15), and he has an entire vocabulary for the kinds of deviations which his material takes including weaving, distorting, entwining, spoiling, damaging, replacing, corrupting, assembling, braiding, combining, transforming, decomposing and reconstructing (Ibid., p. 17). Discussing his *Piano Etudes*, he says that he begins composition by producing unconnected fragments or sections which arise by themselves and which are then adjusted and connected, separated and assembled, as he places them together (Ibid., pp. 62, 64, 70).

As Jacques Amblard shows, Dusapin's melodic lines are based on speech-like modes which follow the same kinds of modal rules that are observed in speech intonation (Amblard 2002, p. 31).[2] Speech in many languages, it is observed, is often based on quasi-modes made up of a few (four or five) pitch degrees which recur unpredictably. On the basis of this insight, Amblard identifies and sets out a range of 'modal criteria for intonation' in Dusapin's treatment of musical pitch (Ibid., p. 63). In terms of *Faustus, The Last Night*, we can consider the pitch make-up of the first of the work's eleven numbers, which is relatively short at 54 bars. This section of the piece is composed of long-held, shifting harmonies and rhizomatic modal lines in instruments and voices, with pitches that develop in ways that are consonant with the kinds of processes described by Amblard. Ultimately, there is something rhizomatic about Dusapin's entire output. Many of his works make use of material from earlier ones, and he writes of 'secret and furtive links' connecting all of his works, or sometimes particular works, for example, his piano *Études* (1997–2001), the opera *Perelà Uomo di fumo* (2001) and the piano concerto Á quia (2002) (Ibid., 77–8).

Contemporary operatic/music theatre assemblages

Dusapin, apart, the field of contemporary opera and music theatre is one that benefits greatly from consideration in terms of Deleuzian assemblages of heterogeneous forces. This is not something new since opera, at its origins, is recognized widely as being the result of the happy confluence of a number of productive forces including the Florentine *intermedi*, the Renaissance *instrumentarium*, late-sixteenth-century stagecraft and scenography, the rediscovery of Aristotle's *Poetics*, Greek tragedy and the role of the chorus, the Florentine Camerata, a new ideal of song, pastoral drama, monody, declamatory delivery of text and the development of the madrigal (Kimbell 1991, pp. 19–62). It seems that opera is always, by necessity, constituted as a heterogeneous assemblage and that this is no less true of contemporary operatic/music theatre works.

As has been noted throughout this chapter, assemblages are composed of all kinds of heterogeneous elements, drawn from a variety of milieus, which are the distinctive parameters or dimensions of a phenomenon. Contemporary operatic/music theatre works, for example, are formed from an unprecedented array of forces from different milieus, including developments in vocal writing, experimental approaches to narrative and text, plurality of interpretation, mobile elements, multiple stages, lighting, multimedia, electronic sound, dance, new musical idioms, variable instrumental forces and so on. While Wagner in the nineteenth century conceptualized the music drama as the 'total work of art', it remains to early twenty-first century practitioners and theorists to consider the workings of the assemblages that comprise contemporary operatic/music theatre pieces. It is clear that a number of composers working in the field think of their works as assemblages of heterogeneous forces, held together by precisely that quality which Deleuze and Guattari refer to as consistency or consolidation and, in which, musical sound will be only one component among a number of others drawn from various milieus. Part of the problem of contemporary opera and music theatre is the struggle for supremacy that can occur when these competitive art-forms and media possibilities are brought together. Bertolt Brecht in 1930 had already identified the 'great struggle for supremacy between words, music and production', for which his response was to radically separate the elements and resist any kind of fusion which he thought of as a 'muddle' and as the degrading of each art (Brecht 1964, p. 37–8).

For Luciano Berio, who prefers the designation 'musical action' to that of opera, 'music can filter texts in a much more radical way [than before]. It can decide what in a text can be "thrown away", and what should instead take on a dominant role: for example, what can be reduced to acoustic material and what can instead be highlighted with its network of significances intact' (Berio 1989, p. 2). Music can also 'establish the same relationship with the action', there being 'various ways in which it can identify itself with what you see on stage, but it can equally remain indifferent to it'. Ultimately, for Berio, while 'text and music must each have their autonomy, and an analogous degree of complexity and dignity. . . . music must have the upper hand' (Ibid., p. 4).

Aperghis and *Avis de tempête*

The music theatre or operatic works of Georges Aperghis form unique assemblages of components from a wide range of heterogeneous milieus, including images, actions, sounds, music, language, literary texts and technological interventions. Since the foundation of ATEM (*L'Atelier théâtre et musique*) in 1976, Aperghis has developed and experimented with new methods and techniques for the creation of music theatre works in terms of literary construction, musical composition and stage production, each work starting with no fixed plan and in an empirical, experimental way. These works are the result of the molecularizing of musical, sonic, linguistic, gestural and visual material in ways that are consonant with Deleuze's work, so that Evan Rothstein writes of the rhizomatic nature of his music theatre assemblages and of an Aperghis abstract machine (Rothstein 2003, p. 1).[3]

Aperghis's works are multiplicitous assemblages which defy any kind of unilinear reading, and there is always much more happening at any given moment than any human listener or viewer can grasp completely or make conventional sense of. Despite the complex and seemingly anarchic surfaces of his pieces, Aperghis generally employs systematic procedures in generating basic material and, as Rothstein notes (following Daniel Durney), this material is often organized, for the individual aspects of a work, by means of 'oulipian' organizational principles which, while systematic in process, serve nevertheless to destabilize communication (Ibid., pp. 4–5).

Each work has its origins variably in improvisation, in elements that are deterritorialized from a previously composed piece, from aspects of scenography pertaining perhaps to staging, lighting or technological possibilities, from a text, or from all of these at once, and this is then worked on and fixed in more or less definitive form during an intensive period of rehearsal (Rothstein 2003, p. 7). Multiple lines of thought can proceed simultaneously within a work, the various media and parameters in operation either reinforcing one another or in conflict. No order of events is fixed at the outset, since these are assembled in the course of rehearsals through exploration of a great number of possible juxtapositions of materials until the piece emerges. The texts that are used may be original, taken from elsewhere or a mix of the two, in existing language or composed of sounds that belong to no known human language, in paragraphs, sentences, words or merely phonemes (Ibid., p. 8).

Aperghis works with the individual members of a team of disciplinary specialists in developing each aspect of the work independently with their interaction coming later through the 'juxtaposition, modification or transformation' that is worked on during rehearsal time, a period during which particular codes or rules may evolve only to then be modified or discarded altogether (Ibid., pp. 8–9). All of the work that takes place in the studio is geared towards the discovery and exploration of 'lines of connection or of flight between texts, sounds and gestures' and the possibilities they offer. Consequently, each of the participants is a partner in the creation of what is a collective work. Working in this way, a 'Deleuzian "patchwork"' is formed through variation of a restricted number of elements, including the kinds of sounds, words and objects that are often rejected as lacking in value, and Aperghis likes to misappropriate objects, ideas, texts, language, sounds, images and the rest, deterritorializing them from their ordinary contexts and watching as they reterritorialize in new and unexpected ways (Ibid., pp. 9–10).

Avis de tempête ('Storm warning') from 2004, described by Aperghis as a 'real opera' and not musical theatre, is an assemblage that results from collaboration with a librettist, video artist, computer technicians, scenographer, conductor, four performers (two men, two women) and instrumental musicians. It is an assemblage in a state of constant deterritorialization, in which the heterogeneous elements leap from one milieu to another and, where, 'an abstract sound becomes the voice of an actor, a phoneme becomes running water, a character may be divided up and then reconstructed elsewhere' (Aperghis 2005, p. 16). Aperghis's idea at the outset was the creation of a spectacle dealing with all kinds of storms, pertaining not only to meteorology but also to war, the human passions and the financial markets (Houdart 2007, p. 53). While the philosopher and musicologist Peter Szendy was invited to write a text for the work, and he in fact produced an essay on tempests, it seems that the text for the completed work was really conceived by Aperghis featuring, as it does, fragments of texts by Melville, Kafka, Baudelaire, Shakespeare and Hugo.

Szendy's essay which takes Melville's *Moby Dick* as its general starting point, and which was delivered in instalments, allowed Aperghis to clarify the purpose of the piece as he set to work on the production of electronic sound material with Sébastien Roux at IRCAM. Consequently, when he came to write the score, the electronic material had already been produced and Szendy's essay, which became a book in its own right, was almost finished (Ibid., pp. 53–4). While Aperghis describes *Avis de tempête* as a 'fetish reading' of *Moby Dick* (Ibid., p. 66), for Szendy, 'Melville's universe impregnates the entire spectacle' (Ibid., pp. 25–6).

Célia Houdart provides an excellent description of what occurs during a performance of *Avis de tempête*, in which a sense of the piece's rhizomatic working is apparent.[4] The stage setting includes screens, which hang over the stage, as fragments of a presumably shattered sphere. Images of either the faces of the performers or of landscapes are projected onto these screens, become distorted and vanish. Quasi-distress signals are sent from what could be the top of a mast. For Houdart, the whistling and breathing of the orchestra suggest the presence of a beached whale while the figurative and abstract images on the screens may be the real and imagined goings-on inside a human head. A woman spins while speaking of fear and of a storm and the orchestral conductor performs in a scat-like manner. There is a tower which may be a lighthouse or a lightning conductor which a man climbs up onto. Instrumental and electronic sounds pass imperceptibly from one to the other. A solemn choral piece is performed with a detail from the Sistine Chapel relayed onto a screen. The soprano circles round addressing herself to the camera while reciting a fast, rhythmic text. A moment of calm is called for before war-like sounds are heard and 'the performers metamorphose into the electronic components of a video game'. The woman is overwhelmed with a torrent of words and fragments of phrases in French and English, with two cordless cameras in her hands. Everything on the stage seems to swirl round in the image that is projected and she becomes the sole 'fixed point'. There is the sound of a pinball machine, 'phonemes shatter', 'clusters of chords', a foghorn, 'high-pitched notes', 'thunderclaps' and 'explosions'. The conductor announces that 'the text is written on his forehead' and it ultimately 'is written . . . on the bodies of the performers and . . . the spectators', Houdart concluding that 'the end [of the piece] is the beginning of a living book' (Ibid., pp. 18–22).

In terms of the gestation of *Avis de tempête*, which Houdart has documented in a book with extended statements from each of the main co-workers, video artist Kurt D'Haeseleer describes how he and Szendy, stimulated by Benjamin Franklin's essays on lightning, reached a starting point which was 'to construct a sort of exploded sphere with a lightning conductor tower at the centre which would transmit and receive information' (Ibid., p. 27). Movement in the work is 'automatic' and the 'semi-opaque screens are simultaneously windows and membranes'. The images 'form an autonomous system' with its own logic. The actions produced by the singers give the impression of being 'dictated' by the video installation with which they are surrounded while, paradoxically, the video representations are often created by their movements (Ibid., pp. 27–8).

D'Haeseleer describes how in one sequence, the image of actress Johanne Saunier 'is mixed live with a flux of video material' producing 'a purely electronic tempest, an attack of pixels', so that the decisive elements within the image are distorted with 'numerical errors and viruses' (Ibid., p. 28). The video images are often exaggerated or blurred, subjects are not completely identifiable and images shift. Houdart describes how an image of 'flat blue sky' swirls and becomes abstract until we realize that we are actually looking at a mouth. Faces and landscapes exchange properties as 'a lake becomes an eye, an eyelash a fern' (Ibid., p. 77). The performers carry mini-cameras in order to film live images that are mixed with recorded images to the extent that it is unclear where the live and pre-recorded sequences begin and end. The images produced by D'Haeseleer emanate not from real-life dramas but are 'fragments of fictitious catastrophes replayed in socially identifiable and ludic surroundings' (Ibid., pp. 77–80) and, as Houdart notes, the screens are shaped in 'the form of a broken cranial box', which suggests that in viewing the work, the audience member penetrates into her or his own mental space (Ibid., p. 80).

Sébastien Roux, who worked on the production of electronic sounds, describes how the piece mixes material for acoustic instruments and voice with electronic material. The electronic sequences were created in advance of the instrumental part and inform it, punctuating the score and providing a 'timbral and spatial counterpoint to the orchestra' (Ibid., p. 33). Instrumental and vocal samples are transformed electronically in ways suggesting 'malfunctioning', and Aperghis established a vocabulary of themes which Roux could use to create 'computer tools' or 'storm machines'. Drawing on the notion of a 'virus', and William Burroughs's cut-up techniques, a number of processes were decided upon including the use of granular synthesis in which sound samples are cut up into fragments of a millisecond and then rearranged aleatorically to form complex sound objects. Other processes include the virus-like introduction of numerical errors into the instrumental samples; the modification of instrumental timbres using artificial multiphonics and vocal/instrumental sonic hybrids and, finally, the production of noise through manipulation of the partials of sounds (Ibid., pp. 35–6).

A lengthy period of experimentation followed in which Aperghis and Roux manipulated the sound samples produced by the four soloists and the instrumentalists in different ways. Combinations of the procedures were tried out on the samples resulting in several hours of sounds, which were then assembled and superposed until they arrived at satisfactory sequences for diffusion in performance (Ibid., p. 36). Outcomes were favoured where the sound blocs cut into one another in such a way that a sound develops only to be cut off by another sound, where sounds bump into and respond to one another, and where order is disturbed to the point of being destroyed altogether (Ibid., p. 53).

The literary text for *Avis de tempête*, which cannot be summarized, was formed simultaneously with the music, Aperghis describing its gestation as 'instinctive' (Ibid., p. 56). There is no linear narrative, and all narrative continuity or sense of cause and effect is avoided. A wide range of vocal possibilities is used, including speech, singing, murmuring and yelling to the point that the instrumental and the vocal are not always clearly distinguishable. Signification in the work operates precisely in non-semantic ways, and it is not important whether words or phonemes are spoken or sung since they are capable of being understood, for the most part, to a minimal degree (Ibid., pp. 88–9). The staging consists purely of screens, mini-cameras, a tower and a ladder, and while the score consists in the proliferation of fragmented and agitated gestures, Aperghis wanted staging that was 'calm' and reduced (Ibid., pp. 60–1). The performers who are equipped with mini-cameras, operate according to the principle that 'they never address themselves to the public', addressing themselves only to the cameras and making sure throughout that they are 'in the frame' (Ibid., p. 64).

In all of his operatic/music theatre works, Aperghis recognizes the possibility of a 'polyphony, consisting of many micro-languages, capable of creating a physical or emotive energy resulting in violent confrontations between the meaning of an image or a sound, and a significance which is purely formal' (Aperghis 1993, p. 113). This leads him to take on 'the uncertainties of arranging sounds in relation to images, texts [and] gestures', and he suggests the need to replace the traditional notion of the libretto with a new kind of score which co-ordinates everything, directing both primary and secondary events, text, lighting and gestures, and arranging not just 'sound' but rather all of the components in the assemblage from their respective milieus (Ibid., p. 114).

Goebbels and Neuwirth

Like Aperghis, Heiner Goebbels, who is not interested in institutional opera on the grounds that it has too many constraints and conventional divisions of responsibility, works from the beginning of a project with an entire team of specialists, including a camera operator, sound, light and stage designers and others, developing all of the elements simultaneously. Following Brecht, Goebbels subscribes to the 'separation of elements', and he prefers to develop individual theatrical elements which are then introduced piece by piece. To take only the case of 'light', his goal is to work not only with the visibility of the performers in mind but more fundamentally 'in a way that respects the light bulb as a sculpture or that is able to develop the force of a light itself as an artistic force' (Goebbels, in Tusa 2003). This means that he has 'to work with light from the very beginning, from the very first rehearsal' since if he were to introduce this or any other element later in the process, it would lose importance and become merely 'illustrative'. All of this is achieved practically through improvisations, pictures, sounds, scenes, and over a period of several months, after which he brings some order to the piece, to its words, costumes, staging and so on, all the time trying to avoid producing any kind of hierarchy between the components. In this way, he produced a series of brilliantly innovative music theatre works including *Eraritjaritjaka* (2004) for string quartet which works its way through the twentieth-century string quartet repertoire, with one actor who enunciates selected texts by Elias Canetti, spoken throughout in French translation. Again, this is not story-telling, but, as Goebbels says 'letting an audience have an experience' (Goebbels 2007). There is a complete separation of text and body, and voice and image are seemingly independent resulting in what Goebbels identifies at one point as an 'irritating separation of hearing and seeing'. For Goebbels, theatre is a 'reality shift', not a way of making statements about reality, and he cites Canetti, for whom 'the different arts should live together in the most chaste relationship'.

In a similar way to Aperghis and Goebbels, Olga Neuwirth explains that in her music theatre piece *Lost Highway* (2002–03), based on the film by David Lynch, she played 'off the various levels against one another (stage area and persons "against" video projection, narrative fiction "against" non-narrative fiction, music played live "against" recorded music, objective "against" subjective), i.e. closing the gap between the elements', and she states that her interest lies in the deconstruction of 'images and sounds/music by means of a discourse about perception, as a way of showing that there are images and sounds that work according to a certain logic and can also be manipulated' (Neuwirth 2006, p. 38). While neither Goebbels nor Neuwirth invoke Deleuze in theorizing their work, it seems clear that their music theatre pieces involve assemblage type processes every bit as much as those of Aperghis. Indeed, while a more extensive discussion of their distinctive cooperative working methods would undoubtedly be instructive, it is beyond the scope of the current chapter.

Bernhard Lang, assemblages, difference and repetition

The final example of a musical assemblage that we will consider in this chapter is the music of Austrian composer Bernhard Lang, who integrates elements from a range of styles and sound worlds within his compositions including free jazz, DJ culture, noise music, electronic music as well as aspects of contemporary classical music. Not only are his compositions innovative assemblages uniting elements from a range of heterogeneous musics, but many of them are also based explicitly on Lang's understanding of Deleuzian difference and repetition. To this extent, they demonstrate very well the intrinsic relations linking difference, repetition, the rhizome and the assemblage.

Sharing Schoenberg's aspiration that musical material should be varied continually, Lang avoided repetition in the music he composed before his encounter with Deleuze's *Difference and Repetition* in 1995, an event he describes as having awoken him from his 'dogmatic slumber' (Lang 2002, p. 1). This discovery transformed his understanding of repetition and stimulated the creation of a series of around 30 pieces composed between 1998 and 2013 with the titles *Differenz/Wiederholung* or *DW*, after the German title of Deleuze's book. While the DW pieces relate also to the cut-up/fold-in techniques of William Burroughs, the poetry of Christian Loidl and the videos of Martin Arnold, Deleuze's ideas are of undoubted importance for them.

Lang refers to himself as a 'repetition-perpetrator'. Having begun to transcribe improvisations around 1994, by around 1997, he was improvising and transcribing DJ culture-based loops, a practice he describes as 'a mutual process of transcribing and re-transcribing improvised repetitions and written out repetitions' (Lang 2002, p. 2). He was fascinated by the possibilities presented by 'erratic, asymmetrical loops' particularly as the result of a jump by a turntable needle or the unexpected vibration emanating from a malfunctioning CD player (Lang 2004, p. 7). His first essays in transcribing loop sequences produced by turntable artists such as Phil Jeck and film-makers such as Martin Arnold into notated material for classical instruments coincide with the beginning of the *DW* series. Of *DW 1* (1998), where he attempts to transcribe vinyl loops for a trio of flute, cello and piano, he draws attention to 'the interplay of different repetitions, of repeated differences contained within the loose form of a notated improvisation: found structures, tiny objects, brought into view by the augmenting effect of repetition, continuously being forgotten and recovered' (Lang 1998).

As with many of the pieces in the series, Lang revised *DW 1* in 2002 as *DW 1.2* for the new combination of flute, tenor saxophone and piano and the piece featured prominently in the 2002 *SWR New Jazz Meeting* at Baden-Baden where it was adapted and remixed by various combinations of jazz musicians (including soprano saxophonist Steve Lacy), classical improvisers and performers on turntables and electronics. This meeting resulted in a large number of versions of *DW 1.2* and the production of three CDs containing Lang's original composition along with 17 remixes for various combinations including solos, duos, trios and quartets made up from the various jazz, new music and electronic forces, as well as a nonet featuring all of the participants.[5] Three musicians from each genre were involved, producing what Reinhard Kager describes as 'a fluctuating dialogue between jazz, new music and electronic music'. Attempts were made to 'overcome the mutually felt shortcomings' in terms of the 'formal vagueness' that sometimes results with free improvisation and the lack of spontaneity that is sometimes the case with contemporary composition as 'jazzy grooves, electronic sounds and formal coherence were allowed to intermingle' (Kager 2003). As Kager notes

> remixing . . . essentially meant that the loops inherent in the composition took a new, decisive turn depending on the creativity of the improvising jazz instrumentalists, the tonal feeling of the electronic musicians, and the integration of the three "classical" musicians, who not only interpreted Lang's original composition but also took part quite freely and naturally in the remix improvisations (Kager 2003).

Having worked intensively with *DW 1.2* at first individually and then collectively for a week in the studios in Baden-Baden, the three trios then performed the material live in concerts in Tübingen, Freiburg and Karlsruhe where they followed certain principles whereby

> in each concert the jazz trio was to play alternately with one of the three electronic musicians; secondly, each evening all nine musicians were to play together once; thirdly and most importantly in the order of events, each evening *DW 1.2* was to be performed in the original version, divided into four parts, to draw attention to the difference between the improvisations and the original (Kager 2003).

The experience of *DW 1.2* suggested to Lang the further possibility of integrating these methods within a notated score thus 'using compositional material to combine improvisatory methods and actual performing practices' (Lang 2004, p. 7). He relates how

> *DW8* draws on passages from *DW11* played by the Symphonieorchester des Bayerischen Rundfunks and recorded to vinyl before being mixed by the two turntable artists in live performance, their entries being given a defined structure. The orchestra becomes a kind of gigantic record player, the plethora of loops and more well-known sounds emerge in a context of repetition and may be perceived or understood anew (Ibid., p. 7).

Lang describes his approach to the creation of loops in some detail, identifying key elements of his practice and providing a taxonomy of loop types. Loops are formed from recorded samples from within which a brief segment of around 200ms to 7000ms is defined and repeated (Lang 2002, pp. 3–4). Samples can be manipulated substantially by the variation of the speed of their unfolding, being either stretched or compressed. He reveals that the *DW* pieces feature 'several phenomenological types of loops' according to 'technical differentiation', amount of silence, circularity, symmetry and 'the modulation of the loop within the repetitions', each of these types being further differentiated into even more precise sub-categories (Ibid., pp. 4–6).

In addition to the development of loop techniques, *DW2* contains short texts by Burroughs and Loidl as well as a number of brief citations from the text of Deleuze's *Difference and Repetition* referring to difference, repetition, habit, contraction, 'a single clamour of Being for all the beings' and the 'living present' (Lang 2000, pp. 8–13). Difference is palpable in multiple ways in *DW2* including the apposition of contrasting musical styles and types of sound in each movement, with elements of free jazz, free improvisation, noise music, experimental electronic as well as contemporary classical music. There is also the difference produced by the sounds of three heterogeneous vocalists where, as Jan Jagodzinski notes 'the incomprehensible voice of a Kurdish singer, the stuttering, yet trained voice of a classical singer, and the rapid fired verse of a rapper, form a mix of difference which *forces* us to feel the contours of the words as sound images by their stuttering, repetition, and pithy alliteration' (Jagodzinski 2000, p. 6).

Conclusion

Throughout this chapter, it has been suggested that all innovative music is formed from numerous kinds of unexpected rhizomatic connections, the coalescence of heterogeneous forces from a variety of milieus including musical form, social practice, the development of instruments and instrumental techniques, musical systems, notation, performance styles and practice, developments in technology, the specificity of performance spaces, the possibilities within particular musical institutions, the means of recording and reproduction of music, music's relationship with literature, visual arts and philosophy and innumerable other factors.

Rhizomatic thought and the Deleuze-Guattarian assemblage have been considered in relation to a range of musicians and writers who draw explicitly on Deleuze as well as those who do not. We have considered Stoïanova's classification of assemblages as musical enunciations, including graphic score works, 'impulsion texts', 'scores of programmed actions' and gestural compositions. Cimini has highlighted the Spinozan origins of the Deleuzian assemblage as an encounter between bodies or sound-particles. Quaglia, after Berio, suggests that the musical assemblage can be the product of multiple texts. Nesbitt and Gilbert have shown how we can conceive aspects of progressive jazz in terms of the assemblage while Hemment uses it as an explanatory tool in discussing several generations of sound recording technologies. We have discussed the impact of the Deleuze-Guattarian rhizome on Dusapin's music and theory, including the production of the libretto and melodic writing for the opera *Faustus, The Last Night*. Finally, we considered the multi-disciplinary music theatre assemblages of Aperghis, Goebbels and Neuwirth and the difference/repetition-based assemblages of Bernhard Lang. By necessity, the discussion has been selective, and while it is hoped that it has shown the working of the assemblage in relation to a wide range of musics and repertoires, it has not been possible to take account of the great number of references to the Deleuze-Guattarian assemblage that have been made to date in music studies. Perhaps no other Deleuze-Guattarian concept has been embraced so enthusiastically by writers on music.

In positing the concept of the assemblage along with a rhizomatic image of thought, Deleuze and Guattari direct attention away from the agency of the composer to the mobile and transient forces active within a particular musical artwork or repertoire. In doing so, they offer an alternative to music histories which account for innovation in terms of evolutionary change that is linear and progressive, the result perhaps of successive mutations or logical deductions. Nor is music history to be conceived of as the result of any kind of Hegelian dialectical negation, where elements of a previous aesthetic are rejected through the agency of a revolutionary event. Nor again are works to be explained in terms of a Marxist base-superstructure model where aesthetic materials are always subsidiary to contemporary economic systems and the means of production pertaining within a given situation.

It may be that musical assemblages can be classified into types along the lines of Deleuze's classification of cinematic montage types. It is also possible that the Deleuze-Guattarian assemblage could be taken in conjunction with Jacques Rancière's concept of the sentence-image, which offers a way to think the play of specific aesthetic forces in relation to one another. Once again, all of this lies beyond the scope of the current study. While rhizomatic thought and the assemblage are implicit throughout all of the discussions in this book, we will return to the assemblage explicitly in Chapter 5 where we will consider it this time in relation to semiotics, sign functioning, multiple regimes of signs and the planes of content and expression that, for Deleuze and Guattari, are produced within assemblages.

3

Rethinking musical pitch: The smooth and the striated

One of the most important preoccupations linking Deleuze with his great predecessor Henri Bergson is a fascination with the ideas of continuity and discontinuity and, like Bergson, Deleuze takes up this opposition in relation to the dimensions of space and time. In Chapters 3 and 4, a range of music will be considered in relation to Deleuze's post-Bergsonian thinking of spatiality and temporality in terms of the continuous and the discontinuous. The core idea in Chapter 3 is centred on the way in which music at times may be said to inhabit striated, that is variably divided and discontinuous, pitch spaces that contrast with the possibility that pitch space may be smooth, undivided and continuous. In a similar way, Chapter 4 is concerned with approaches that theorize and attempt to actualize variably discontinuous and continuous notions of musical time.

The concepts of the smooth and the striated that are used by Deleuze and Guattari in *A Thousand Plateaus* are taken explicitly from the work of Boulez but, as always, they are developed in unexpected ways. While this chapter will focus almost exclusively on the smooth and the striated in terms of pitch spaces, the philosophical reflections presented by Deleuze and Guattari show that these concepts can also be useful to music studies in other ways.[1]

In *A Thousand Plateaus*, smooth space is opposed to any number of traditionally striated spaces, understood as two distinct models or images of thought. Consideration of any important English language musical dictionary or encyclopaedia shows the extent to which music is, at any given time, thought in terms of concepts that are largely determined historically and culturally, and that are far from exhausting everything that we might understandably refer to as music. Comparison of fairly recently published work in the areas of musicology, music theory and history shows that the conceptual fields for dealing with music in English, French and German language studies, to take only some key examples, are by no means the same. Each philosophical and musicological culture and language favours certain ways of thinking about music over others and seems, for the most part, oblivious to the conceptual divisions of the others. In a sense, each culture may be said to striate the musical totality rather differently in terms of conceptual thinking. The subject matter of Chapters 3 and 4 therefore concerns topics that are more often dealt with in French language publications than in English language studies.

Defining musical space

While music may be said to exhibit spatiality in two discrete senses, which we can characterize as (1) interior spatiality (the pitch space continuum) and (2) exterior spatiality (the arena in which a musical performance occurs), the present study restricts itself to those aspects of interior pitch space that are conceived of as some kind of continuous or discontinuous spectrum of sounds.[2] While the spatiality of sound goes beyond pitch and can also be understood to include the distinctive timbre of instruments or other sound sources, this chapter focuses for the most part on pitch space and the notion of a pitch spectrum.

In a study devoted to interior spatiality in music from Schoenberg to Cage, Francis Bayer identifies musical spatiality as a major, but nevertheless neglected preoccupation of many twentieth-century composers, both in their theoretical writings and in their compositions. He recognizes that all music may be said to take place within or to form an individual pitch-space since modality, tonality and chromaticism can all be viewed from this perspective as a variety of ways of exploring pitch space. From a spatial perspective, tonal music can be thought of as tracing paths through pitch space by means of the system of keys and their modulation to distinct, but related regions. Analogous with this, dodecaphonic music, as theorized and practiced by Schoenberg, Webern and Berg, traces alternative paths through pitch space, by means of the 12-tone series with its 12 transposed forms, retrogrades, inversions and inverted retrogrades. These can be manipulated whole, as in Schoenberg, or motivically, as in Webern, whose series exploit particular intervallic characteristics in order to enable the generation of entire pieces.

Bayer is fundamentally correct in affirming that, while spatiality is an inherent quality within all music, contemporary music brings the idea to our attention more clearly than any previous Western music (Bayer 1981, p. 9), and his purpose is to account as precisely as possible for the varied musical spaces which are formed in the acoustic (non-electronic) music of several key figures from Schoenberg to Cage. This undertaking stems from the conviction that Modernist music reveals music's spatial qualities in ways that are not quite the case in most other music. Instead of confirming old listening habits and revisiting familiar sound spaces, Modernist music often seeks to open up new, perhaps previously unimagined, musical spaces for the listener (Ibid., p. 201).

Regina Busch, who has explored the place of interior spatiality in the writings of the Second Viennese composers, acknowledges it as one of a number of terms that are used innovatively in their work. While Schoenberg, Webern, Berg, Spinner, Stein and Rufer all make mention of pitch space, it is never defined clearly, and Busch suggests that it would be problematic to presume that Schoenberg always used the term in the same way (Busch 1985, pp. 4–6). In the 1934 version of the essay 'Composition with Twelve Tones', for example, he writes of 'the law concerning the unity of musical space', and in the 1941/50 version, he distinguishes the properties of this musical space from those of the physical world (Ibid., p. 8). Schoenberg's notion of a unified musical space was important also for Webern who, in turn, developed his own metaphorical spatial understanding, which he discusses in his lectures.

Smooth and striated pitch space

It seems that the microtonal theorist and composer Ivan Wyschnegradsky (1893–1979) is responsible for the introduction of the concepts of musical space, of simultaneity, and the notion of a continuum of sounds, into the musical sphere, certainly in a French context. In the article 'Musique et Pansonorité' (1927), an early formulation of his views, he declares that 'the principal problem in music' is '*the antithesis of the continuous and the discontinuous*, an antithesis which is manifested nowhere (except perhaps in higher mathematics) with greater clarity and relief than in musical art' (Wyschnegradsky 1927, p. 144). He acknowledges, furthermore, that this antithesis has been treated 'magisterially' by Bergson (Wyschnegradsky 2005, p. 62).

Unlike Deleuze, Wyschnegradsky's reflections are embedded in an essentially dialectical account of music history, and in *Une philosophie dialectique de l'art musical* (1936; 2005) and *La Loi de la Pansonorité* (1953; 1996), two posthumously published versions of his theory, Western music is conceptualized as having developed through three successive stages, each of which is transitory and preparatory. Accordingly, medieval modality is replaced dialectically by tonality, which is itself replaced by a number of supratonal forms (atonality, metatonality, ultratonality or microtonality) which find their consummation in pansonority (Jedrzejewski 2005, p. 8; Wyschnegradsky 2005, p. 14). Without entering into the details of Wyschnegradsky's quasi-Hegelian notion of a dialectic containing within itself moments of negation and *Aufhebung* (overcoming) (Wyschnegradsky 1996, p. 60), the key point in relation to Deleuze is the idea that music can aspire to the condition of pansonority understood as a 'new constructive principle' centred on the concept of musical spatiality (Ibid., p. 71). Furthermore, this pansonorous opening up of the pitch space is inextricably linked at various points in time with a number of significant cultural assemblages, of which it is the product. While Deleuze rejects dialectical philosophy outright along with its historicist and progressivist narrative, it is in Wyschnegradsky's Bergsonian opposition of the continuous and the discontinuous, his explorations of ever smaller pitch denominations and his quest for a completely smooth pitch space (Boulez's term) that we find material that is Deleuzian *avant la lettre*.

More specifically, it is interesting to view the taxonomy of pitch spaces, which Boulez set out in his Darmstadt lectures under the rubric of the smooth and the striated, in the light of the codification of spatial types produced earlier by Wyschnegradsky. In *La Loi de la Pansonorité*, the 1953 version of his study, the Russian composer distinguishes between total and partial spaces, where partial space is further divided into regular (or uniform) spaces and irregular spaces, and where this last category also includes semi-regular spaces. There are also periodic and composed spaces (Wyschnegradsky 1996, pp. 159, 189), and he defines the three essential properties of musical space as 'uniformity, infinity and continuity' (Ibid., p. 118). Where Boulez proposes the possibility of a curved space, Wyschnegradsky had already noted that if the more standard octave is thought of as constituting a straight line throughout the pitch space, then the replacement of the octave with the interval of a seventh or ninth has the effect of curving the pitch space, and he suggests that a non-octave space is always richer than an octave space (Ibid., pp. 164, 172).

Wyschnegradsky is Boulez's most explicit predecessor in presenting a morphology of musical spaces, and there was no shortage of avenues whereby he would have become familiar with the older man's ideas. It is interesting to note that Deleuze was also aware of Wyschnegradsky's work through the auspices of Pascale Criton, who became involved with the philosopher's seminar quite by chance in 1975. While Deleuze drew on her knowledge of chromaticism and the sound continuum for his seminar,[3] Criton also met and studied with Wyschnegradsky from 1976. In the early 1990s, Deleuze read several drafts of the essay which she later published in 1996 as her introduction to *La Loi de la Pansonorité*, and which she dedicated to the philosopher (Dosse 2007, pp. 525–6).

In his Darmstadt lectures, which are undoubtedly the most systematic formulation of his ideas, Boulez identifies 'the conception and realisation of a *relativity* of the various musical spaces in use' as an urgent objective (Boulez 1971, p. 83).[4] He calls for the exploration of musical pitch space and says that the musical space-continuum 'is *manifested* by the possibility of *partitioning* space according to certain laws' (Ibid., p. 85). He acknowledges two main pitch space states, which he terms striated space and smooth space. Striated space is marked by a standard, regular measure, which creates clear perceptual landmarks for the ear to orient itself, whereas smooth space is free, irregular and dispenses with all points of reference. While Western music, including serialism, has mostly retained the traditional 12 semitonal striations of tempered space, any number of alternative ways of striating pitch space could theoretically be adopted, allowing for the limitations of human perception, and the restrictions imposed by the state of conventional instruments, which were designed with traditional tempered space in mind. Boulez envisages any number of possible striations being enacted upon untempered sound space, and he acknowledges the possibility that the pitch series, as he has expounded it, can be used in 'any tempered space, according to any temperament, and to any non-tempered space, according to any module, whether it be the octave or some other interval' (Boulez 1971, p. 83; 1991, pp. 117–18). Series could thus be formed of intervals which no longer conform to any homogeneous measure, such as the semitone, and could include any number of intervals.

The possibility of structuring music on the basis of alternative intervals and temperaments was of course not original to Boulez. In non-Western music, for example, Indian music, the minute subdivision of pitch space and the notion of an unpartitioned continuum are commonly accepted, while in Western music, the minute subdivision of pitch space and the possibility of a seamless continuum were taken up not only by Wyschnegradsky, but also by Carrillo, Hába, Varèse, Partch and others, and it stimulated their microtonal explorations. Varèse, for example, who described equal temperament scathingly as 'the octave's cheesewire' (Boulez 1991, p. 174), used sirens in works such as *Amériques* as a way of producing a smoother space than was enabled by the semitones of the tempered scale (Varèse 1998, pp. 204–5).

In the Darmstadt lectures, having elaborated the principle of striated space, Boulez next lays out a taxonomy of possible striated spaces, such as straight spaces, where an 'unvarying module reproduces the basic frequencies over the whole range of audible sounds ... *curved spaces* ... which depend on a regularly or irregularly variable module ... *regular spaces* ... which always adopt the same temperament whatever the module', and *irregular spaces* which do the reverse (Boulez 1971, pp. 86–7). While he theorizes the possibility of such variably striated spaces, it is not known whether these ideas have ever been actualized in compositional terms, and it may be that they have remained within the realm of speculative theory.

Smooth space, in contrast, 'can only be classified in a more general fashion ... by the statistical distribution of the frequencies found within it'. The smaller the partitions or the micro-intervals within a striated space, the closer it will be to being conceived of as an unbroken smooth continuum. Boulez was realistic in acknowledging, at the time of writing in the early 1960s, the practical difficulties involved in attempting to produce such smooth musical spaces, given a situation where music theory was in advance of instrumental technology. He looked admiringly, at least in 1952, to Cage's experiments in producing non-tempered sound spaces with already existing instruments, courtesy of his prepared piano with its eccentric appendages. Likewise, Pierre Schaeffer's *musique concrète* appealed at first to him, on the basis that it would allow him to work with non-tempered sound spaces. Beyond the studio, however, there simply were no instruments at that time capable of transferring ideas of smooth space and various types of striations (pitch divisions) from the realm of theory to that of live performance practice.

Despite such logical and consistent theorizing, most of Boulez's compositions are in fact restricted to the exploration of striated space and, at that, the traditional striations of equal temperament. The opposition of smooth and striated pitch spaces occur in his own compositions primarily as a means of articulating form, and he perhaps comes closest to achieving a smooth pitch space, or at least a more flexibly striated one, in *Répons* where the pitches of the solo instruments are transformed electronically. While striated space is clearly marked out through the conventional use of tempered instruments, smooth space is suggested through the complex simultaneities produced by the resonant tuned percussion, through the dense abundance of trills and lastly, through the electronic transformation of pitch.

Smooth and striated space in Deleuze and Guattari

Whatever the practical musical difficulties, Deleuze and Guattari picked up Boulez's concepts of smooth and striated space in *A Thousand Plateaus* as they had done with the notion of the pitch diagonal. According to Brian Massumi, '*A Thousand Plateaus* is an effort to construct a smooth space of thought' (Massumi 1988, p. xiii), and an entire plateau (chapter) is devoted to 'The Smooth and The Striated'. The Boulezian origin of the concepts is acknowledged followed by discussion of a variety of models of smoothness and striation in technological, maritime, mathematical, physical and aesthetic contexts (Deleuze and Guattari 1988, pp. 474–500).[5] Such models represent merely a few of the multifarious 'aspects of the two spaces and the relations between them' which Deleuze and Guattari could have chosen (Ibid., p. 475). They contrast the vertical and horizontal striations of embroidery with the smooth, amorphous nature of felt. They refer to the sea as the 'smooth space par excellence' that becomes increasingly striated for navigational purposes. The sea is consequently described both as 'the archetype of smooth space' and as 'the archetype of all striations of smooth space: the striation of the desert, the air, the stratosphere', and it is contrasted with the city, the paradigmatic striated space (Ibid., pp. 479–81).

For Deleuze and Guattari, Boulez makes these fundamentally different spacing types perceptible through music, and he is said to be:

> concerned with the communication between the two kinds of space, their alternations and superpositions: how a 'strongly directed smooth space tends to meld with a striated space', how 'a striated space in which the statistical distribution of the pitches used is *in fact* equal tends to meld with a smooth space'; how the octave can be replaced by 'non-octave-forming scales' that reproduce themselves through a principle of spiraling; how 'texture' can be crafted in such a way as to lose fixed and homogeneous values, becoming a support for slips in tempo, displacements of intervals, and *son art* transformations comparable to the transformations of *op art* (Ibid., p. 478).

While Deleuze and Guattari describe Boulez's theory of pitch space beautifully, their reflections are in fact far from purely musicological and serve their own distinct and very different purpose. They use Boulez's opposition of smooth and striated pitch space (and all of the other smooth and striated spaces) as models to enable them to articulate two distinct images of thought, smooth thought and striated thought. They wish to oppose traditional striated representational philosophy which they term 'State philosophy' with what they call 'Nomad thought'. In Massumi's words

> The space of nomad thought is qualitatively different from State space. Air against earth. State space is 'striated', or gridded. Movement in it is confined as by gravity to a horizontal plane, and limited by the order of that plane to preset paths between fixed and identifiable points. Nomad space is 'smooth', or open-ended. One can rise up at any point and move to any other (Massumi 1992, p. 6).

In other words, nomad thought is the smooth, rhizomatic thinking of difference that is opposed to the striated, arborescent thinking of identitarian State philosophy. They say that Boulez 'makes palpable or perceptible the difference between non-metric and metric multiplicities, directional and dimensional spaces', rendering them 'sonorous or musical' (Ibid., p. 477). Deleuze articulates this special relationship between music and philosophy when he says that philosophy is 'an unvoiced song, with the same feel for movement that music has . . . . not a matter of setting philosophy to music, or vice versa' but rather of 'one thing folding into another: "fold by fold," like Boulez and Mallarmé' (Deleuze 1995, p. 163).

It is important to acknowledge once again that Deleuze and Guattari use Boulez's musical concepts for their own philosophical purposes. They seem to equate striated pitch space with the production and organization of 'horizontal melodic lines and vertical harmonic planes' while smooth space is said to constitute 'the fusion of harmony and melody', in other words, the diagonal dimension (Deleuze and Guattari 1988, p. 478). Whatever the philosophical validity of conflating Boulez's ideas of smooth and striated space with the concept of the pitch diagonal, the resulting conjunction of concepts produces only musical confusion. Boulez's pitch diagonal is the result of compositional processes which result in music which is neither primarily melodic nor harmonic in the sense of horizontal or vertical. The diagonal dimension is consequently independent of whether or not a composition is based upon the fixed or variable intervals of a striated space, or instead upon the kind of smooth pitch continuum made possible by electronic and computer technology.

Despite a lack of specificity in their reflections on music, with Deleuze and Guattari, the concepts of the smooth and the striated move beyond the Boulezian universe and become more widely applicable concepts for thinking music. While they appropriate Boulez's terms to theorize smooth and striated spaces of thought, when these terms are re-appropriated for the musical sphere, they no longer refer to Boulez's work in any privileged way, becoming instead rather elegant concepts for thinking all kinds of music in terms of the continuous and discontinuous treatment of pitch. The concepts go beyond the musical sphere and indicate that the play of the continuous and the discontinuous at work in the variable treatments of musical pitch space has much also to tell us about peoples, societies, politics and culture in terms very similar to those employed by Deleuze and Guattari when they oppose traditional and striated representational philosophy or 'State philosophy' with 'Nomad thought'.

Tonality as the dominant Western system for striating and organizing musical pitch

Central to this chapter is the contention that the distinction of State philosophy and Nomad thought, as the striated and the smooth, presents us with two productive concepts for considering a range of issues relating to musical pitch. What is common to the discussions that follow is that in each case, a dominant tradition or practice is in operation that is often thought to be the most authoritative, the most important system available, and against which all contenders are generally judged unfavourably.

From a Deleuzian perspective, there is a problem with any kind of pitch system that is promoted over all others, thus permitting only one model of striated pitch space without even considering the possibility of smooth space. While modality and chromaticism have an assured place in music's past and present, this is not at the expense of other possibilities. The situation is very different with tonality which, as a developing phenomenon, is common to all European art music from the late seventeenth to the early twentieth century, informing music from Bach to Brahms and Wagner. Even today, tonality is still by far the most prominent musical system for all kinds of Western music from popular music to the work of those contemporary composers who pride themselves on a return to tonality, sometimes articulated as the reinstatement of true values after the unfortunate adventures of musical modernism.

The growing chasm between the majority of listeners and the various streams of modernist, avant-garde or experimental composition, is testimony to the problem and gives seeming support to those who wish to argue that the discrepancy arises in part from a failure to acknowledge the natural basis of tonality and its consequent superiority over what are seen as merely ersatz, human constructs. Such scholars and composers posit that tonality cannot be compared with other musical systems since, unlike them, it is natural. Composer and theorist Paul Hindemith claims that it is 'a natural force' (Hindemith 1942, p. 152), that the triad 'corresponds to the force of gravity' (Ibid., p. 22) and that in his own work he was working with timeless musical laws derived from nature.

Already in the nineteenth century, the physicist Hermann Helmholtz could state, on the basis of his unprecedented research into acoustics, that there is no more justification for accepting the diatonic major scale as a 'natural product' than for holding the same of the 'gothic pointed arch' since 'both are necessary and *natural* consequences of the principle of style selected' (Helmholtz 1954, p. 236). For Schoenberg, the major-minor system, despite its greatness, is nevertheless a historical product that is subject to change. It is not the telos or end-point of musical development, and it is only one of an indefinite number of possibilities. For Boulez, 'lack of respect for the natural order', in other words, for tonality, is one of five main arguments that 'unrepentant fetishists' use against modern music (Boulez 1986, p. 33). He responds by noting that 'neither the minor triad nor equal temperament are "natural" so much as familiar to our ears' and that all musical systems are simply working hypotheses developed in response to the problems facing individual historical periods (Ibid., pp. 41–2).

While acoustics and elementary arithmetic would seem to offer some support to claims that tonality is based in nature, the science of sound is not so straightforward, and those properties that are often lauded as the greatest benefits of tonality are shown to be not so much the result of nature in its pure state as the product of human ingenuity. Without denying the great value and effectiveness of the system of equal temperament, the form in which we most often encounter tonality today, this, as we will see, is far from being a neutral value. The reflection on the smooth and the striated that we find in Deleuze and Guattari goes well beyond Boulez's laying out of a seemingly neutral taxonomy of pitch spaces and is charged with ideological force in a move that seeks to unmask all dominant values as authoritarian, thus promoting what we might call minor, nomadic musical spaces.

Where tonality has at times been presented as the acme of an evolutionary movement stretching from the Middle Ages to the late Baroque/Classical and Romantic periods, this narrative poses a number of problems which will be tackled in the course of this chapter. This progressivist, teleological view fails to acknowledge that tonality did not emerge in any kind of definitive form and that it has been constantly changing and developing. The assertion of tonality as natural and superior to all other systems is hopelessly ethnocentric in its favouring of Western musical values and its denial of the resources that facilitate the microtonal sophistication of other ethnic musics.

Without using the term, Kenneth Levy identifies certain aspects of 'ideology' in what is most often presented as a seemingly disinterested, scientific justification of tonality. Tonality is valued in this view as a sustainer and reinforcement of a security that goes beyond the musical to encompass what are often termed conservative or traditional values. This is the case with neoromanticism or with the kinds of approaches favoured formerly by composers and pedagogues such as Leonard Bernstein and today by figures like John Adams. As Levy notes, tonality is also often used as the basis for certain types of religious music that seek to kindle religious 'fervour', to which we could add the predominance of tonal means in overtly political music. Ultimately, as Levy points out, the continued popularity of tonality generates colossal amounts of money within the capitalist system (Levy 1988, pp. 301–2). Despite all of this, Levy proposes that the physics of sound, history and anthropology all undermine the idea of tonality's inevitable return since within history it is primarily change that is inevitable (Ibid., p. 302).

Even if we acknowledge the inevitability of change and the historically conditioned nature of tonality, there are certain ambiguities in Deleuze's relation to the principle of the 'emancipation of the dissonance' whereby Western music history has not been working towards tonality but rather towards the ever-increasing emancipation of dissonance or of Wyschnegradskyan pansonority. Steven Shaviro picks up on this point in a study of Deleuze and the philosopher Alfred North Whitehead, where he questions 'Deleuze's implicit endorsement of the modernist narrative of the progressive expansion and liberation of harmony in Western concert music', culminating in the work of 'composers like Boulez' (Shaviro 2009, p. 26). This is found most explicitly in *The Fold* where Deleuze writes of 'the musical model' as 'the most apt to make clear the rise of harmony in the Baroque, and then the dissipation of tonality in the neo-Baroque: from harmonic closure to an opening onto a polytonality or, as Boulez will say, a "polyphony of polyphonies"' (Deleuze 1993, p. 82). Again in *What is Philosophy?*, together with Guattari, he writes of 'not only the enlargement of chromatism to other components of pitch, but the tendency to a non-chromatic appearance of sound in an infinite continuum (electronic or electro-acoustic music)' (Deleuze and Guattari 1994, p. 195). It is perhaps a fault line in Deleuze's work that his forcibly non-historical and overtly non-historicist philosophy seems in fact to endorse some kind of progressivist narrative in relation to the opening up of pitch space.

The exploration of this possible aporia will not be taken further within this study which instead will focus on a number of ways in which pitch space has been treated in terms of the two central values that form Deleuze's thinking of the smooth and the striated. We will consider a number of issues relating to pitch in terms of the continuous and the discontinuous, the smooth and the striated, though evidently these terms are most often not employed. While doing this, the discussion will also focus on the distinction of State philosophy' and 'Nomad thought' in the conviction that, as Deleuze and Guattari suggest, the smooth and the striated are not neutral, ideologically free terms. The formation of Western scales along with equal temperament and the equally tempered semitone may be described as the state-sponsored paradigm of a contemporary scale, in relation to which all other contenders are deemed defective. Composers working in the fields of microtonality, electroacoustic and computer music may also be thought of as Deleuze-Guattarian nomads, charting new coordinates in more finely striated pitch fields, sometimes to the point of almost smoothness. This music, which again can be contrasted with more traditional models, very often fails to register in the paraphernalia of the state concert hall apparatus and is often not included in standard histories of contemporary music. The historic, alternative striations of pitch space that are encountered in other musical cultures, for example, in Javanese and Indian music, have not always been understood in sufficiently independent terms, at times being subjected to the idiosyncrasies of essentially Western theory. Once again, we are not dealing with disembodied musical phenomena, but rather with the formation of significant cultural forces which undergo all kinds of transformation as a result of transversal processes of deterritorialization.

Striated space: Alternative striations

The tempered space of Western music, where the octave is normally divided into 12 equal parts, is only one possibility among innumerable others since the total sound space is capable of being divided in any number of alternative ways. No matter the size of interval chosen for the striation of a given scale or mode, this can always be further divided, at least in theory, to infinity. In other words, the musical sound space, understood as pitch space, is capable of being striated in a great number of ways, and in the areas of musical acoustics, microtonal composition and ethnomusicology, we find some of the most interesting examples.

Equal temperament and its Western others

All musical modes and scales are formed from series of pitches placed on a continuum. The pitch scale can be thought of as deriving from a harmonic series, an acoustical phenomenon in which any given pitch that is sounded produces not only the dominant pitch which is heard (the fundamental) but also a sequence of higher pitches that stand in fixed relations to the fundamental. It is easiest to explain the components of the harmonic series in terms of pitch frequency by which is meant their number of vibrations per second. If the fundamental sound has a frequency of 100 vibrations per second (100 Hertz), further sounds will resonate simultaneously with it at 200 Hz, 300 Hz, 400 Hz and so on, in simple ratios of 2:1, 3:1, 4:1 and so on. In this way, the musical intervals which form the modes and scales customary to Western music can be seen to correspond to simple ratios as follows: octave (2:1); fifth (3:2), fourth (4:3); major third (5:4); minor third (6:5). There are also two intervals which lie between a minor third and a whole tone (7:6 and 8:7); a large whole tone (9:8), a small whole tone (10:9) and after that increasingly smaller intervals which go on to infinity, producing ever more remote overtones (Duffin 2007, p. 21).

Despite the simplicity of these frequency relationships and their ratios, the formation of satisfactory modes and scales is not so straightforward, hence the multiplicity of systems that have been developed. Pythagorean tuning, for example, favours the ratio 3:2, in other words, the interval of the fifth. Beginning on a low note on the piano, for example, the lowest pitch class 'C', it is possible to form what is a called a circle of fifths by progressively tracing a continuous sequence of fifths until one arrives back at pitch class 'C', 12 fifths later, at the other end of the piano keyboard. In this way, the following sequence of pitch classes [C-G-D-A-E-B-F#-C#-G#/Ab-Eb-Bb-F-C] is formed. This process can be completed (though not on the piano) beginning from any given note.

The theoretical and practical problem for the formation of scales arises from the fact that a series of 12 acoustically pure fifths of ratio 3:2 does not result in any return to a previously sounded pitch class such as 'C' but rather arrives at a point about a quarter of a semitone too high to be appreciable as being in octave relationship with the initial pitch. A clear discrepancy is noted in number and in sound between the arrival point when seven octaves are traversed (7 x 2:1) as opposed to 12 fifths (12 x 3:2), a discrepancy that is referred to as a 'comma'. While pianos are normally tuned nowadays in such a way that we return to the initial pitch class after the completion of a sequence of 12 intervals of a fifth, this is the result of a system of tempering, of adjusting each of the 12 intervals by the amount of exactly 1/12th of the difference between the two arrival points, that is, the discrepancy between a series of seven pure octaves and 12 pure fifths (Duffin 2007, pp. 23–7). Equal temperament has the effect of narrowing all of the fifths by 1/12th of the overall discrepancy, and in so doing it also widens the fourths to the same degree. Where fourths and fifths are generally acceptable within equal temperament, since they are only about one-fiftieth of a semitone away from the acoustical ideal, it is the interval of the major third which causes the greatest concern, with the major third about a seventh of a semitone wider than the acoustical ideal of a 5:4 ratio, and the minor third equally narrow (Ibid., pp. 27–9).

The system of equal temperament is an efficient solution to the problem of producing a workable 12-note division of the octave, and while it is the one we have become most used to in Western music, it is important to realize that it is not 'natural', that it is a compromise solution for a very difficult problem, and that it is by no means the only available solution. A number of musicians and experts in tuning systems dispute its privileged position, arguing that it does not sound as well as other possibilities and that it entails the loss of other equally important musical qualities. In *How Equal Temperament Ruined Harmony* (2007), Ross Duffin rails against equal temperament as 'a given for generations of musicians through most of the twentieth century and into the twenty-first. They think in ET. They tune in ET. They hear in ET. Notes in ET are "in tune", and everything else is "out of tune"' (Ibid., p. 17). A musical universe in which equal temperament is dominant is, for Duffin, 'the result of decades of delusion, convenience, ignorance, conditioning, and oblivion' (Ibid., p. 16). He notes that it was only in the mid-nineteenth century that equal temperament became a standard to strive for, that it was paid 'lip service' from around 1850 and that 1917 seems to be the pivotal year that marks the beginning of its victory over all other contenders. From this time, 'tempering became a skilled science based on universally accepted mathematical principles' (Jorgensen, cited in Duffin 2007, pp. 104, 112, 138).

While Duffin acknowledges that, in contemporary practice, string quartets and chamber music ensembles often integrate elements of just intonation with its pure fifths, fourths and thirds in preference to the impurity of equally tempered intervals (Ibid., p. 69), this is insufficient to assuage the sense that equal temperament still occupies an unjustifiably dominant place. Despite not working within a Deleuzian framework or referring to the philosopher at any point in his argument, it seems nevertheless that equal temperament exemplifies for Duffin what Deleuze and Guattari refer to as State philosophy.

There are a number of alternatives to equal temperament which can, at least in a contemporary context, be viewed as nomadic alternatives to the dominant 'state' view. The system of just intonation strives for exclusively pure intervals, an outcome which requires that the pitch of notes can be varied flexibly in accord with momentary need, something which is only possible with voices and certain instruments. There are also a number of mean tone temperaments, and tuning systems can also be either regular or irregular in their division of the octave. While equal temperament is the best-known exemplar of a regular temperament, where all of the intervals are the same size, in irregular temperaments, the intervals can be of different sizes (Ibid., p. 39). Irregular temperaments include among their number the so-called 'good temperaments' or 'well temperaments' which can be employed without adjustment for a range of keys. There are also 'circulating temperaments' which do not need to be adjusted for use in any of the 12 keys, albeit that by definition, the irregularity of the intervals entails that all keys do not sound the same, having their own distinctive characteristics and qualities (Ibid., pp. 36–7).

In just intonation, unlike equal temperament, there is no enharmonic equivalence so that each member of the following pairs of pitches is a distinctive pitch [C#/Db, D#/Eb, F#/Gb, G#/Ab, A#/Bb]. Furthermore, music theorists, going beyond the limitations of the 12-note equally tempered scale, recognize the existence of major and minor semitones which are small intervals within the span of the whole tone in non-equal tuning systems. This introduces the difference between diatonic or major semitones and chromatic or minor semitones, where the former denotes intervals such as D#-E and the latter refers to intervals such as Eb-E, the former being larger than the latter. In other words, between pitch classes D and E, an instrumentalist or singer can choose either D# or Eb depending on context (Ibid., pp. 51–3).[6]

The octave can in fact be striated into any number of equal parts, the main tuning systems being those that divide it into 12, 19, 24, 31, 43, 53 and 55 intervals (Duffin 2007, p. 55; Benson 2008, p. 217). The composer Lou Harrison has used a 16-tone just scale. Vincentino (1555), Christiaan Huygens (1691/1724) and Adriaan Fokker (1945) worked in different eras with the 31-tone equally tempered scale, and Charles Claggett divided the octave into 39 parts (1788). While it seems that the Pythagoreans knew of the 53-tone equally tempered scale, Robert Bosanquet produced a keyboard harmonium with 53 notes to the octave in 1876. Beyond 53, 'the next good denominator' is an equally tempered 665-tone scale which, while giving 'a remarkably good approximation to the perfect fifth', falls down on the fact that 'the adjacent tones are so close together . . . as to be almost indistinguishable' (Benson 2008, p. 217). One of the most detailed ways of thinking the possible striations of pitch space is the division of the octave into 1200 cents, an infinitesimal denomination based on a logarithmic scale, introduced by Alexander Ellis in 1885, and an alternative to the previous system where intervallic values were enumerated in terms of commas. In Ellis's system, the equally tempered scale can be enumerated as having 100 cents in a semitone, 200 in a whole tone, 400 in a major third, 700 in a fifth and 1200 in an octave. At this point, we approximate to smoothness and to the molecularity of Deleuzian thought.

Microtonality in music from Carrillo to Partch

The resources we have considered from the point of view of tuning systems have been explored in all kinds of ways by a number of twentieth- and twenty-first-century composers who work with microtones, understood as all intervals smaller than the semitone. As we have seen, microtones are not a twentieth-century invention. Aristoxenus in the fourth-century BC mentions a chromatic modal scale with two intervals in quarter tones, and intervals smaller than a semitone are found in a range of vocal music from around the world. While microtones occur in the production of vibrato, glissandi and the miniscule pitch inflections employed by singers and string players, these are not truly microtonal, and the term is generally reserved for musical systems which employ intervals smaller than a semitone.

A small number of composers and theorists working in the first half of the twentieth century became all too conscious that the traditional tempered system of 12 tones was an arbitrary grid or striation of musical pitch space, which entailed the systematic neglect of the multiplicity of achievable pitches nestling between the semitones. The Mexican Julián Carrillo, the Czech Alois Hába and the Russian Ivan Wyschnegradsky are the three most important figures experimenting with microtonality in these years. Carrillo, who first worked on micro-intervals around 1895, managed to produce micro-intervals as small as a sixteenth of a tone on his violin, and he writes in his treatise *Sonido 13* (1948) of how he was 'seized' in 1895 with the 'supreme aspiration of filling the space with an infinite number of sonorities' (Bayer 1981, p. 110). Indeed, his sixteenth-tone music entails an octave that is striated into 96 equal divisions.

Hába and Wyschnegradsky, who it seems knew nothing of Carrillo's work, began their own independent research into micro-intervals. Hába, who produced a *Treatise on harmony, for diatonic, chromatic systems, in quarter, third, sixth and twelfth-tones* (1927), was particularly interested in quarter-tones which he saw as simply an enlargement of the equally tempered scale of semitones and which had the effect of providing 24 quarter-tone pitches within the octave in place of the standard 12. Like Hába, Wyschnegradsky, whose taxonomy of musical spaces has already been noted, also conceives the use of microtones as a way of extending tempered chromatic possibilities. He favours scales with numbers of octave divisions related to the number 12, a restriction he insists upon on the basis that it involves no break with Western music's 12-tone chromatic past, while enabling him to develop it further. However, in the course of his development, he works also with conventional tunings with third-, quarter-, sixth-, eighth- and twelfth-tones (Ibid., 114–15).

Hába and Wyschnegradsky are both engaged primarily in extending the pitch resources bequeathed by tradition, and quarter-tone scales become here a development of the traditional, equally tempered scale. Despite the adventurousness of their vision and the new pitch resources they made available, neither was able to compose music that was equally enterprising. Carrillo's compositions, despite their micro-intervallic resources, are written in a late-nineteenth-century idiom that retains fairly traditional means of articulation and Hába's style is almost a rather curious late-Romanticism achieved by quarter-tone means. He was undoubtedly interested in integrating into Western art music, intervals that were already in use in Czech folk music. While Wyschnegradsky's music is perhaps more successful in melding content and form, many of his best pieces seem to recall certain rather perfumed aspects of Scriabin. To this extent, neither Carillo, Hába nor Wyschnegradsky really attain the status of a Deleuzian nomad since the power of the 'state' ultimately proves itself too strong for them, recuperating their exceptional gains within essentially 'sedentary' contexts at the edge of state territory.

This is not the case with the music of Harry Partch, all of which is composed for instruments which he designed and constructed himself and which are tuned to a microtonally extended just intonation scale (Gilmore 1998, p. 2). Two points in particular are striking about Partch's music and theory, namely, the range of scales he worked on and the social reasons for his embracing of microtonality including his defiant rejection of traditional pitch spaces.

Working from the harmonic series and with just intonation as his permanent ideal, Partch decided to make the eleventh partial the 'limit' point for the generation of intervals, which means that all of the intervals he uses can be traced, in the first instance, to those 'between any two of the first eleven elements of the harmonic series, and the inversion of these intervals' (Ibid., p. 63).[7] Starting from a given fundamental, this process generates, in all, 29 microtonal pitches within the octave. Since, however, there are considerable discrepancies in the sizes of adjacent intervals in this scale, with some rather wide gaps and other rather narrow ones, Partch decided to split the wide gaps even further in order to produce a more evenly spaced scale, which he achieved by adding pitches, described later as 'secondary ratios'.

The number of secondary ratios in Partch's scale varied between 1928 and 1935, encompassing, at various times, 29, 37, 39, 41 and 55 tones, before he finally decided on the 43-tone scale that is analysed in *Genesis of a Music*, his great treatise. As Gilmore notes, the numerous changes in the make-up of Partch's scale is much less important than the consistent theoretical framework which underpins his work throughout all of the changes. Having abandoned the imperative for 12 pitches to the octave in the late 1920s, he maintained the importance of a scale with a set number of degrees while, at different moments, changing the number of tones within the octave.

Partch's process for generating new intervals or secondary ratios, by dividing them into ever smaller ones, is theoretically limitless but restricted in practical terms by the limits of human perception (Gilmore 1998, pp. 63–4). His 43-note scale 'contains all the interval relationships found in the twelve-tone chromatic scale, as well as many others derived from the unfamiliar seventh and eleventh partials' (Ibid., p. 65). He stopped at the eleventh harmonic because he believed that the thirteenth harmonic was not really properly perceptible (Ibid., p. 67), but as with many other aspects of psychoacoustics, this very much depends on the capacities of individual listeners.

Partch's rejection of 12 tones within the octave and his quest to open up the pitch space is not solely the result of a disinterested love of acoustics. In Helmholtz's *On the Sensations of Tone* (1885 ed.), he found rational support for the provisional, compromised and imperfect nature of the equally tempered system of 12 tones to the octave and for the legitimacy of his efforts to restore the qualities of pure intervals in just intonation as well as the use of a wider range of intervals. As Gilmore shows, Partch's work arises from a struggle between the musical values of an implanted and alien European culture dating from the eighteenth and nineteenth centuries, with its intonational system, equal temperament and concert traditions and a more fundamental relationship with musical harmony and acoustics which, for Partch, was coherent with a 'deep and abiding tie with peoples and animals and things removed in time and space' (cited in Gilmore 1998, pp. 35–6, 41–2). Equal temperament is dismissed not only as a tuning system but as the conceptual means whereby musical thought is restricted (Ibid., p. 69). The piano keyboard is described as 'twelve black and white bars in front of musical freedom', preventing exploration of alternative pitch resources (Ibid., p. 53). Unlike Hába and others, Partch also refuses the use of quarter-tones since these are simply divisions of equally tempered semitones which in fact support the system that he wants to go beyond (Ibid., p. 88).

It is difficult not to make connections between Partch's innovative striations of musical pitch space and the itinerant nature of his life, particularly during the years 1935–41 when he wandered throughout the Western part of the United States. The collective title *The Wayward* was given in 1956 to the works *Barstow*, *San Francisco*, *The Letter* and *U.S. Highball*, which all feature 'spoken and written words of hobos and other characters' picked up during his time on the road (Ibid., p. 155). To this extent, a certain nomadism is evident in both Partch's life and in his attitude to Western musical culture and its pitch spaces which suggests that his life and music exemplify very well the kind of nomadic spaces theorized by Deleuze and Guattari in opposition to state spaces or sedentary spaces. No other composer seems to have argued so explicitly against tonality, the equally tempered scale and the entire Western musical apparatus in a way that is so concordant with Deleuze's work.

Striating pitch space in Indonesian and Indian music

The idea that pitch spaces can be thought of as Deleuzian nomadic or sedentary/state spaces with political and cultural as well as musical value is one that emerges equally from ethnomusicological studies of pitch. In contrast with Western tonality, microtonality has historically been integral to many non-Western cultures including music from India, Arabia, Persia, Turkey, Indonesian gamelan music, Byzantine liturgical music, as well as Middle- and Eastern-European folk music.

In Southeast Asia, and most particularly Java and Bali, gamelan tuning has an elasticity which means that it varies significantly from ensemble to ensemble in terms of both pitch and interval size. There is no one authoritatively standard tuning for the pitches that comprise the two main scale-types, the five-note *sléndro* and the seven-note *pélog*. This elasticity or variability in tuning is to some extent the result of seeming indifference to any concept of absolute pitch, as well as the product of particular tuning practices and the gradual changes which take place within the metals used for the manufacture of instruments (Rahn 1978, p. 69). Furthermore, in Balinese gamelan, pairs of instruments are tuned 'slightly apart from one another' producing a 'beating' effect (Kartomi 2007–13). In terms of the striations of the two main scale-types, it is normally the case that five-note modal selections are made from the seven pitches of the *pélog* scale, and in Central Java, both scale-types are usually divided into smaller modes. In the five-note *selisir*, the most frequently encountered Balinese tuning, the pitches are unequally spaced.

For over a century, differences in gamelan and other non-Western scales have been calculated for the most part in terms of Alexander Ellis's unit of the cent, a practice which putatively enables the measurement and conceptualization of 'the intervallic structure of nonharmonic scales' in a way that is generally considered both scientific and objective. It is a method which seems to bring 'mathematical purity' to the task of studying the tuning systems of societies and cultures separated by place and time, and it seems that the approach has been used in relation to Javanese gamelan music much more than with any other musical culture (Vetter 1989, p. 217).

As Vetter notes, Ellis's cent system stimulated a scientific and speculative approach to non-harmonic tuning systems which concentrated primarily on 'the analysis of numerical data generated from tone measurements of artifacts, i.e., fully-tuned gamelan sets'. Vetter suggests that a 'different perspective' may be attained if instead of calculating cents, ethnologists were to focus on the 'study of tuners in the actual process of tuning' (Ibid., p. 218). The work of previous scholars is questioned to the extent that it presumes that gamelan tone measurements are static and consistent facts rather than something in a process of slow evolution, facilitated by natural changes in the materials and the interventions of those engaged with tuning. Ultimately, Vetter fears that scholars have been more concerned with 'abstract numbers' and insufficiently attentive to 'tuning as an artistic and functional aspect of musical behavior' (Ibid., pp. 219–20).

As Hardja Susilo notes, Javanese musical culture is more tolerant than Western practice in allowing greater variation in tuning systems, and intervallic relationships are considered as 'not comfortable', 'not quite comfortable', 'more comfortable', 'comfortable' or 'very comfortable' in place of their binary Western differentiation in terms of right and wrong (Ibid., p. 220). Ultimately, Vetter argues that Javanese tuning systems are incapable of being explained solely in terms of cents and that reducing them to 'numerical representations' and subjecting them to 'Western patterns of analytical logic' are not likely to yield genuine insight (Ibid., p. 226). It may be that Vetter's judgement applies just as well for many other attempts to think non-Western music in terms of essentially reductive Western scales of measurement. While Ellis's system is invaluable in allowing miniscule measurements of pitch to be made, it is important to recognize the degree to which such measurements remain exogenous Western constructs that are often alien to endogenous understanding of pitch striations. Ellis's model becomes once again the means by which all kinds of heterogeneous pitch spaces are homogenized or are judged deficient in relation to a Western exemplar. The expectation is that all systems or practices should submit to one form of rationalization, thus making all pitch spaces comprehensible in terms of one homogenous 'state' model.

The political import of what Deleuze and Guattari have to say on the smooth and the striated is found also in the work of Lewis Rowell for whom 'the history of musical tunings is at the same time a history of politics, imperialism, colonialism, resistance, and submission, in which there were both winners and losers'. He judges that 'we delude ourselves if we believe that some musical systems disappear and others survive solely on the strength of their intrinsic excellence or the ingenuity of their proponents' (Rowell 2000, p. 150). This insightful remark is made in the context of a study of 'Scale and Mode in the Music of the Early Tamils of South India', where he attempts to account for the importance of the pitch collection of 22 tones that is found there. He discovers 'a series of nested pitch collections' comprising 5 pitches within 7 within 12 within 22, which he believes may be the only surviving example of such a pathway within an early civilization (Ibid., p. 153).[8]

Rowell infers that the importance of 22 lies not in its divisibility or its resistance to division but rather in 'its ability to represent the pitch relationships inherent in the diatonic scale' (Ibid., pp. 147–8), and he suggests that this early Tamil system with its numerical pathway of 22, 12, 7 and 5 pitches may be symptomatic of a 'political compromise' between the ways in which the then indigenous Tamil population and the incoming Indo-Aryans envisaged and experienced their music (Ibid., p. 150). For Rowell, the advent of early modal systems is in need of much greater elaboration, and he judges that 'our confidence in the inevitability of the systems and grammars of pitch organization in Western music is shaken – or ought to be shaken – whenever we come in contact with the radically different scales and modes of the old high musical cultures of Asia' (Ibid., p. 136).

Transformation is not just the case in South India, and Rowell has also charted the development of pitch resources across the Indian subcontinent. The distinction is made in ancient Indian music theory between a *svara* and a *śruti*, a *svara* being either 'an abstract pitch class, a scale degree' or 'a melodic element, a scale degree in a melodic context' (Powers and Widdess 2007–13). *Srutis*, in contrast, are 'the potential divisions of the pitch continuum, an unheard musical substratum of background sound' in which the octave is divided into 22 'unspecified microunits' (Rowell 1992, pp. 145–6). While there is no agreement as to the exact size of the *śrutis*, some argue for an equally divided octave into 22 *śrutis*, others hold that the *śrutis* were unequal and a third group claim that the question was never settled, the interval sizes being determined approximately in the process of oral transmission (Rowell 1992, pp. 146–7).

Invoking, like Bergson and Deleuze, the opposition of the continuous and the discontinuous, Rowell thinks of the *śrutis* as constituting a kind of background pitch continuity in relation to which the *svaras* become manifest (Ibid., p. 150). In practical terms, each scale degree or *svara* is identified with the upper limit of a pitch band consisting of two, three or four *śrutis*, a rather different conception from the Western notion of a pitch as a point (Ibid., p. 151). As Sathyanarayana states, the *śrutis* 'are not regarded as discrete, self-contained and independent entities but as the locus traced by the *śruti* moving vertically in a tonal continuum' and the *svaras* 'are regarded as those regions of the continuum where there is manifestation, illumination, or expression'. For Rowell, this amounts to 'subtle motion along a continuum of pitch' which 'becomes manifest in the form of individual sound events, each a microworld of sound variations, oscillations and transitions', the paradox of a music which is at once 'both atomistic and continuous – projecting the illusion of a sensuously moving stream of sound while traversing a network of fixed points' (Ibid., pp. 151–2). Accordingly, scale degrees in early Indian music are not 'fixed positions' but rather 'bands of tolerance' which allow for a great deal of variation. Citing an important but unnamed Indian musician, Rowell notes that 'a note is not a point. It is a region to be explored' and that perhaps 'to be a note' entails working within a small frequency range rather than striking a precise point (Rowell 2000, p. 153). In identifying the importance of the concept of pitch band for early Indian music, Rowell highlights the specificity of particular pitch spaces which are not at all homogeneous, and he makes clear in the process that the atomized pitch conception that is prominent in the West is not the only way.

Spatial continuity (glissandi, clusters and clouds)

While the introduction of micro-intervals indisputably narrows the gaps between pitches, it also results in sound spaces that are much more concentrated in their striations. Even where the intervals separating adjacent pitches become so infinitesimally small as to be imperceptible to the human ear, this still does not result in an absolutely smooth sound space, and it is clear that in many cases both temperament and spatial discontinuity are maintained. Consequently, it can be said that all scales and modes, no matter how small the intervals involved, subscribe by definition to an 'aesthetic of discontinuity' that can never be overcome, since an intervallic gap is capable of being divided even to the point of infinity (Bayer 1981, p. 122).

While it is impossible to produce a truly smooth sound space, composers have succeeded in creating a sense of pitch continuity in a number of ways, though this has not always been their manifest intention. Francis Bayer is correct in recognizing the possibility of an 'aesthetic of continuity' which is contrasted with the 'aesthetic of discontinuity' that has been the case with the musical systems discussed to this point (Ibid., p. 122).

Independent of the temporal unfolding of the musical work, Iannis Xenakis's conception, perhaps unsurprisingly for a composer who was also an architect, is primarily a spatial one in which pitch structures are key. In contrast with the essentially linear and punctual nature of serial structures, Xenakis produces spatial structures in which the individual sound is unimportant in its own right acting instead as an infinitesimal particle in a global mass of sound. The listener focuses on the general global movement of the sound mass as it shifts register within the ensemble without being able to follow the movement of the individual particles.

In *Pithoprakta* (1955–56), the Maxwell-Boltzmann theory of gases is drawn upon to form a music in which individual sound molecules are distributed within the complex sound mass in a manner akin to the speed and movement of gas molecules. Pitch and duration are distributed probabilistically in the form of glissandi as the work progresses by means of the continuous and gradual transformation of the sound material. The 46 string instruments in the score were chosen on account of their capacity to produce smooth glissandi, the possibilities they offered for the production of sound masses and their wide timbral range, especially when the percussive sounds yielded by the bodies of the instruments are added to their more traditional palette. In addition to glissandi, clusters are also employed and in bars 60–104, a large single cluster is sustained in which each string instrument has a different pitch, and a continuous texture is maintained in bars 122–71 (Matossian 1990, pp. 102–3).

An aesthetic of continuity is also discernible in the micropolyphony or 'saturated polyphony' of the works composed by György Ligeti between 1958 and 1968, most notably *Apparitions* (1958–59), *Atmosphères* (1961) and *Lontano* (1967). Following his arrival in Cologne in 1956, and stimulated by the experiments undertaken in the electronic music studio of West German Radio, Ligeti transferred something of the sonic textures made available by the electronic medium to the orchestral sphere. What he came to call, micropolyphony is first found in the second movement of *Apparitions* where the counterpoint is so dense that individual voices can no longer be heard for the most part and the listener's attention is focused instead upon changes in texture and register. At certain points in the score, there are 63 staves to accommodate the individual parts given to each instrument.

In *Atmosphères*, Ligeti produces a micropolyphonic sound space in which clusters and glissandi are prominent, the work opening (bars 1–13) with a vast chromatic cluster which traverses over five octaves and which is held statically before decreasing gradually in magnitude until only the violas and cellos are left in a reduced sound space of just over one and a half octaves. Out of this reduced cluster, an even bigger cluster forms throughout the entire orchestra in bars 13–22 over a span of almost six octaves which, while registrally stable and static in terms of pitch content, has constantly changing dynamics and timbre. This second cluster, which begins at the end of bar 13 with the entire mix of strings and wind instruments, is reduced in bar 20 to a string cluster, and we become aware of two key components, a diatonic cluster and a pentatonic cluster which emerge in turn from the saturated texture before amorphousness is restored.

Glissandi are used by Ligeti as a means of shifting gradually from one bounded cluster to another, and in bars 63–4 of the first movement of *Apparitions*, for example, he engineers, by means of bands of glissandi, a registral shift in the strings from one pitch cluster which saturates almost a three-octave space to a lower cluster which spans around two and a half octaves (Iverson 2009, pp. 68–9). In this way, clusters change shape as their registral limits are altered to the extent that in *Atmosphères* the contour of the cluster is more significant than the identity of its individual pitches (Ibid., p. 73).

Bayer is correct in seeing in Ligeti's use of clusters and glissandi a concern with continuity that is paradoxically constituted by 'infinitesimal sound events' and therefore by 'micro-discontinuity' (Bayer 1981, p. 137). Ligeti's sound masses are much more mobile with their infinitesimal changes than the more monolithic and steady sound blocks of Penderecki's sonoristic scores such as *Threnody to the Victims of Hiroshima* (1960) for 52 string instruments and *Polymorphia* (1961). Unlike Ligeti's finely calibrated micropolyphony, in which every note is chosen as the result of careful composition, the score of *Threnody* contains for the most part symbols which direct the instrumentalists to play at particular points within their range or to focus on textural effects. While Penderecki opposes continuity and discontinuity in a 'creative and enriching dialectical conflict', in Ligeti's micropolyphonic works, discontinuity is integrated within the continuity of the surface (Ibid., p. 139).

As Bayer notes, both horizontally conjunct and vertical presentations of micro-intervals can create the effect of a continuous sound space. This can be achieved by means of horizontal glissandi, which can sound to the human ear as traversing a smooth unbroken continuum or, on the vertical plane, by means of certain micro-intervallic sound clusters built, for example, from thirds of a tone or quartertones. The massive quartertone string cluster at the end of Penderecki's *Threnody* is a good example of this, where a distinct sense is given of the dense occupation of a continuous segment of pitch space (Ibid., p. 123).

In order to achieve this kind of continuous effect, it is necessary that all sense of distance between a given sound and its closest neighbours, whatever the module (semitone, third-tone, quartertone, etc.) is suppressed, a challenge in which success and failure may depend on a number of factors including the perceptual capacity of listeners and the speed and density of musical events. For the most discriminating musical ear, it may always be the case that the simultaneous or successive sounding of two or more neighbouring pitches will result in discrepancies, in identifiable gaps between the sounds, which relegate continuity to the realm of the ideal. While it may be easier to create the sense of a pitch continuity through the successive sounding of pitches, for Bayer, the concept of a sound continuum seems to be an unrealizable one since 'two notes heard together are always necessarily separated by a certain interval' (Ibid., p. 124). Despite this obvious difficulty, it seems that perception can still be convinced of the experience of pitch continuity when clusters are built from sufficiently small intervals packed densely enough together to annihilate all discrimination of individual pitches or particular pitch combinations, the sense of a filled sound space being the primary effect. While the threshold of appreciable pitch differentiation varies from listener to listener, the figure of five to six cents difference between sounds is often cited as the critical point for many. It is also the case that we do not listen to pitch in abstraction from the other parameters of the musical sound and timbre can be a highly significant factor in affecting recognition and discrimination of pitch.

In the estimation of Bayer, glissandi, clusters and clouds of sound are 'three basic archetypes' which make possible 'an aesthetic of spatial continuity' in certain strands of music after 1945 where 'the massive effect of a brute and unarticulated sound matter' is opposed to the aesthetic of discontinuity with its pitch modes, scales and series (Ibid., p. 129). While he does not refer to the reflections of Deleuze and Guattari on the smooth and the striated, he suggests that contemporaneous forms of glissandi, clusters and clouds restore 'a savage, primitive sound experience' which subverts all systemization and all attempts to contain it within any kind of discursivity. In doing so, it recaptures 'expressive power' that in general had been 'neutralized and imprisoned' by rules that are ultimately artificial and cultural in origin (Ibid., p. 130). He also recognizes that this kind of approach was rejected by composers he considers to have been over-concerned with 'formal rigour and Cartesian logic' (Ibid., p. 133). Paradoxically, in this discussion, it is Boulez who stands charged with promoting a dominant state space in opposition to the nomadism of the cluster, the glissando and the cloud.

Conclusion

Despite the vast range of possible ways of dividing up pitch space, whether the unit of measurement be tones, semitones or microtones, a comma or an infinitesimal cent, it remains the case that two different pitches are always separated by a spatial interval and the passage from one to the other always entails a qualitative discontinuity. This is not a problem for all composers and theorists, and Wyschnegradsky considers the interval of 1/12 of a tone as the limit of ultrachromatic possibility, almost imperceptible to the human ear, and so small as to amount to the practical attainment of the spatial continuum (Wyschnegradsky 1996, pp. 111, 213).[9] As Deleuze and Guattari acknowledge 'the two spaces in fact exist only in mixture: smooth space is constantly being translated, transversed into a striated space; striated space is constantly being reversed, returned to a smooth space' (Deleuze and Guattari 1988, p. 474).

The present chapter has not been a pretext merely to revisit some of the most important moments in the history of pitch development in twentieth- and twenty-first-century music, although it has in fact done so. Nor has it aimed simply to unfold some of the implications implicit within Boulez's distinction of smooth and striated space. Both of these goals, entirely worthwhile on their own account, could have been achieved without reference to Deleuze and Guattari, from whom they need no justification. While something of the origins of the terms smooth and striated space has been laid out, a process that inevitably led to some consideration of their use within Boulez's theoretical writings, the terms mean much more when taken up by Deleuze and Guattari.

Beyond the brute fact that musical pitch may be thought of as inhabiting a spatial continuum that we can think of as alternatively smooth or striated, Deleuze and Guattari introduce into this seemingly rather disinterested topic the philosophy of difference and the play of Nietzschean forces that has already been discussed in the first two chapters of this book. Viewed in terms of the Deleuze-Guattarian opposition of State Philosophy and Nomad Thought, tuning systems are caught up in and constituted by a play of forces in which they participate as dominant or dominated, active or reactive forces. Lewis Rowell makes this point forcefully in terms of geography, the history of migrations and ethnomusicology, and it is not too difficult to imagine that histories of conquest and migration may have effected or shaped the survival, disappearance or development of tuning systems and the pitch spaces they map out.

While microtonality including the use of quartertones is generally nomadic in orientation, escaping from the dominant system at work in the musical West, we have seen from the work of individual composers and theorists that within microtonality, there are active and reactive forces, progressive and regressive figures. Where Partch strives to adopt new means for new ends, Carrillo, Hába and others adopt new microtonal means for essentially old purposes. The play of Nietzschean forces and the philosophy of difference are at work even in the conception of the chromatic or the diatonic scale where, as we have seen, the compromise solution of the equally tempered scale, excellent though it be in itself, can be used as a dominant system in the service of musical ideology. In this case, particular musics may be canonized speciously as corresponding to natural law. Misused, the equally tempered scale, at its worst, is used to justify a dominant Western conception of music which pays scant attention to the degree of compromise involved in its successful use and which entails that we forget that tuning, tonality and Western listening habits are excellent cultural constructs and examples of learnt behaviour.

4

Thinking musical time

Music is a temporal art which, unlike the visual arts, exists by necessity in time. The positing of alternative temporalities is a hallmark of modernism in philosophy and literature, and in music, time and temporality have become the focus of reflection for a great number of composers and music theorists. Debussy, Stravinsky, Messiaen, Boulez, Stockhausen, Carter, Ligeti and Grisey, to name only some key protagonists, share considerable interest in compositional questions concerning rhythm, duration, tempo, time and temporality. One of the most interesting aspects of their music is the prominence given to more variably pulsed times and to almost unpulsed temporalities, which create the effect of suspending time, arresting all feeling of forward movement.[1]

To some extent, the renewed interest in time and temporality in twentieth- and twenty-first- century music relates to developments in the field of rhythm, for which Stravinsky's experiments in masterworks such as the ballet *The Rite of Spring* (1913) must be acknowledged as pivotal. Messiaen's catalogue of rhythmic devices, as found in his compositions and musical treatises, take rhythmic experimentation in further innovative directions, and he tries to underpin his rhythmic theory with more overarching reflections on time and temporality, cobbled together from a great panoply of sources. While Boulez's reflections are less overtly philosophical, he nevertheless goes beyond the traditional rhythmic vocabulary in setting out the temporal possibilities for contemporary music as existing between the poles of what he calls pulsed and unpulsed time or smooth and striated time, concepts that are taken up by Deleuze and Guattari in *A Thousand Plateaus*. Equally important in the recent history of time and temporality in post-war music is the temporal layering in works by Stockhausen from the late 1950s as well as his concept of 'Moment-form', Elliott Carter's experiments with metric modulation and polyrhythms, the temporal implications of Ligeti's micropolyphony and the new possibilities explored in Gérard Grisey's spectral experiments.

As with smooth and striated space, there is again a certain recursiveness in Deleuze's treatment of musical time as pulsed and unpulsed. While once again taken from Boulez, the terms are appropriated idiosyncratically, and are related by Deleuze and Guattari to the opposition of Chronos and Aion, two distinct, yet complementary conceptions of time which Deleuze discovered in Victor Goldschmidt's 1953 study of Stoic philosophy and which he had, to some extent, already expounded in *The Logic of Sense* (1969).[2] These concepts, it seems, became to some extent fused with Boulez's pulsed and unpulsed times, Deleuze having been impressed by Boulez's reflections on time in the music of Wagner.[3]

Boulez, Wagner, Proust and Deleuze

While a more extensive account of Boulez's variable conception of musical time will be given later in the chapter, we can note for the moment that in 'Time Re-Explored' (1976), he draws attention to the temporal 'malleability' of Wagner's musical motives which have no definitive tempo, are not limited to the tempo or speed of their original sounding, and whose transformations obey no other imperative than 'the expressive needs of the moment at which they are employed' (Boulez 1986, pp. 266–7). The simple nature of the components that make up Wagner's motives, arpeggios and dotted rhythms, for example, makes them easily adaptable to great variability in musical treatment. In this way, the idea of variation is pushed beyond anything achieved previously, a development which entails an equally important transformation of the concept of musical time which becomes more 'supple', 'malleable' and 'ambiguous' (Ibid., p. 268). Wagner's motives seem 'infinitely capable of expansion and contraction', their temporal aspect becoming momentarily fixed only to then decompose and reform in line with a work's musical and dramatic unfolding. For Boulez, this kind of transition with its constantly shifting temporalities became Wagner's 'chief obsession' and his 'real subversive achievement' (Ibid., p. 277), necessitating a different kind of listening (Ibid., p. 270).

Boulez recalls how Deleuze approached him with a view to participating in the IRCAM seminar on time, which he [Boulez] was organizing in 1978.[4] 'Making Inaudible Forces Audible', the position paper which Deleuze delivered, and in which he primarily considers the concepts of pulsed and non-pulsed time, and how Boulez makes both temporalities audible (Deleuze 2006, pp. 156–60), was later described by the composer as 'a fantastic development'. In his paper, Deleuze reflects on the nature of time and temporality that is displayed in each of the five musical works that were performed as part of the seminar. He acknowledges that while the works are not directly related to or dependent upon one another, they nevertheless 'begin to react to one another' when placed together, producing a particular 'profile of musical time' (Ibid., p. 156). An alternative set of works, he suggests, would produce different reactions and another 'unique profile of musical time or of a different variable than time'. This is not the formulation of some abstract and generalized concept of musical time but rather an approach in which it is recognized that time in music can only be treated nominalistically with due respect for the variability and specificity of the multiple times and temporalities embodied within contemporary musical works, which all adds up, for Deleuze, to a 'cartography of variables'.

Recognizing that the question of musical time is only addressed partially by any particular musical work, Deleuze pinpoints something of the temporal particularities of the five works chosen for the IRCAM seminar in relation to Boulez's concepts of time as pulsed and non-pulsed. Of Ligeti's *Chamber Concerto*, he notes that 'a non-pulsed time rose from a certain pulsation' while Messiaen's *Mode de valeurs et d'intensités*, Boulez's *Éclat* and Stockhausen's *Zeitmasse* 'developed or showed different aspects of this non-pulsed time'. Finally, Carter's *A Mirror on which to Dwell* is judged to have shown how 'a non-pulsed time could lead to a new form of original pulsation' (Ibid., pp. 156–7). Despite the impression made on Deleuze by the experience of these works, there are no references to time or temporality in Carter, Stockhausen, Ligeti or Grisey in *A Thousand Plateaus* or elsewhere in his writings and interviews.

For Deleuze, pulsed and unpulsed time go beyond the musical, and non-pulsed time in particular is judged as approximating to Proust's 'time in its pure state', to 'duration' and to freedom from measure. Ultimately, 'non-pulsed time puts us first and foremost in the presence of a multiplicity of heterochronous, qualitative, non-coincident, non-communicating durations' (Ibid., p. 157) and, drawing again on Boulez, he notes the autonomous and transformational character of Wagner's motives which exist in a 'non-pulsed floating time' (Ibid., p. 159).

In 'Occupy without Counting: Boulez, Proust and Time' (1986), Deleuze picks up explicitly on Boulez's alternative whereby we can either 'count to occupy space-time, or occupy without counting' (Deleuze 2006, p. 292), and Boulez's concept of the 'time bubble' now becomes a duration block (Ibid., pp. 294–5). As with smooth space, Deleuze is thinking here of a nomadic time in which number escapes all sense of measurement, a 'musical Nomos', distinct from measured number. Pulsed and non-pulsed time, however, just like smooth and striated space, are of less value as a division than as a continuum, since they can be alternated or superposed (Ibid., pp. 294–5), a phenomenon that is found, for example, in sections of Boulez's *Répons*. Music and sound, for Deleuze, enable us to perceive 'time in its purest form' (Ibid., p. 298), a project he recognizes in the music of Messiaen and which is continued by Boulez in a serial context. The temporal dimension of Boulez's work recalls, for Deleuze, aspects of Proust's temporal explorations in that both are concerned with capturing 'the forces of time' and with rendering them perceptible, and he recognizes that for both Proust and Boulez, time and temporality are 'multiple'.

Deleuze and Guattari on time

Deleuze's two essays on music and time form only a small part of the much more extensive philosophy of time found in both his solo writings and in those with Guattari. Again, it is in *A Thousand Plateaus* primarily that time is discussed in relation to music and Boulez's twin concepts, and Deleuze and Guattari write there of 'the "pulsed time" of a formal and functional music based on values versus the "nonpulsed time" of a floating music, both floating *and* machinic, which has nothing but speeds or differences in dynamic' (Deleuze and Guattari 1988, p. 262). They pick up on Boulez's

> proliferations of little motifs, accumulations of little notes that proceed kinematically and affectively, sweeping away a simple form by adding indications of speed to it; this allows one to produce extremely complex dynamic relations on the basis of intrinsically simple formal relations. . . . A clock keeping a whole assortment of times (Ibid., p. 271).

Such musical processes with their distinctions of pulse seem to describe very well the perpetual movement which Deleuze and Guattari believe is at work in their new image of thought with its flows and forces. This is why they claim that it is not a question of 'the ephemeral and the durable' or 'the regular and the irregular', but rather of 'two modes of individuation, two modes of temporality' (Ibid., p. 262). Once again, they are not writing primarily about music, and they are using Boulez's musical categories to communicate the operations taking place within two distinct images of thought. Ideas of pulse are related to the plane of consistency on which 'there are only relations of movement and rest, speed and slowness between unformed elements, or at least between elements that are relatively unformed, molecules and particles of all kinds' (Ibid., p. 266).

As already noted, the distinction of pulsed and non-pulsed time is related by Deleuze and Guattari to that of Chronos and Aion, two distinct, yet complementary conceptions of time which Deleuze, after Goldschmidt, believes originate within Stoic philosophy.[5] Where Chronos '*is composed only of interlocking presents*', Aion '*is constantly decomposed into elongated pasts and futures*'. Aion is defined as time which is 'infinitely subdivisible' in a situation where 'each present is divided into past and future, ad infinitum' (Deleuze 1990, pp. 61–2). This event 'has no present. It rather retreats and advances in two directions at once, being the perpetual object of a double question: What is going to happen? What has just happened?' (Ibid., p. 63). Deleuze writes of it as being 'unfolded' and becoming 'autonomous' as it 'flees in both directions at once, toward the future and toward the past' (Ibid., p. 62). It is 'the past-future, which in an infinite subdivision of the abstract moment endlessly decomposes itself in both directions at once and forever sidesteps the present' (Ibid., p. 77).

If Aion divides past and future in relation to an infinitesimal instant, Chronos, in contrast, is an 'eternal present', something like God's view of time in which past, present and future are held together as one (Ibid., p. 150). Chronos is therefore 'the always limited' and 'variable living present' (Ibid., pp. 61–2) or 'the present which alone exists' (Ibid., p. 77). With Chronos

> only the present exists in time. . . . whatever is future or past in relation to a certain present (a certain extension or duration) belongs to a more vast present which has a greater extension or duration. There is always a more vast present which absorbs the past and the future. Thus, the relativity of past and future with respect to the present entails a relativity of presents themselves, in relation to each other. God experiences as present that which for me is future or past, since I live inside more limited presents. Chronos is an encasement, a coiling up of relative presents (Ibid., p. 162).

In *A Thousand Plateaus*, Chronos and Aion are connected by Deleuze and Guattari with Boulez's twin conceptions of musical time. Chronos, as 'the time of measure that situates things' and 'develops a form', is said to correspond to Boulez's striated or pulsed time (Deleuze and Guattari 1988, p. 262). Aion, corresponding to Boulez's smooth or non-pulsed time, is

> the indefinite time of the event, the floating line that knows only speeds and continually divides that which transpires into an already-there that is at the same time not-yet-here, a simultaneous too-late and too-early, a something that is both going to happen and has just happened (Ibid., p. 262).

In this way, something central to musical modernity more generally, the sensible opposition of smooth and striated, of pulsed and non-pulsed time, is recognized as relating to the new Deleuzian image of thought. While pulsed time, perhaps as chronometry is for the most part readily perceived, the experience of what Deleuze, after Proust, calls 'time as a *force*, time itself, "some time in its purest form"', is much more difficult to capture (Deleuze 2006, p. 298). It is precisely this normally inaccessible aspect of time, its 'mute force', which Deleuze finds in Proust and Boulez and more generally in significant strands of late musical modernity.

From a Deleuze-Guattarian viewpoint, Boulez's pulsed and non-pulsed times are encountered in musical compositions as percepts. The percepts of pulsed and non-pulsed time no longer make music audible in time, but rather make time audible in music. In this music, we become conscious of time and of the contingent nature of temporality, recognizing that it is not a unitary phenomenon. Modernist music no longer plays, for the most part, with the topoi of Classical music or the mythic semes of the Romantic era but often takes musical time itself for both its form and content, a notion that is also found in Susanne Langer for whom music more generally 'makes time audible'(Langer 1953, p. 110).

Deleuze's three passive syntheses of time

While pulsed and unpulsed time are related by Deleuze and Guattari to Chronos and Aion, in *Difference and Repetition*, Deleuze provides an alternative and completely independent temporal schema which goes beyond the binary times of *The Logic of Sense* and *A Thousand Plateaus*.[6] Time is conceptualized here as three passive syntheses, the first of which is the 'living present', in which the past and future are dimensions that are contracted into the present (Deleuze 1994, p. 76), in other words, each present is enlarged back and forwards in time, and time becomes a collection of different and more expansive presents. Where the events of the past are maintained through retention in the living present, the future is manifested through anticipation (Williams 2011, p. 25). What makes this approach different from previous, phenomenological explanations is that neither of these dimensions is psychological in nature or the result of any act of consciousness, being instead constituted as subjectless processes

(Ibid., p. 29). Nor does Deleuze produce a monistic reduction of temporal experience since the living present unites past and future around itself and there are 'many and multiple living presents' (Ibid., p. 37), 'durations or stretches' which overlap irreducibly to produce a fragmentary situation 'with jumps, returns, gaps and resonances resistant to a satisfactory situation on a single continuous line' (Williams 2011, p. 70; Deleuze 1994, p. 83).

In the second synthesis, the present is now a dimension of the past, 'its most contracted leading tip' (Williams 2011, p. 3), and the focus here is on the fact of the passing present and the constantly reorganized relationships in the pure past it enacts, as each passing present instant now takes its place as the most recent point of the past, resynthesizing or reformatting the entirety of relationships between all other past events in the process (Ibid., p. 14). In this second passive synthesis, the past is revealed not as something fixed but as a constantly fluid, continuously reordered synthesis of all former presents. Taking his cue here from Bergson's *Matter and Memory*, Deleuze terms this idea the 'pure past' in which the entire past accompanies the arrival of each present moment (Ibid., pp. 63–4).

In the third synthesis, 'a pure and empty form of time' (Ibid., p. 84), the past and the present are now dimensions of the future but, unlike the first two syntheses, the third is marked by cuts and caesurae in which each new present/event organizes all of the others anew. It is a static present that is 'determinable yet undetermined' (Ibid., p. 86), a synthesis in which a temporal cut or caesura separates past and future and 'the past becomes a dimension produced by the future' (Ibid., p. 94).

With all of this, Deleuze sets out a theory of time as multiple and irreducible processes in which past, present and future are not separate but rather closely interrelated dimensions that interact in variable ways (Williams 2011, pp. 9, 16–17). For Williams, the apparent discrepancy between the two times of *The Logic of Sense* and the three passive syntheses of *Difference and Repetition* does not undermine Deleuze's work on time (Ibid., p. 154). While Chronos closely resembles the first passive synthesis, the third relates strongly to Aiôn, leaving the second as a situation in which 'the relation between Aiôn and Chronos' is 'mediated through intensity'

(Ibid., p. 138), and it seems clear that whatever taxonomy of times is adopted, 'all of these times coexist' in a way that is absolutely irreducible to any one model or to any operational code (Ibid., p. 140).

Deleuze and his philosophical predecessors: Bergson, Husserl and Whitehead

Given that the manifest intention of this chapter is to demonstrate the value for music of Deleuze's philosophy of time, it is important to show where his work stands in relation to that of his predecessors, some of whom address themselves explicitly to significant aspects of music.

In opposition to the reduction of time to the individual moments of clock time, a view which he rejected as a spatialized misrepresentation, Bergson (1889), who as we have seen is an important figure for Deleuze, posited a concept of time as duration, as an indivisible and continuous experiential flux. In doing so, he pointed to musical melody as exemplifying the continuity within temporal duration, in that to appreciate a melody, memory must somehow grasp all of its notes as a unity, as an instant (Bergson 1910, p. 100ff.).[7] Bergsonian duration is therefore an experience of time, a temporality, in which time is no longer conceived in fragmented units that can be measured, but rather as a 'mutual penetration' or 'interconnection' of successive states of consciousness.

Bergson's position was not uncontested, and in 1925, Gabriel Marcel argued convincingly that Bergsonian duration does not accurately encapsulate musical experience. Of course, Bergson had not set out to develop a theory of musical time or duration, and he used the example of melody only metaphorically (Marcel 2005, pp. 86, 88–9). Marcel, who appreciates that Bergson's account of musical experience is entirely passive, rejects it in favour of a more participative hypothesis, in which the listener exercises 'a kind of mastery' in apperceptively grasping the internal coherence of a musical phrase or composition (Marcel 2005, p. 90). Aesthetician Boris de Schloezer, whose work on music anticipates significant aspects of

1960s structuralism, further qualifies Bergson's account stressing that music has an 'immanent sense' and that its existence is independent of our apprehension, our mental states and of whatever physiological and psychological processes it may elicit within us (Schloezer 1947, pp. 30–1).

Further criticism of Bergson's position was forthcoming in Charles Koechlin's article 'Le Temps et la musique' (1926), which distinguishes musical time from the quantitative time of physics and mathematics, from psychological time and from Bergson's qualitative duration. Musical time has its own character, which Koechlin relates to the flow of sounds and to the unfolding of melody (Emery 1998, pp. 491–2). Gaston Bachelard (1936), who supports Bergson in most respects, disagrees with him in holding that melody also contains elements of discontinuity, and that its continuity is in fact metaphorical, an illusory and 'sentimental reconstruction' which the mind of the listener has learnt to perform (Bachelard 2001, p. 116). Pierre Souvtchinsky writes in 1932 of an aesthetic conjunction linking Bergson, Proust and Debussy, honouring the composer as the first to extend the musical instant in terms of sound duration (Souvtchinsky 1990, p. 248). Distinguishing between 'psychological time' and 'ontological' or 'real time', in which the multifarious manifestations of the former are rooted ontologically in the latter, it is suggested that music provides 'one of the most pure forms of the ontological sensation of time' (Souvtchinsky 2004, pp. 241–3). While individual composers present their idiosyncratic experiences of musical time, the spectrum of temporal possibilities is typified generally by the alternative of the chronometric (ontological), characterized by a sense of 'dynamic calm', and the chrono-ametric (psychological), which relates to the 'secondary notation of primary emotive impulses'. Stravinsky and Wagner are identified as respectively exemplifying each tendency.

While it is into this mostly French, post-Bergsonian strain of theorizing that we must place Deleuze's discussion of time, Husserl's *On the Phenomenology of the Consciousness of Internal Time* (1893–1917), which like Bergson, uses the experience of listening to a melody as a central example, is of equal importance. For Husserl, the present moment of auditory experience is connected intimately to what is just past and to what is imminent for perception. While I hear a note in the present, I also retain something of what directly preceded this present note so that the present is widened to include within itself a series of retentions of past notes. The present is further thickened by anticipation of what is to follow the present note. According to Husserl's understanding, when listening to music, the present that presents itself to perception 'is a complex form of consciousness comprising my present impression of the current note together with a series of present retentions of immediately past notes and a series of present protentions of immediately future notes' (Smith 2007, p. 212). Retention is not to be equated with memory or recollection, properly speaking, protention is not the same as anticipation, and both retention and protention are distinct aspects of perception (Ibid., p. 214). While Deleuze's philosophy draws in certain ways from Husserl, there are also important differences. Ultimately, Husserl, from Deleuze's perspective, is insufficiently free of identity and subjectivity, as is evident in the prominence he gives to intuition and to consciousness (Williams 2008, pp. 101, 132).

Deleuze's philosophy of time also shares certain elements in common with that of Alfred North Whitehead, who uses the term 'prehension' for the temporal process in which past, present and future are linked, so that every event is a prehension of other events. For Whitehead, the immediate past of 'between a tenth of a second and half a second ago' is retained or prehended in the present moment (Whitehead 1967, p. 181) so that 'the present moment is constituted by the influx of *the other* into that self-identity which is the continued life of the immediate past within the immediacy of the present'. Consequently, 'the past has an objective existence in the present which lies in the future beyond itself' (Ibid., p. 191). In a similar way, 'the future is immanent in each present occasion' not as the actual existence of a particular future event but nevertheless having 'an objective existence in the present' (Ibid., pp. 193–4). This rich concept of temporal experience is contrasted with what Whitehead refers to as the 'specious present of the percipient" (Whitehead 1978, p. 169) by which is meant the psychological phenomenon of the temporal instant of perception which is variable and not at all a strictly definable quantity.

While no reference is made in *A Thousand Plateaus* to Whitehead's philosophy of past, present and future with its prehensions, Deleuze and Guattari refer approvingly to Husserl's retentions and protentions in connection with the novella (Deleuze and Guattari 1988, pp. 192–3) but not in relation to music, and no attempt is made to relate Husserl's concepts to either the twin times of Chronos and Aion or to the three passive syntheses.

Music, time and temporality

Within this rich spectrum of views, what we take from Deleuze's philosophy of time is the multiplicity of temporal possibilities it acknowledges. While this is something that could be inferred without reference to Deleuze from the great wealth of experiments in temporality undertaken by numerous writers and composers working in the twentieth- and early-twenty-first centuries, Deleuze, arguably, perhaps more than any other figure, gathers all of this up and gives it philosophic expression as time's fundamental dimensions of past, present and future are reconfigured in paradigmatic ways that are sufficiently flexible and multiple to allow for innumerable configurations. At the most fundamental level, this is seen in the play of Chronos and Aion, pulsed and non-pulsed times and in the variety of intermediate temporal states that their interplay allows.

In terms of music's history, whether we are dealing with art music, rock, pop or jazz, Western music is for the most part metred. Musicians working in Paris in the thirteenth century developed the first example in Western art music of an elementary notation that also indicates duration. This early system, which is described in the treatise *De mensurabili musica* (c. 1250), attributed to Johannes de Garlandia, comprises a series of six rhythmic modes, each with its own distinctive metre and rhythm. Since then, Western music, in all genres, forms and styles, down to the twentieth century, has, for the most part, existed within the developing conventions of what we are calling here pulsed time, albeit that some music has subverted the seeming constraints of time signature, regular metre and pulse. Beyond art music, all rock'n'roll, for example, is rooted in dance rhythms with regular metre, meaning that it invariably works within 'the standard metres (2/4, 3/4, 4/4, 6/8, 9/8, 12/8) and four-, eight-, twelve- and sixteen- bar rhythmic groupings of Western dance forms' (Bogue 2004, p. 104).

Looking beyond the West, ethnomusicologist Martin Clayton notes that while 'all music has "rhythm"; some, but not all, has a perceived pulse; of this "pulsed" music some but not all has this pulse organized periodically; and some, but not all forms of periodic organization may be described as "metre" (Clayton 1996, p. 329). The boundaries between categories are not always clear since not all listeners may perceive musical pulse in certain musics or whatever pulse is there may be irregular or discontinuous, and Clayton expresses some doubt over the extent to which any music can ever be completely free from pulsation, given the uncertain nature of the boundary separating the pulsed from the unpulsed. He suggests that the inclination to perceive musical pulse is so powerful that it is difficult to find music which does not at least suggest it.

While Clayton is undoubtedly correct in identifying what might be called a will to pulse in both the performer and the listener,[8] this in itself is insufficient to nullify the force of the alternative temporalities forged by a number of significant composers working in the twentieth and twenty-first centuries. The creation of alternative temporalities has been of central importance for these composers and, whatever the limitations and ambiguities that surround the possibilities of creating completely unpulsed music, one of the most interesting aspects of their work is the prominence given to new static temporalities.

Temporal flexibility is already a feature of late romantic music, and the malleability of Wagner's motives was acknowledged earlier in the chapter. Wagner is not alone however among the late romantics in creating a musical fabric that is much more flexible in its treatment of rhythm, pulse and metre. Like Wagner, Brahms was also developing a proto-modern rhythmic sensibility which displays equally astonishing rhythmic and metrical flexibility as he plays with the putative constraints of time signatures, the placing of accents and the length of phrases. This, as Paul Zukofsky suggests, results in music with great 'plasticity' in which Brahms is able 'to engineer a conflict between the length of the phrase, and its internal metric' (Zukofsky 1997/2004). A number of scholars have discussed the 'metric irregularities' in his music with terms such as metric and rhythmic 'dissonance' and 'metric displacement', noting 'the bivalence of [its] metric clues', its ambivalence and the coexistence within a given passage of 'multiple rhythmic impulses' (Smith 2001, pp. 191–3). Despite all of this, while the music of Wagner and Brahms contains a wealth of ingenious treatments of pulse and each, in its own distinctive way, may be said to embody the kinds of speeds and slownesses envisaged by Deleuze and Guattari, it is perhaps only with Debussy that composition moves at significant moments beyond playing with pulse to something which creates the sonic illusion of a static music.

Debussy, Bergson and Jankélévitch

While the temporality of Debussy's music has been highlighted as one of its most distinctive and innovative aspects, it also marks an important turning point in how time is conceived in Western composition. Later composers such as Messiaen, Boulez, Stockhausen and Grisey, for whom consideration of musical time is also pivotal, have shown a great deal of interest in the temporality of his music, Boulez stating, for example, that with Debussy's *Prélude à l'après-midi d'un faune* 'the art of music began to beat with a new pulse' (Lesure and Nichols 1987, p. 50).

The distinctive sense of time of Debussy's music has been placed by some within the wider context of a late-nineteenth-century predilection for 'statism' in the symbolist, pre-Raphaelite and impressionist painters, the symbolist poetry of Mallarmé and drama of Maeterlinck and a more pervasive questioning of time as something primarily homogeneous or measured (Fleury 1996, pp. 207–10). While Boulez acknowledges that an interest in Eastern cultures had been perceptible in certain aspects of European music since the eighteenth century, he suggests that this is particularly the case with Debussy, and the importance of his encounters with Javanese gamelan at the World's Fair in Paris in 1889 and Balinese gamelan in 1900 is evident from remarks made by the composer and his friends. Despite a lack of explicit reference, there seems to be little doubt that much of Debussy's own music shares something of the static temporality of gamelan, for example, in its employment of short ostinato figures which inhibit all sense of progress.

In terms of philosophical reference, the temporality of Debussy's work has long been linked with that of Bergson, with Bergson's one-time pupil Vladimir Jankélévitch producing a book-length study titled *Debussy et le mystère de l'instant* (1976). As Jann Pasler notes, Bergson referred to Debussy's work in an interview from 1910 as 'a music of *durée*', acknowledging also that he had 'an 'intuitive predilection' for it. Debussy's friend Louis Laloy also suggests that the work of Bergson and Debussy is linked by 'secret correspondences' and that 'such a music could not be produced except in the same environment as such a philosophy, and vice versa' (cited in Pasler 1982, p. 74). At the end of her study of Debussy's ballet score *Jeux*, a composition in which 'a different sense of time' is manifest in each section, Pasler concludes that despite certain parallels linking Debussy and Bergson, there are also significant differences, principally in relation to the notion of 'cinematography' with its 'juxtaposition of contrasting ideas'. While this notion is rejected completely by Bergson, it nevertheless co-exists in the music of Debussy alongside Bergsonian duration (Ibid., p. 75). It may be that this cinematic link suggests an interesting avenue for further exploration of the work of Debussy in relation to that of Deleuze.

In *Debussy et le mystère de l'instant*, Jankélévitch takes up the refusal of progression and development in Debussy's music and relates it to the very slow values found in Liszt's late works (Jankélévitch 1989, p. 137). In doing so, he enumerates a long list of Debussy's compositions where the temporality is static, including the end of the *Prélude* from *Pour le piano*, the *Études* for repeated notes, eight fingers and chromatic degrees, *The Snow is dancing* and *Jardins sous la pluie* (Ibid., pp. 130–1). For Jankélévitch, *Parfums de la nuit* 'sprawls voluptuously as if time no longer existed' (Ibid., pp. 133–4), and of the piano prelude *Des pas sur la neige*, the first *Ballade de Villon*, the third part of *En blanc et noir* and the *Colloque sentimental*, he judges that 'here nothing develops nor becomes, here becoming is at a standstill and is bogged down'. Similarly, the repeated notes which are used within the first movement of the *Violin Sonata* and the interlude from the *Sonata for flute, viola and harp* are described as 'hypnotic' and as suspending all progress (Ibid., p. 133).

These static elements in Debussy's music are described by Jankélévitch as 'eternal presents' or 'the instant' (Ibid., p. 300), and he notes that:

The twenty-four *éternités instantanées* which are called 'Preludes' correspond to twenty-four immobile visions which fix for us as many static images of the total presence; each Prelude immobilizes a minute of the universal life of things, a moment from the history of the world and it arrests this universal life in the *aeternum Nunc* of a vertical cut, that is to say, outside of all becoming and of all succession, without relation to either before or after; nothing evolves, develops or is transformed (Ibid., pp. 290–1).

Following Jankélévitch, Steven Rings theorizes the temporality of Debussy's piano prelude *Des pas sur la neige* as 'a snapshot of an instant of *lived experience*, one in which the vertical density of a psychological moment is sliced up and unfolded horizontally, given temporal extension within the music'. Beyond this, Rings identifies at different points in the piece, the possibility of a kind of 'temporal polyphony', moments of 'temporal expansion and contraction, in which different phases of the music suggest different rates of temporal unfolding', and he suggests that a sense of 'temporal stasis' is produced by the ostinato figure and the decay of the piano tones (Rings 2008, pp. 189–90).

Pasler's study of *Jeux* focuses on 'the shaping of time' as the primary factor in the work's organization (Pasler 1982, p. 61), and she notes that each of the ballet's three characters inhabit three distinctive 'metric areas – 3/4, 3/8 and 2/4', the changing metres serving to reflect the quickly shifting relationships between characters (Ibid., p. 64). As Pasler notes, a number of post-war composers identify *Jeux* as a pivotal work for the development of what Stockhausen later called moment form, where each moment is '"something individual, independent, and centred in itself, capable of existing on its own" rather than the consequence or cause of any surrounding moments'. However, as Jonathan Kramer points out, the moment forms composed later by Stockhausen and others go well beyond what Debussy was able to do in *Jeux* (Ibid., p. 68). In more general terms, Pasler suggests that where Bergson theorizes duration in relation to melody, Debussy thinks it in relation to musical form, a shift that she also notes in the work of the spectral composer Gérard Grisey (Pasler 2008, p. 90). While Pasler draws on Deleuze's reading of Bergson to explain just how the latter's work may be appreciable in Debussy, Brian Kane notes that it is Deleuze's rehabilitation of Bergson that has created a climate in which Jankélévitch's Bergsonian connection seems less 'idiosyncratic' (Gallope et al. 2012, p. 216).

Messiaen and time

Like Debussy, Olivier Messiaen recalls the profound and lasting effect of the Balinese gamelan which he first encountered in Paris at the *Exposition Coloniale* in 1931. Whatever influence may derive from the exposure to gamelan is only one and is certainly not the most significant, among many sources from which his conception of time and idiosyncratic rhythmic practice are fashioned. He had shown himself to be a rhythmic innovator in his compositions in the 1930s and 1940s, producing an account of his procedures in the treatise *Technique de mon langage musical* (1944). In contrast with Debussy, Messiaen is much more explicit in detailing the temporalities embodied within his music, and his posthumously published seven volume *Traité de rythme, de couleur, et d'ornithologie* (1949–92) begins with a significant chapter on time, which considers the phenomenon from a great variety of musical and non-musical perspectives.

Messiaen's twin conceptions of time, the progressive and the static, embody the contrast of time and eternity or the earthly and the eternal, and static music is said to suspend our normal experience of the passage of time, communicating a sense of the eternal which is beyond time. This static temporality is opposed to linear progressive music, analogous to the human experience of lived time on earth, and Messiaen grounds this conception with the support of a series of texts from the Bible and St Thomas Aquinas in which 'time is the measure of the created, eternity is God himself' and is 'indivisible' (Messiaen 1994, p. 7). He cites *Sept Haïkaï* (1962) as an example of a work which has resulted from his interest in the 'static character' of Gagaku, telling us that it was this 'static, hieratic, and sacred atmosphere' which he tried to emulate 'while trying to give it a Christian dimension' (Samuel 1994, p. 137). Other pieces which feature temporally static elements include *Visions de l'Amen* (1943), the *Turangalîla-Symphonie* (1946–48), *Cantéyodjayâ* (1948), *Livre d'orgue* (1951), *Chronochromie* (1960) and *Couleurs de la cité céleste* (1963). While Steven Shaviro is correct in noting that Deleuze, like Nietzsche, Whitehead and Bergson would reject any kind of 'Platonic separation' of time and eternity, understood as the opposition of 'a higher world of permanence and perfection ("a static, spiritual heaven") against an imperfect lower world of flux' (Shaviro 2009, p. 38), Deleuze does not raise this objection explicitly against Messiaen. As with the other composers whose work is discussed in this chapter, the two temporalities, in practice, are often found in Messiaen's compositions in mixtures that preclude their strict separation.

Messiaen's concepts of structured time and duration (Messiaen 1994, pp. 9–12) are broadly similar to Boulez's smooth and striated time in that both composers set up an opposition between non-pulsed and pulsed times. While Boulez's account remains mostly at the level of musical technique, Messiaen attempts to provide a more explicit philosophical basis for the temporalities underlying his rhythmic practice. Quoting extensively from Bergson's statements on duration, he presents a framework comprising two distinct conceptions of time which he terms lived duration and abstract or structured time. In doing so, he draws directly upon the digest of Bergsonian and post-Bergsonian thinking which he found in Armand Cuvillier's school philosophy text book and which sets out the two temporal viewpoints systematically. No attempt is made by the composer to develop or to apply the two temporalities, and it is not absolutely clear that he is recommending them to us as indicative of his temporal conception. Despite this, lived duration is defined as concrete since it 'merges our successive states of consciousness' into a perceptible unity. It is heterogeneous, in that it can have fasts, slows and every possible intermediate tempo, depending upon the number of events which merge within it. It is qualitative which means that it is not quantifiable or measurable, and it is subjective since it is purely within us. Structured time, in contrast, is abstract, 'an empty frame in which we include the world and ourselves'. It is homogeneous, since all of its moments are identical, quantitative in that it is measurable and numbered in relative terms and objective since as a measure it exists outside of us (Cuvillier 1972, pp. 230–1).

Invoking a great panoply of sources, time is discussed by Messiaen in terms of the expansion of the universe, the age of the stars, the geology of the earth, the physiological and psychological 'times' of human beings down to the microphysical time of particles within quantum physics. When Messiaen discusses rhythm in chapter two of the treatise, he again draws upon an extremely wide range of sources, linking musical time with the sounds of nature, birdsong, the mineral, vegetable and animal kingdoms, dance, language, poetry and the plastic arts. He perceives rhythmic value in terms of the organization of stones and mountains, of trees, flowers, leaves and so on. Rhythms are associated with the movement of animals, as in Hindu tradition, accentuation within spoken language, 'the rhythm of volumes in sculpture', of colour in painting and the effects of stained glass windows (Messiaen 1994, pp. 65–6). All of this is described by Deleuze and Guattari as the presentation of 'multiple chromatic durations in coalescence', and this rhythmic multiplicity is related by them to the refrain and to 'a power of deterritorialization permeating nature, animals, the elements, and deserts as much as human beings' (Deleuze and Guattari 1988, p. 309). They cite Gisèle Brelet for whom Messiaen's durations alternate 'between the longest and the shortest, in order to suggest the idea of the relations between the infinitely long durations of the stars and mountains and the infinitely short ones of the insects and atoms: a cosmic elementary power that . . . derives above all from the labor of rhythm'. To this extent Messiaen, in his exploration of musical time, characterizes vibration as something that music shares with everything else in the universe. His compositions with their malleable durations and additive rhythms molecularize duration and embody for Deleuze and Guattari the kind of pulverization of the molar and the valorization of the 'elementary and the cosmic' that they desire for thought. *Chronochromie* with its heterophony of eighteen birdsongs is cited as an example of 'autonomous rhythmic characters' which 'simultaneously reali[ze] an extraordinary landscape in complex counterpoint' (Ibid., p. 320).

Boulez, Stockausen and musical time

Boulez, who acknowledges Messiaen's importance as an original thinker of musical time, produces his own reflections on musical time in his Darmstadt lectures in terms of pulsed and non-pulsed time (Boulez 1971, pp. 88–9). In pulsed or striated time, regular durations are associated with chronometric time as signposts, while in amorphous, non-pulsed or smooth time there are no regular pulses or landmarks.

Smooth time is only connected with chronometric time in an overall way since, in such a temporality, durations (with or without precise proportions) occur within a broad 'field of time'. Speed, acceleration and deceleration are consequently only features of striated time, while only the density of events within a chronometric time limit can vary in the passage of smooth time.

For Boulez, the regularity or irregularity of pulsation within striated time will be determined by the 'fixed or variable' nature of its divisions (pp. 91–2). The most important factor concerning pulsations that are irregular and irregularly divided is the fundamental question of their realizability which, for Boulez, is dependent upon their not going beyond a given degree of practical difficulty in terms of both their proportions and divisions. Nevertheless, as he makes clear in the later Collège de France lectures, the mere fact that a musical passage is arhythmic does not necessarily guarantee the production of a slow, suspended music or smooth time since frenetically, agitated music, which is too complex for perception to unravel, may be arhythmic without producing a sense of musical stasis (Boulez 2005b, p. 101).

He provides a detailed classification of musical times in which only striated time is divided into a variety of types since smooth time has 'neither partition nor module' (Boulez 1971, p. 93).[9] Straight time is defined, regardless of partition, as having a 'constant module', which means that its initial values operate between two boundaries, while the values which are derived from it will be placed, accordingly, 'between the multiples of the relationship defined by these two limits'. Curved time provides the opposite possibility in that the derived values will 'depend upon a function of the relationship defined by these two limits', and Boulez provides an example in which 'all the values will . . . be augmented or diminished according to the direction of the time-register which is followed'. With regular time 'whatever the module . . . partition remains fixed', while with irregular time 'partition varies (according to a defined numerical proportion or to the tempo)'.

Boulez suggests that smooth and striated time are 'capable of reciprocal interaction, since time cannot be *only* smooth or *only* striated', and he states unequivocally that his treatment of time from a formal point of view is based solely on these two categories (Boulez

1986, p. 87). Smooth and striated time are described, respectively, as 'filling time' and 'counting time', and smooth time is defined as 'that over which the performer has no control' (Boulez 1971, p. 94). Finally, Boulez introduces the concepts of homogeneous and non-homogeneous time, in which the time within a composition can be homogeneously smooth or homogeneously striated. A piece will be composed exclusively of either smooth or striated time, but not both. Alternatively, the time may be non-homogeneous, in which case striated and smooth time can be alternated or superposed upon one another, and it is this last possibility which is the case in Boulez's compositions (p. 93).

It is clear that the two temporalities have been elements within Boulez's compositional practice from his earliest published works. While early works like the *Sonatine* for flute and piano are really only anticipations of his later temporal practice, smooth, unpulsed time is clearly perceptible, almost uniform and rather amorphous in *Le Marteau sans maître*. From the mid-1960s onwards, Boulez begins to play with his temporalities and to structure compositions around them so that pieces often feature a number of intermediate states between the homogeneously smooth and the homogeneously striated. Ultimately, temporality is used by Boulez as an envelope, and he opposes the two temporalities as an effective means of articulating form, of playing with perception and of establishing or inhibiting orientation and direction.

In the 1960s, like Debussy and Messiaen, Boulez acknowledges the influence of Eastern temporality in his thinking of time, particularly in the production of smooth, non-pulsed time, and he declares his interest in the precise 'organization of rhythmic structures' in the music of Bali and India (Boulez 1986, pp. 421–2). He contrasts the richness of an Asian conception of time with that more utilitarian Western approach which prefers to move from A to B in a straight line, his preferred option being to integrate delight in sonority and developmental logic in a unified conception. Again, like Messiaen, Boulez has also drawn attention to the 'stretched time' and the 'long unmetered tones' of Japanese Gagaku as a model offering alternative temporal possibilities for composers and, as Joji Yuasa explains, where European music works within a framework of precisely measured time signatures, Japanese music rests on an 'uncountable temporality' that is 'based on breathing' (Kawabata 2003). Once again, Deleuze and Guattari pick up on this, referring to Eastern music in terms of an 'immanent plane of consistency . . . composed of speeds and slownesses, movements and rest' (Deleuze and Guattari 1988, p. 270).

A sense of stasis is also found in the music of John Cage and Morton Feldman, and while Karel Goeyvaerts describes his own early compositions as 'static music' (Maconie 1976, p. 7), of the Europeans it was Stockhausen who made the most sustained theoretical effort to rethink the place of time in music. In an article from 1955, he explores the connection between 'structure and experiential time' (Stockhausen 1958, p. 64), while in '. . . how time passes . . .' (1957), processes are applied to duration in line with the 12-tone treatment of pitch, and which correspond to the acoustical facts in the pitch domain of fundamental pitches and their harmonic spectra (Stockhausen 1959, p. 20). Without naming particular works, he is clearly describing *Gruppen* (1955–57) when he discusses the possibility of three orchestras, which on the basis of three different fundamental durations and their duration-spectra, form separate 'time-strata' which unfold independently of one another (Ibid., pp. 25, 29). Referring no doubt to *Zeitmasse* ('Time Measures') (1955–56), he describes a process in which 'a first duration-formant has a constant tempo, a second is "as fast as possible", a third speeds up and a fourth slows down, and all are to be played simultaneously; and only the fundamental duration of such a time-spectrum is exactly measured as a single value' (Stockhausen 1959, p. 32; 1989, p. 49). Finally, he presents the idea of 'a serialisation of successive proper times', an idea which is accomplished in *Klavierstück XI* (Stockhausen 1959, pp. 36–7).

Like Stockhausen, Deleuze and Guattari refer throughout *A Thousand Plateaus* to 'differential speeds and slownesses' (Deleuze and Guattari 1988, p. 267), to 'simultaneous accelerations and blockages', 'comparative speeds' (Ibid., p. 55) and to 'a clock keeping a whole assortment of times' (Ibid., p. 271). In doing so, their work seems to indicate that the kinds of multiple, simultaneous speeds that we find in the music of Stockhausen, but also in Carter, Grisey and others, go beyond music, and it is yet another example of how music exemplifies thought.

With the concept of the 'moment' and 'Moment-form', Stockhausen formulates a type of musical structure in which each 'moment' has its own distinguishing features and is perceived as a distinct 'implicit eternity' and not as a stage in a developmental process. He compares Moment-form with particular aspects of Eastern cultural traditions, such as the Japanese Noh theatre or haiku verse, forms which concentrate upon the immediately present moment with 'no thought for the past or future' (Stockhausen 1989, pp. 59–60). Moment-form, which was first used in *Carré* and *Kontakte* (both 1959–60), is responsible for the formal structure of most of his compositions from the 1960s. He describes its use in *Kontakte* in terms of a 'concentration on the NOW – on every NOW – as if it were a vertical slice dominating over any horizontal conception of time and reaching into timelessness, which I call eternity: an eternity which does not begin at the end of time, but is attainable at every *moment*' (Griffiths 1995, pp. 144–5).

While Stockhausen's innovations regarding musical time pre-date the formulation of Deleuze's philosophy of time, the philosopher does not draw attention to the specifics of this composer's contribution. Despite this, Stockhausen's concept of moment-form and the 'moment' seems to be close to what Deleuze and Guattari mean by a 'haecceity'. This medieval philosophical concept, pertaining to the 'thisness' of something, becomes for Deleuze and Guattari yet another means of describing the assemblage. In temporal terms, a Deleuze-Guattarian haecceity can be 'a season, a winter, a summer, an hour, a date', all of which 'have a perfect individuality lacking nothing' (Deleuze and Guattari 1988, p. 261). The haecceity is exemplified even more poignantly in the words of the great Spanish poet Lorca, who writes of '"five in the evening" when love falls and fascism rises'. The haecceity is 'the entire assemblage in its individuated aggregate' (Ibid., p. 262) and, extending Lorca's image, Deleuze and Guattari encapsulate it brilliantly as 'we' who 'are all five-o-clock in the evening, or another hour, or rather two hours simultaneously, the optimal and the pessimal, noon-midnight, but distributed in a variable fashion' (Ibid., p. 263). While not reducing one to the other, all of this brings us into the territory of the Stockhausian 'moment', a veritable slice of time of variable composition and duration.

Elliott Carter, metric modulation and temporal multiplicity

Perhaps no twentieth-century composer has thought more about the working of time in musical composition than Elliott Carter who, having become particularly interested in the subject in the 1940s, continued to explore music's temporal possibilities for the rest of his career. Carter's explorations are to some extent stimulated by the rhythmic experiments of Charles Ives, Henry Cowell's *New Musical Resources* (1930) and Conclon Nancarrow's series of Studies for Player Piano, which explore a vast range of novel possibilities in the realms of polyrhythm, polymeter and polytempi.[10] His compositional precursors aside, Carter's innovations are rooted not just in an interest in rhythmic development but in the nature of musical time, and he discusses the philosophical contributions of Bergson, Husserl, Heidegger, Whitehead and Langer as well as Koechlin, Souvtchinsky and Brelet (Carter 1997, pp. 187, 262–80, 313–18).[11] Having grappled with philosophical theory and compositional practice, he quite understandably concludes that the question of musical time is a 'confusing one' with no agreed conceptual vocabulary. Despite this, he suggests that within his own music, 'some of these concepts of time can affect even small details and make them able to participate in larger constructions' in so far as his work is concerned with the multiplicity of ways in which the dimensions of present, past and future, understood as the moment, what has gone before and what is anticipated, can be related (Carter 1997, p. 318).

While Deleuze is not cited by Carter, one of the most striking points that emerges from this composer's work is the overwhelming sense that time in music is multiple and unlimited in its manifestations, something that is evident in all of his compositions from the Sonata for Cello and Piano in 1948, generally acknowledged as the first fruits of his temporal explorations. When he reveals that in the first movement the piano presents the steady rhythm of 'chronometric' time with the cello simultaneously working within a much freer 'chronoametric' time, it is unclear whether this is the straightforward introduction of Souvtchinsky's philosophical opposition into the compositional arena or an ironic take on the production of such conceptual categories (Carter 1997, p. 266; Bernard 1995, p. 648).[12]

From the sonata to the *Double Concerto* (1961) almost all of Carter's pieces signal further developments in the treatment of musical time, the earlier pieces focusing primarily on rhythmic succession rather than simultaneity. The Cello Sonata sees the introduction of the technique which is often known as metric modulation and through which he is able to produce music that is a function of different but related speeds, and in which it is possible to move smoothly from one speed to another by means of changing time signatures and redivision of the beat. While there are places where speeds overlap, metric modulation is primarily concerned in this piece with the composition of 'a *series* of different speeds, each precisely related to its immediate predecessor and its immediate successor' (Bernard 1988, pp. 167–8).

Where the Cello Sonata, in Carter's judgement, uses metric modulation 'too schematically – "modulating" from one speed to another with each phrase – at times – or each large section', he tries in the *String Quartet No. 1* (1951), to produce a constantly shifting work in which changes in speed are embedded within the work's material. While this is not achieved with complete success in the quartet, he manages nevertheless to produce layers of different speeds which gradually appear and disappear (Meyer and Shreffler 2008, p. 118), there being 'four main and several subsidiary themes each in a different speed and each having a different character' (Carter 1997, p. 226).

Concerned now with the production of notated accelerandos and ritardandos, the first example of a notated accelerando which speeds up consistently from the opening to the close of a piece occurs in the sixth variation of the *Variations for Orchestra* (1955) (Carter 1997, pp. 274–5). In the fifth section of *String Quartet No. 2* (1959), the cello material accelerates and decelerates freely in contrast with the insistently strict time of the other instruments, the two violins with persistently strict speeds and the viola departing from its initially strict speed to inhabit the border between freedom and strictness (Bernard 1988, p. 185). The introduction to the *Double Concerto for Harpsichord and Piano* (1961), informed by a notion of 'organized chaos', features 'the superposition of ten rhythmically divergent textural layers' which results in a 'dense polyrhythmic texture' (Meyer and Shreffler 2008, p. 167).[13] In the *Concerto for Orchestra* (1969), which fuses four distinctive movements within a continuous piece, Carter assigns a different tempo to each movement and, as Meyer and Shreffler note, 'the work's underlying conception lies in the fading-in and fading-out of these contrasting layers' (Ibid., p. 197). Carter, who describes chords and intervals in the piece as 'nows', relates them to Husserl's 'internal time-consciousness' in which:

> The sensible nucleus . . . is 'now' and has just been and has been still earlier, and so on. In this now there is also retention of the past now of all levels of duration of which we are now conscious . . . . The stream of lived experience with its phases and intervals is itself a unity which is identifiable through reminiscence with a line of sight on what is flowing: impressions and retentions, sudden appearance and regular transformation, and disappearance and obscuration. This unity is originally constituted through the fact of flux itself; that is, its true essence is not to be, in general, but to be a unity of lived experience (Husserl, cited in Carter 1997, p. 278).[14]

Carter, who is concerned in his music with the complexities of the human experience of time, believes that it must consequently 'be organized by a musical syntax that takes direct account of, and thus can play on, the listener's time sense' (Schiff 1983, p. 23). Relating this kind of experiential time to his reading of Joyce and Proust, he writes of wishing 'to express this situation in [his] music' (Meyer and Shreffler 2008, p. 255). He had become familiar with Whitehead's philosophy at Harvard in the late 1920s and, according to Bernard, he 'retained Whitehead's conception of actual entities, or events, as processes, while also . . . allowing . . . for the possibility of many strands contributing simultaneously to this process' (Bernard 1995, pp. 649–50, 655). Whitehead is, nevertheless, not mentioned by Carter for the most part in his discussions of the philosophy of time.

Carter's temporal experiments continued throughout his career. The *String Quartet No. 3* (1970–71) has four discrete rhythmic layers. Each orchestra in the *Symphony of Three Orchestras* (1976) often plays against the others with several different layers of speeds (Meyer and Shreffler 2008, p. 258). The three duos of the *Triple Duo*

(1982–83) are clearly distinguished with the woodwinds moving 'in eighth-note triplet subdivisions, the percussion and piano in sixteenth-note quintuplets, and the strings in regular sixteenths, producing a rhythmic counterpoint of 3 against 4 against 5' (Ibid., p. 248). Having been interested from the mid-1970s in producing large-scale polyrhythms which would operate throughout an entire movement or work, the 88 bars of *Esprit rude/Esprit doux I*, for flute and clarinet (1984) present the simultaneous development of two 'rhythmic pulses' which unfold in a ratio of 21:25, the flute taking the slower pulse, the clarinet the faster, with no coincidence of the two at any point (Ibid., p. 261). In *Esprit rude/Esprit doux II* (1994), 'the flute moves in quintuple sixteenth values (and their multiples) throughout, the clarinet in triple eighths, and the marimba in sixteenths' (Ibid., p. 291). While his music is for the most part pulsed, there are nevertheless occasional moments of stasis in certain pieces such as *Esprit rude/Esprit doux II* (Ibid., p. 293).

Grisey and a multiplicity of musical times

Like Carter, musical time was a career-long preoccupation for Gérard Grisey and in the article 'Tempus ex machina: a composer's reflections on musical time' (1980; rev. 1985), he distances himself from many previous conceptions of musical time, including those of Messiaen and Boulez, setting up instead a tri-level model which he terms the 'skeleton of time', the 'flesh of time' and the 'skin of time'.

In 'Tempus ex machina', the 'skeleton of time' refers to the 'temporal divisions' employed by the composer for the organization of sounds (Grisey 1987, p. 239). This will not be immediately apparent to the listener, being at best 'sensed beneath the "flesh of time"', and in Grisey's model, it operates in chronometric time and has the second as its unit of measurement. He rejects those approaches to rhythm that have no reference to pulse on the grounds that they lack 'perceptual reality', contemporary systems organizing duration often fail to do justice to 'sound as it is perceived', and Boulez's distinction of smooth and striated time is dismissed as 'merely the invention of a conductor bereft of any phenomenological awareness' (Ibid., pp. 239–40).

For Grisey, the listener cannot perceive the difference between time which is divided up by a virtual (presumably shifting) pulse and non-pulsed smooth time, when the rhythms in such pieces are often layered, thus removing all sense of periodicity anyway (Ibid., p. 240). Far from having any global, rhythmic sense of the work, perception, it seems, can only extend to the duration which is grasped at the moment and, at best, to those that immediately surround it. The tempi in his own music, consequently, and unlike those in Boulez and Stockhausen, are rarely structural in function, serving instead to condense or elaborate musical sequences, and the emphasis is placed on the complete duration of a sequence rather than on any durational unit of measurement (Ibid., p. 242).

Grisey assembles a table of temporal categories termed 'a scale of complexity', which is intended to replace previous 'arbitrary and generally dualistic categories' and classifications of durations such as 'short/long, ternary/binary, rational/irrational values, symmetry/asymmetry' (Ibid., p. 244). Acknowledging that his own classification is most likely just as arbitrary, it is formulated with the intention of relating to 'phenomena of musical times as they are perceived' while allowing us to grasp something of their continuity. While Grisey's scale operates between the periodic and the smooth, the continuous and the discontinuous and order and disorder, the table is not the whole story and the 'degree of complexity' along the path from maximum to zero predictability relies equally on 'musical context' and on the perceptual capacities of the individual listener (Ibid., pp. 244–5).

Continuous-dynamic time marks the passage from the regularity of the periodic to either a continuous acceleration or a continuous deceleration, perceived either as a blurring of sounds or as their slowing down (Grisey 1987, p. 249), and periodicity, acceleration and deceleration are associated by Grisey with the changes in human cardiac and respiratory rhythms that occur in the discrete phases of a normal night's sleep (Grisey 1987, p. 252). Discontinuous-dynamic time can entail accelerations and decelerations which progress step-wise but which skip over segments in a sound's development. Alternatively, it can involve 'statistical accelerations and decelerations'. This is a case of 'composing with continuity and discontinuity, with dynamism and stasis, [in] an unstable and perpetually renewed play' that results in perceptual unpredictability (Ibid., p. 253). Statistical time is described as 'the probabilistic distribution of a vast scale of durations' leaving us 'no possibility of prediction'. It entails maximum disorder in which attention can only remain fixed for a very limited period upon discontinuity (Ibid., p. 256). Finally, smooth time is described as '(non)-rhythm, seamlessness or lack of all temporal division' which can be either 'entirely perceptible, the rhythms being only operative, or [it] can be perceptible *and* conceptual, a rare case of the total absence of any event, single sound or rhythmic silence' (Ibid., pp. 256–7). Having theorized this scale of complexity, Grisey then notes that its categories are merely referential and that an indefinite number of other classifications lie between those that he has identified.

To get closer to what he calls 'musical reality', Grisey goes beyond the skeleton to the 'flesh of time', which is more 'qualitative' and in which sounds 'inhabit and envelop the temporal skeleton with their density and complexity' (Ibid., p. 257). Closer to phenomenology and psychology, the flesh of time is the 'unacknowledged part' of composition, what is normally left to performers, what it is sometimes claimed cannot be learnt or what is put down to intuition. It pertains to the 'immediate perception of time in its relationships with the sound material', whereby a single temporal skeleton is capable of being enveloped and perceived differently depending on how the musical flesh is distributed on it (Ibid., p. 258).

Grisey's third level, the 'skin of time' is described as a 'zone of immediate contact between the listener and the music' (Grisey 2008, p. 236) and as a membrane connecting 'musical time and the listener's time' that is mostly off-limits to the composer (Grisey 1987, p. 272). It pertains to the domains of psychoacoustics and sociology, to how a sound's complexity is organized and structured by the listener, to how memory chooses what it perceives, to the roles of culture and music education in the shaping of choice and to the time in which the listener 'live[s] and breathe[s]'. Ultimately, for Grisey, 'real musical time is only a place of exchange and coincidence between an infinite number of different times' (Ibid., p. 274) and, in a circumstantial text from around 1985, he adds to the mix each interpreter's time, each listener's time, concert hall resonance time, 'socio-cultural time, planetary or galactic time', the time of the work's inspiration, of 'composition and realisation', and the 'coded time' within scores, magnetic tape and computer programmes, the composer's art consisting of putting these different times in phase with one another (Grisey 2008, pp. 179–80).

In practical terms, we can note the place of 'stretched time' in Grisey's earlier works (Ibid., p. 133), of superimposed pulses and tempi and transformation processes in the composition *Tempus ex machina* (1979), as well as the juxtaposition and superposition of different temporalities in his later compositions. In *Le Temps et l'écume*, (1988–89), for example, three times – 'normal', 'extremely compressed' and 'extremely stretched', are indicative of the temporal frames of humans, insects and whales and follow one another successively in the formal unfolding of the work (Grisey 2008, pp. 247–8, 154). In *Vortex Temporum* (1994–96), the same material is presented in different times, described as 'ordinary', 'more or less dilated' and 'more or less contracted', again related to human language and breathing, whale time and that of birds or insects (Ibid., pp. 158–9).

Composer and theorist Pascale Criton, who assisted Deleuze in matters musical, studied composition with Grisey and introduced Deleuze to aspects of his work. François Dosse goes so far as to maintain that Deleuze was a reference point for Grisey, 'the only philosopher whose writings helped him to think music'. While Dosse notes that Criton also brought Grisey's theoretical writings to Deleuze's attention (Dosse 2007, p. 526), it is not yet known which writings and compositions Deleuze was aware of or how they might have affected his thinking of musical time. Criton confirms that she 'passed onto him the work of Gérard Grisey and expounded to him the details of the spectral movement' (Criton 2005).

While interesting work remains to be done in relation to Grisey and Deleuze, Deleuze is cited briefly in 'Tempus ex machina' where Grisey states that 'the composition of process springs ['sort'] from everyday gestures and, even by that, frightens us. It is inhuman, cosmic and provokes a fascination with the Sacred and the Unknown, reaching out to what Gilles Deleuze defined as the splendour of ON: a world of impersonal individuations and pre-individual singularities' (Grisey 1987, p. 269). For André Pietsch Lima, Grisey's *Vortex Temporum* is an example of such Deleuzian individuation in which the composer makes the 'heterogeneous times' of whales, humans and birds 'swirl', the individuation of the human emerging 'like the actualization of a potential and the establishing of communication between disparates', in this case the extreme scale set out by the macro-time of whales and the micro-time of birds (Pietsch Lima 2006; Deleuze 1994, p. 246).

Conclusion

There has been little agreement regarding the nature of time in art music since 1900 and, in the course of the chapter, a range of idiosyncratic philosophical positions and compositional approaches has been explored. Deleuze explicitly associates his own philosophy of time as Chronos and Aion with Boulez's opposition of pulsed and non-pulsed times, a distinction with applications outwith Boulez's music. Beyond the particularities of this opposition, Deleuze's rich philosophy of time, as encapsulated variably in the opposition of Chronos and Aion, but also in the three passive syntheses, seems to set out the parameters within which it may be possible to place a great variety of times, including aspects of the work of Bergson, Husserl and Whitehead, whose work, as has been seen, has been connected with that of Debussy, Messiaen, Carter and possibly Grisey.

The question then is the extent to which Deleuze's temporal theory may offer a philosophical gathering up of multiple possibilities or better, a temporal virtuality from which innumerable experiences of time are actualized. While it is not a matter of forcing every distinctive artwork into a handful of paradigmatic stances, the objection could well be raised, is this not precisely what is done when a range of music is considered under the rubric of the pulsed and the unpulsed? The answer must be no since, as Deleuze (and Boulez) make clear, the pulsed and the non-pulsed are more general conditions – polarities which most often take form in variable mixes and combinations rather than two fixed oppositions. Likewise, the three passive syntheses and the pairing of Chronos and Aion offer extreme points which stretch the coordinates made possible by the dimensions of past, present and future, in such a way that all of the music that has been considered can be located within this cartography of possibility.

Perhaps all of this post-phenomenological theorizing of time and of the experience of time is banging against the limits, the boundaries of possibility, as previously unconceived temporalities are theorized or find actuality in musical artworks and philosophy. As with striated space, the condition of completely unpulsed time is more an aspiration than something that is achieved definitively in any artwork. It can be suggested to perception as composers employ innumerable devices to disorient the sense of time passing or pulse. Bergson, Husserl, Whitehead, but also Heidegger, Bachelard, Koechlin, Langer, Souvtchinsky, Brelet and others, open up the time scale. Deleuze is not, however, some kind of Wyschnegradskyan endpoint, the temporal equivalent of pansonority, where a completely smooth or unpulsed time is laid out as the end of music. While Deleuze's work is without this kind of historicism, it may be possible to interpret it as the tracing of time's multiplicity, understood not as an already accomplished laying out of all possibilities but rather as the placing of parameters which amount to a temporal virtuality and from within which a great multiplicity of individual times can emerge.

Deleuze seems to go beyond his 'predecessors' in a number of ways. While he undoubtedly takes his cue from Bergson, who starts off this entire discourse, Bergson, merely uses the idea of melody to illustrate something about time per se rather than about musical time in particular, albeit that the concept of duration is an important one within a musical context, particularly as nuanced and amended by later thinkers. If Langer pre-dates Deleuze in telling us that time becomes palpable in music, Deleuze goes further to state that not 'time' but a multiplicity of 'times', all kinds of mixed times, become palpable in music. Like Bergson, Husserl focuses almost entirely on melody, albeit that he presents an exemplary analysis of the workings of the past and future as retention and protention, within the extended, thickened present. It seems clear that Deleuze's conception draws also on Husserl's work with significant differences. Intentionality, intuition and the operation of the reduced, phenomenological subject are no longer found in Deleuze who, while not using the term, seems closer to Whitehead on this point in thinking time as process, or rather, as processes. Once again, Whitehead's work seems closer to Husserl in its emphasis on the retention of immediately past moments and protention as the anticipated, immediate future in the thickened present, albeit that these are now termed prehensions.

Unlike Bergson, Husserl and Whitehead, Deleuze is much more interested in what music has to offer thought by way of creative possibilities than merely how we can study music in order to exemplify and illustrate philosophical thought. Music, as the other arts, is not subjected to philosophy by Deleuze. Music assumes the condition of thought, new thought, albeit in the realm of the percept rather than the concept. Here again, the adoption of Boulez's terminology of pulsed and unpulsed time as well as the time-bubble makes clear that while music may be perceptual rather than conceptual, musicians do create and employ concepts in the creation of their music.

The composers whose work has been considered in this chapter present a wide range of temporal possibilities from Messiaen's eclectic gathering of insights to Boulez's much leaner paring down of possibilities; from Stockhausen's temporal experiments, Carter's polyrhythms, poltemporality, metric modulation and experiments with temporal succession and simultaneity to Grisey's phenomenological cartography, not of pulses but of layers of time and temporal time worlds. The enquiry could, of course, go on to even more recent experiments, for example in the work of Claus-Steffen Mahnkopf (Coulembier 2013).

The gathering of possibilities that is designated here under the name of 'Deleuze' in no way arrogates all innovation in the thinking of musical time for Deleuze, and it is clear that most of the composers whose work is considered here produced their temporal innovations independently of Deleuze. Nor does it aim to give him the credit for the important work on time undertaken by other philosophers, composers and musicologists. 'Deleuze', in this context, is a name for a collective assemblage of enunciation, not to be confused with the historical Gilles Deleuze. This is not to say that the name 'Deleuze' is synonymous with everything and anything pertaining to musical time and important limits, in this regard, have been already acknowledged. Carter notes the multiplicity of approaches and the seeming impossibility of integrating them within a coherent framework, as well as the extent to which they seem to be mutually incomprehensible, presenting what Lyotard would term a 'differend'. Deleuze, in a sense, dissolves this problem by removing the 'either . . . or' logic within which it is most often framed, replacing it with the 'and . . . and . . . and' logic of the disjunctive synthesis. A post-Leibnizian logic now prevails where, as with the heterophony of Chapter 1 or the temporal simultaneity of Chapter 4, a series of possibilities, that need not be compossible with one another, can inhere at the same time without fear of exclusion on the grounds of contradiction.

5

A Deleuzian semiotics of music

In the fields of music analysis and aesthetics, a key area of research that developed as a result of the structuralist vogue in France is that of the semiotics and semiology of music. While the broad range of semiotic or semiological theories is incapable of simple methodological reduction, they all share a concern with music as a sign-based discourse. For Kofi Agawu, the semiotics of music is 'a plural and irreducibly interdisciplinary field' which provides a framework for thinking music structurally and stylistically, and which is exemplified in the multiplicity of approaches pioneered by Jean-Jacques Nattiez, Eero Tarasti, Kofi Agawu, Márta Grabócz, Raymond Monelle, Robert Hatten and others (Agawu 2009, p. 9).

Where the semiotics/semiology of music developed very much within a structuralist context, Deleuze is a post-structuralist philosopher. He acknowledges that it was in Umberto Eco's *The Open Work* that he discovered the absence of any kind of centre or point of convergence in 'modern' art works, as attention shifted from structures and codes to fluxes and multiplicities (Deleuze 1994, p. 313). His own semiotics is a mix of that of Charles Sanders Peirce and the linguistic theory of Louis Hjelmslev, both of whom take up positions at odds with the semiology of Ferdinand de Saussure, the initiator of that field. As Brian Massumi notes, Deleuze, alone and together with Guattari, rethinks semiotic theory a number of times in his work (Massumi 1992, p. 24), perhaps most notably in the books

Proust and Signs, Anti-Oedipus, A Thousand Plateaus and the two volumes on Cinema.

Semiotics is preferred by Deleuze to semiology on the grounds that where the latter is primarily linguistic in conception, devaluing the non-linguistic or attempting to think it in linguistic terms, the former seems better suited to thinking pre- and non-verbal signs, images and sounds (Deleuze 2005a, p. xi). In Peirce, he finds 'the most complete and the most varied' classification of signs and images (Ibid., p. xix). Despite valuing Peirce's work highly, Deleuze and Guattari recognize in *A Thousand Plateaus* that his distinctions are nevertheless founded on 'signifier-signified relations', an opposition they are devoted to overcoming (Deleuze and Guattari 1988, p. 531). While they continue to use his terms, they alter their connotations so that Peirce's three most basic sign types, namely, indexes, icons and symbols, are now understood in terms of territoriality-deterritorialization relations, instead of signifier-signified relations.[1] Indexes now become territorial signs or 'territorial states of things constituting the designatable', icons are 'operations of reterritorialization constituting the signifiable' and symbols mark a 'relative deterritorialization', in 'a constant movement of referral from sign to sign' (Ibid., p. 112). In addition, the 'diagram', which in Peirce is 'a special case of the icon', is given a more specific function in *A Thousand Plateaus* that is 'irreducible to either the icon or the symbol' (Ibid., p. 531). Diagrams, according to Deleuze and Guattari, produce relations rather than represent them, and the agents of such deterritorializations are termed abstract machines. It is the abstract machine which extracts 'destratified particle-signs' which 'constitute unformed traits capable of combining with one another' (Ibid., pp. 144–5).

In one of his many definitions of the sign, Peirce states 'I define a Sign as anything which is so determined by something else, called its Object, and so determines an effect upon a person, which effect I call its Interpretant, that the latter is thereby mediately determined by the former' (Peirce 1998, p. 478).[2] With the act of signification in this way divided into three distinct elements, the sign, the object and the interpretant, Peirce now expands his semiotic lexicon so that icons, indexes and symbols pertain exclusively to the 'object'; qualisigns, sinsigns and legisigns pertain to the 'sign'; and rhemes, dicents and arguments pertain solely to the 'interpretant'. This becomes even more complex since Peirce then combines elements from each of these three trichotomies with one another to produce, in all, ten distinctive sign types such as a rheme-icon-qualisign or a dicent-symbol-legisign. The reader should not be perturbed at this point with the density of Peirce's terms and his taxonomy of signs since understanding of this chapter does not presume any detailed knowledge of them or of their operation within Peirce's system.

In his two books on Cinema (*The Movement-Image* and *The Time-Image*), Deleuze, convinced that 'the image gives rise to signs', takes up Peirce's rich taxonomy to discuss the multiplicitous array of image types that are employed in the history of cinema, holding that 'a sign appears to be a particular image which represents a type of image, sometimes from the point of view of its composition, sometimes from the point of view of its genesis or its formation (or even its extinction)', and he suggests that 'there are several signs – two at least for each type of image' (Deleuze 2005a, p. 71).

Once again, Deleuze is clear in stating that while he uses Peirce's terms to designate particular signs, the sense for each term is sometimes retained, sometimes modified and sometimes changed completely, with the result that he presents 16 discrete cinematic sign types in *Cinema 1* (Semetsky 2010, p. 244). Where, in Peirce's taxonomy, the 'dicisign' or 'dicent' designates the proposition in general and the 'rheme' stands for a predicate, for Deleuze, the dicisign, in a cinematic context, is 'a perception in the frame of another perception' and the rheme is the sign of a more liquefied perception which passes or flows beyond the frame (Deleuze 2005a, p. 82). To this, he adds the 'gramme', the 'engramme' and the 'photogramme' which designate a more gaseous, molecular perception. All of this, in Deleuze's semiotic scheme, maps out a continuum from 'a solid state, where molecules are not free to move about (molar or human perception)' through 'a liquid state, where the molecules move about and merge into one another', to 'a gaseous state, defined by the free movement of each molecule' (Ibid., p. 86). It should become apparent as the chapter progresses that this distinction of solid, liquid and gaseous signs in cinema resonates very well with the work of a number of contemporary composers, in whose work musical material is similarly dissolved and molecularized.

A number of authors have considered the usefulness of Peirce's semiotics in musical contexts including Nattiez, (1990), Monelle (1991), Hatten (1994), Grant (2003) and Curry (2012). While Nattiez suggests that 'Peirce's thought is so complex, and so often contradictory, that reconstruction of *the* coherent Peircian doctrine seems at present nearly impossible' (Nattiez 1990, p. 7), he recognizes that Eco's adoption of Peirce's interpretant entails that the sign becomes a 'virtual object' blocking 'any structuralist theory of communication'. The cosy pairing of signifier and signified with its correspondence of sign and object is overtaken by unlimited semiosis, unleashed by an 'infinite chain of interpretants' in a process that is now open-ended and ongoing (Ibid., pp. 22–3). While this realization does not lead Nattiez to shift from a structuralist to a Deleuzian post-structuralist position, his critique of Eco's development may nevertheless be taken as corroboration of the openness that Deleuze finds in the Italian semiotician's theory, and which is important for his own work.

While Peirce regards music primarily as an iconic sign, Monelle argues that 'the musical work, in its most typical form, is a *rhematic indexical legisign*', 'the actual performance, or a copy of the score, is a *rhematic indexical sinsign*' and within music's textures, we can find 'qualisigns of theme, rhythm, harmony, style [and] evocation, some of which may function iconically or symbolically' (Monelle 1991, p. 107). Once again, in the context of the present discussion, the important point to grasp here is simply the analogous adoption of Peirce's semiotic classifications in a musical context and not a detailed understanding of the meaning of his terms. Where in Hatten's account the indexical stands for 'representations by conventional association, such as patriotic tunes or chorale melodies' (Hatten 1994, p. 242), Grant, in contrast, invokes the indexical as a category capable of relating justly, and in Peircian terms, to the specificity of experimental music. She suggests that contemporary experimental music is marked by 'a change in the dominant mode of signification from the symbolic to the indexical' as it focuses on a 'general, indexical tendency of presentation as opposed to representation' (Grant 2003, p. 173). This switch in significatory mode is explained with the example of the interval of a major third which, being denied its more usual symbolic role within a coherent musical system, is here framed in such a way that our response to it becomes more significant than the fact of its intervallic content. In this situation, attention is drawn from the object's habitual function to the object itself and to 'the way we otherwise perceive it and relate to it' (Ibid., p. 178).

This leads Grant to the question of musical material, where it is noted that musicological discussion has generally favoured 'a historicised understanding of "musical material"' as 'preformed' material (Ibid., p. 186). Certain musical elements have generally been treated as primary and essential while others have been dismissed as peripheral, at times being reduced to no more than pre-material. In discussing this question, Grant draws close to the degree of molecularity expected by Deleuze in the formation of both artworks and signification. Consequently, when we discuss the semiotic potential of contemporary musical material later in the chapter, we will do so with Deleuzian molecularity in mind and not in terms of preformed, conventional associations, operating at the level of the molar. It is this molecularity that we find in Deleuze and Guattari and, as we shall see, in the musical work of Lachenmann, Aperghis and Levinas.

Hjelmslev, expression and content in recent music theory

Alongside this interest in Peirce's semiotics, Deleuze and Guattari produce, following Hjelmslev, a theory of content and expression in which the 'content plane' and 'expression plane' are purely arbitrary and functional in status and are recognized solely in relation to one another. Where a structuralist approach generally seeks to analyse a phenomenon in terms of underlying codes and signs, the post-structuralism of Deleuze and Guattari is unconcerned with such meta-languages and eschews the reduction of a phenomenon to an essential core, seeking instead to map its surface forces.

While the term 'expression' is often used in the context of aesthetic Romanticism, the rejection of which is most often associated with the work of Eduard Hanslick, Deleuze and Guattari draw on the distinction of content and expression theorized in Hjelmslev's *Prolegomena to a Theory of Language* (1943), a study of language and sign-functioning.

They are not the first to do so, since Hjelmslev's opposition has been taken up by a number of theorists and, in Nattiez's view, it is a reinterpretation of Saussure in which 'the signified becomes the "content" and the signifier becomes the "expression"' (Nattiez 1990, p. 4). For Eco, Hjelmslev's definition, which envisages the sign-function as a reciprocal relation between two 'functives' namely, the expression-plane and the content-plane, may be thought of as a more precise elaboration of Saussure (Eco 1984, p. 14). Hjelmslev, according to Eco, tells us that it is '"more appropriate to use the word sign as the name for the unit consisting of content-form and the expression-form and established by the solidarity that we have called the sign-function" (1943: 58). A sign-function is realized when two *functives* (expression and content) enter into a mutual correlation' (Eco 1976, p. 49).

For Hjelmslev, '"the decisive point for the question of whether or not a sign is present is" . . . whether there are *two* planes and these planes are not *conformal*'. In Hjelmslev's words, 'two functives are said to be conformal if any particular derivate of the one functive without exception enters the same functions as a particular derivative of the other functive, and vice-versa'. Eco adds that 'in the case of "pure games", as well as of music, formal logic and algebra, "if the two planes are tentatively posited the functional net will be entirely the same in both". Therefore these structures are not called "semiotic" for they are interpretable but not biplanar (while languages are biplanar and not conformal)' (Ibid., p. 89).

Monelle demonstrates the content/expression opposition with reference to the particular segmentations of perception produced by individual languages, and how the borders traced by content-forms are situated differently in particular languages. In Welsh, for example, the word '*glas*, meaning "blue", covers also certain shades of green and grey, while Welsh *llwyd* means "grey" as well as "brown"'. This implies that an expression has no fixed meaning and that content and expression are equal partners within a sign function. Indeed, they are said to exist purely because of this sign function (Monelle 1992, p. 44). A musical example of this would be the differences that we encounter in naming the pitches of the chromatic scale in relation to specific pitch frequencies. As was discussed in Chapter 3, the pitch frequency of a given pitch will depend entirely on the tuning system that is adopted, and the same pitch frequency will be identified under different note names depending on the system in use. Where the international standard pitch A4 (the A immediately above middle C on the piano) is set nowadays at 440 Hertz, a number of variations in frequency for this pitch have also been used throughout music's history.

Hjelmslev's opposition of content and expression has clearly not been accepted uncritically into musicology. Considering the extent to which music should be thought of as a language, Baroni suggests that a positive answer to this question would stem from being able to establish a relationship between a musical plane of expression defined as 'audible structure' and a plane of content defined as 'semantic structure'. The plane of expression and the plane of content are said to be related in that 'one "stands for" the other . . . acts as a sign for the other and refers back to it (that is, so that sounds acquire meaning)' in ways that are accepted and recognized through social and cultural conventions or codes (Baroni 1983, p. 181). Baroni is cautious since he believes that the potential workings of such codes and of the planes of expression and content are insufficiently understood. There are problems of psychology, anthropology and epistemology concerning the plane of content while the plane of expression is equally beset with textual, formal and perceptual problems (Ibid., p. 182). Overall, he is unsure of the value of using Hjelmslev's opposition within music theory since he is concerned that it is related to the traditional antithesis of form and content (Ibid., pp. 198–9).

Unlike Baroni, Tarasti (1996) is convinced that a level of expression and a level of content are minimum prerequisites for any musical semiotic, and he theorizes that the level of expression refers to 'the concrete physical-aural stimulus', the technical work of composition, while the level of content deals with all 'emotions, associations, values and meanings joined to music', in other words, the aesthetic response of the listener. These two levels are said to be 'inseparably united with each other – precisely as Saussure presumed that every sign has two aspects: signifier and signified, which are like two sides of the same sheet of paper. Therefore the semiotical analysis of music requires that one pay simultaneous attention to both expression and content' (Tarasti 1996, p. 9).

In an earlier study, Tarasti goes even further and considers expression and content in terms of form and substance. With this model, the substance of expression involves the basic cultural materials of music such as scales, rhythms, dynamics, timbres and so on, and the form of expression refers to the form which is set upon the musical materials. The substance of content refers to 'the associative responses aroused by the composition in a listener', while the form of content refers to the way in which 'a culture determines the patterns and symbols which permit a listener to interpret his responses to a musical work' (Tarasti 1979, p. 31). According to this idea, a composer is not in any way privileged in terms of interpreting the content of her/his own composition and becomes one listener among many, each with their own responses, since 'the content level in art music remains an open, empty place for the shaping of various meanings' (Ibid., pp. 32, 54).

According to Tarasti, the relationship between expression and content in music is completely different from its working in language, and where the relation between signifier and signified in a verbal sign is arbitrary, expression and content are linked inextricably in music so that any change in one results in a concomitant change in the other (Tarasti 1994, p. 11). Ultimately, for Tarasti, music can only be a semiotic process if 'it has at least those two levels of signification' (Ibid., p. 29).

As may be clear from the discussion so far, Hjelmslev has a problem envisaging sign systems that differ greatly from language since with music, for example, 'no analysis of the content-plane can ever be undertaken to prove that it is non-conformal with the expression plane'. To this, Monelle responds by questioning the validity or sensitivity of Hjemslev's criterion, suggesting that a content plane can only be posited for 'certain kinds of language', most specifically for what Roman Jakobson terms referential language (Monelle 1992, p. 46). Furthermore, following Greimas and Courtès, who note that it is often difficult to determine a line separating the content-plane and the expression-plane, Monelle suggests that this distinction, which has been so important for Hjemslev and traditional linguistics, is reduced in force to the extent that music may in fact demonstrate 'the coalescence of expression-plane and content-plane to an even greater degree' (Ibid., p. 238).

While the reception of Hjelmslev's work in Eco, Monelle, Tarasti and Baroni operates primarily within a structuralist semiotic framework, and many aspects of their work are completely at odds with the post-structuralist theory of Deleuze and Guattari, the discussion raises a number of points worth noting. For Deleuze and Guattari, there is no question of thinking of music as some kind of language, of conceptualizing it in terms of audible and semantic structure or of determining its semiotic potential on the basis of criteria such as biplanar[ity] or conformal[ity]. More hopefully, it seems that certain strands from the work of these writers are developed in Deleuze and Guattari including, at the most basic level, Hjelmslev's identification of planes of expression and content and the importance of treating them simultaneously. While Tarasti's identification of 'substance of expression' is an interesting one, it is not elemental enough beginning, as it does, with already pre-formed musical components such as scales, rhythms, dynamics and timbres, all of which, in Deleuze-Guattarian theory, needs to become much more liquefied, gaseous and molecular. In a similar way, Tarasti's concern with the responses of individual listeners is much too subject-focused for Deleuze and Guattari, who work on the micro-scale of the sub-subjective, with collective assemblages of enunciation and molecular intensities. Like Tarasti, Deleuze and Guattari think of the expression plane and the content plane as inextricably linked, albeit that they do not understand these terms in precisely the same way. Finally, like Eco, Greimas, Courtès and Monelle, they reject the monopoly enjoyed by the traditional linguistic model for semiotics while recognizing music's non-linguistic semiotic potential.

More recently, Tarasti (2000) has cast semiotic theory in a rather different light invoking, in the process, a genealogy of first generation semioticians, primarily Saussure and Peirce, followed by a second generation exemplified by Lévi-Strauss, Greimas, Foucault and Lotman. A third, perhaps more problematic generation is identified from the 1980s, in which he includes Foucault's later work, Barthes, Kristeva as well as 'Eco's novels, Derrida's deconstruction, cognitive science, Baudrillard, Bourdieu and so on' (Tarasti 2000, pp. 3, 18). Deleuze and Guattari, perhaps surprisingly, are not mentioned as part of this. Surveying the scene, Tarasti opines the passing of structuralist semiotics noting that its fixed models are incapable of analysing 'universes of flux, where everything is in motion' and where 'nothing is stable, schematic or fixed' (Ibid., p. 3). While he is now searching for what may be 'the most important thing in semiotics; namely, the states *before* the formation of signs, accordingly *"pre-signs"*' (Ibid., p. 7), he attempts to do so by shifting from a structuralist semiotics to an existential semiotics that draws among others on Heidegger. Again, Deleuze, who more than anyone has theorized the sign or the pre-sign at its most molecular, is absent from his account.

Despite this omission, Tarasti now recognizes that 'when the sign has crystallized, there remains almost nothing to be done – on the level of signs themselves', and while he continues to admire Peirce's classification of signs, he has come to the conclusion that 'the most interesting, existential moment of signs is in the moment before or after them, since the life of signs does not stop, of course, with their fixation into objects'. Since he is now of the opinion that signs are 'always in a state of becoming', he allows that a text can be articulated into 'clear-cut units' only in exceptional moments and that

> there are situations in which the continuous becoming flux, and streaming of signs – which hence imitates the inner movement of subjects carrying them – stops, stagnates for a while into a phase of *l'être en soi* (the sign is the same as its concept). There form and substance, matter and mind, communication and signification are united in oneness. However, the pause is always temporary (Ibid., p. 7).

Expression and content: A Deleuze-Guattarian perspective

What Tarasti is proposing in his 'existential semiotics' bears some relation to what Deleuze and Guattari describe as territorialization, deterritorialization and reterritorialization, and he also posits the operation of at least six 'new species of signs' including pre-signs (Tarasti 2000, p. 19). Deleuze and Guattari go much further than this in *A Thousand Plateaus* where they theorize the possibility of multiple semiotic systems or 'regimes of signs' by which they mean 'any specific formalization of expression' (Deleuze and Guattari 1988, pp. 111–12). Acknowledging the arbitrariness of their selections, they enumerate several regimes or semiotic systems including (1) a signifying system or semiology, for which language is the model, but which, they insist, has no privileged place; (2) a 'presignifying semiotic' which promotes multiple forms of expression and in which aspects of 'corporeality, gesturality, rhythm, dance, and rite coexist heterogeneously' alongside language (Ibid., pp. 117–18); (3) a countersignifying semiotic and (4) a postsignifying regime. These are all described in detail, and it is emphasized that all semiotics may be mixed, combining different forms of content and various regimes of signs, given that 'presignifying elements are always active in the signifying regime; countersignifying elements are always present and at work within it; and postsignifying elements are already there' (Ibid., pp. 119, 136). Opposing the reduction of semiotics to signifying signs comprising signifiers and signifieds, Deleuze and Guattari also introduce the concept of asignifying signs or 'pure intensities' which are 'particle-signs' operating 'beneath contents and expressions' (Ibid., p. 70) and which may form an asignifying diagram (Ibid., pp. 138–9).

Deleuze and Guattari follow Hjelmslev in holding that expression and content are purely arbitrary and functional in status and there is no absolute justification for designating one element of a sign as expression and the other as content. It is their 'mutual solidarity' that defines and identifies them, and they can only be recognized relatively in opposition to one another 'as mutually opposed functives of one and the same function' (Hjelmslev, cited in Deleuze and Guattari 1988, p. 45).

Hjelmslev's theory is attractive to Deleuze and Guattari because it bypasses the traditional opposition of form and content and recognizes the arbitrary nature of simple designations of elements as either expression or content. It concentrates instead on the stage prior to the formation and constitution of elements as expressions or contents. Hjelmslev's theory allows the supposition of what Bogue terms 'a material substrate which precedes the formation of the planes of expression and content' (Bogue 1989, pp. 126–7), and Deleuze and Guattari identify this substrate as the plane of consistency or Body without Organs, that is, 'the unformed, unorganized, nonstratified, or destratified body' on which all fixed categories and structures are dissolved or decomposed only to form ever-new formations of heterogeneous elements (Deleuze and Guattari 1988, p. 43).

The level of content and the level of expression are formed from this plane of consistency, and 'between content and expression, there is neither a correspondence nor a cause-effect relation nor a signified-signifier relation: there is real distinction, reciprocal presupposition, and only isomorphy' (Ibid., pp. 502–3). Deleuze and Guattari depart from the already discussed structuralist readings of Hjelmslev's work and consider his opponents to be mistaken in designating the content/expression pairing as a reactionary return to the devalued opposition of signified and signifier (Ibid., pp. 43, 68). In *Nietzsche and Philosophy*, Deleuze approaches the relationship of expression and content from the perspective of force. Slightly modifying Deleuze's text, Brian Massumi posits that 'a thing has as many meanings as there are forces capable of seizing it' (Massumi 1992, p. 10), and signification is consequently 'more a meeting between forces than simply the forces behind the signs'. It becomes 'the encounter of lines of force, each of which is actually a complex of other forces' which resist neat, logical unification (Ibid., p. 11).

Value now becomes a question of the hierarchy of forces manifest within the complexity of a phenomenon. Although we can still distinguish content value and expression value, the distinction is purely functional since both expression and content can be recognized as either the overpowering or the overpowered force. The sign no longer refers to content and is neither a referent nor a signified, but rather refers to the entire complex of forces which are enveloped within it (Ibid., p. 12). In addition to being functional, the distinction of content and expression is 'relative and reversible' since the content in one place can be the expression in another, to the extent that 'the same thing can be both at different times or simultaneously, depending on which encounter is in question and from what angle'. This does not reduce the sign to the subjective, however, since expression and content are not established by the validation of an external observer, being determined by the 'application of an actual force', by a 'power relation'. In their reversibility, they relate to one another in a state of 'reciprocal presupposition' so that they only exist together, are 'mutually determining' and while always in practice mixed, they are 'distinct in nature' (Ibid., pp. 12–13).

In Deleuze-Guattarian terms, meaning is 'an interface between at least two force fields, or more specifically, between a form of content . . . and a form of expression' (Ibid., p. 15) which Massumi explains with an example taken from the carpenter's workshop, namely, the process of making a table. In this case, the 'formal organization of functions' (the carpenter's methods and procedures) is the form of expression, while the series of states undergone by the wood in the process from that of raw material to a table is the form of content (Ibid., p. 13). The distinction of form of expression and form of content facilitates the isolation of the 'dynamic aspect of both formations at their determining point of impact'. Instead of two independent and 'irreducible formations', we have the two aspects of an interface (Ibid., pp. 13–14).

Linking Hjelmslev and Peirce, it may be said that the interface between the form of expression and the form of content presents 'a set of abstract relations between abstract points', what Deleuze and Guattari term a 'diagram'. This is an encounter in which form of expression and form of content become fused. The encounter is dynamic in nature rather than static and consists of the 'interaction between a multiplicity of terms, an interrelation of relations, an integration of disparate elements. It is a diagram of a process of becoming. . . . that enables a real "translation" to take place' (Ibid., p. 14). Again, using the image of the table, Massumi illustrates how 'the interrelation of relations crosses from one substance (the thingness of tools and wood) to another (the ideality of thought)'. The dynamic element of the process within materials is repeated, this time in thought, as 'thought repeats the interrelation in its own substance . . . mimics the encounter' and establishes 'a parallel network of vectors, but between different points (concepts instead of tools and wood)'.

For Deleuze and Guattari, meaning consists in such translational processes. The process first enacted with wood can be repeated in the realm of thought, and what was enacted in thought can be translated into verbal language. The original set of dynamic relations can therefore exist in 'things (tools to wood)' but also in ideas '(concept to concept)' (Ibid., p. 16), however 'if meaning is a process of translation from one substance to another of a different order and back again, what it moves across is an unbridgeable abyss of fracturing. If meaning is the in-between of content and expression, it is nothing more (nor less) than the being of their "non-relation"' (Ibid., pp. 15–16). So it is that 'the interrelation of relations between the wood and the tool bears no resemblance to that between concepts, which bears no relation to that between phonemes or letters: "no conformity or common form, nor even correspondence"' (Ibid., pp. 16–17).

Deleuze, semiotics and music

Pascal Criton translates all of this into a musical context when she notes that 'musical writing' involves movement from the 'autonomization of signs, to the extent that force-form relations circulate from sounds to signs, from gestures to tools and to representations of time and space' (Criton 2011a, p. 241). Writing on how Deleuze's idiosyncratic semiotics operates in the musical sphere, Criton emphasizes, as has already been noted, that he is concerned with the harnessing and capture of material forces and with the play of 'sub-representative dynamisms' that determine 'the intensive experience (individuation)' within an asignifying field (Criton 2011b, p. 2). This is a sub-representational zone featuring the play of 'material-forces, affects and percepts',[3] a question of intensive fields in which 'relations of bodies, signs [and] forces' are configured diagrammatically (Ibid., p. 3). Heterogeneous systems or series from diverse areas are put in communication, resulting in productions that are asignifying and which operate at a 'pre-material' level. Semetsky defines the Deleuze-Guattarian diagram as 'a bridge, a diagonal connection that . . . connects planes of expression and content leading to the emergence of new forms' and in which 'fixed and rigid signifieds give way to the production of new meanings' (Semetsky 2010, p. 243).

For the composer, pre-material components can derive from a great number of milieus including music, literature, painting, cinema, philosophy, the sciences, politics and so on. These are not pre-established, commonly accepted or clearly understood molar categories, but rather molecular, pre-material forces that escape from their previous placements to re-form in new heterogeneous assemblages. These forces meet and enter into relations at a molecular level, below that of representational forms and in such a way that they formulate an intensive diagram composed of music's most molecular properties and components. These range from the relatively molar character of individual chords, pitch aggregates, musical gestures, single pitches, durations, timbres and attacks to the previously unattainable sub-components of sound and pitch, all of which can be connected, disconnected and transposed in multiple ways as a new diagram is traced with its functions reorganized. This means that as the forces comprising the new diagram are rearranged, new matters of expression are produced along with new compositional techniques, materials and micro-materials and the creative redeployment of already existent materials, in what Criton terms 'the overlapping of the semiotic and the material' (Criton 2011b, p. 5). As Criton notes

> The sound element itself is a compound of variables (frequencies, intensities, durations), displaying evolutionary and interactive behaviours. The sound element can thenceforth be considered a decomposable and recomposable *compound* that can always be exposed to transformations. Its imprint is the expression of a state of variables that are conserved . . . or that modulate (modification of only certain variables, i.e. vibrato) or that are transformed into another state of relations . . . . The molecularization of sound material permits access to a variety of continua, to a line of unlimited variation of sound relations (Criton 2011a, p. 247).

In this view, 'sound is an essentially heterogeneous reality, a multiplicity made up of contingencies and determinations, of magnitudes, of dimensions which increase and decrease according to the event that is in process' (Ibid., p. 239). For Criton, this *'acoustic multiplicity* . . . integrates all of the factors that shape the sound and the potentiality of the spatio-temporal variables that will be specified in a particular sound event'. The quest for a musical content that is inseparable from sonic expression results, among other things, in the identification of bundles of non-sonorous forces or becomings, including what Deleuze and Guattari refer to as the becoming-animal, becoming-woman, becoming-child and becoming-machine. While we will look briefly to examples of 'becoming-animal' in recent contemporary music, ultimately, for Deleuze and Guattari, there are no limits to the connective possibilities that can be produced in this way.

The composers whose music and ideas work most within Deleuzian terms are those who first molecularize, deconstruct or dissolve existing musical material, who attempt to empty it of existing connotations or who strive to use familiar sounds or musical gestures in unfamiliar ways. It is the composers who integrate sounds that previously were occluded from the realm of the musical, who work with what might be called the pre-semiotic building blocks of sound or who create new semiotic units through the hybridization of components of existing but previously independent sounds or through the development of new instrumental possibilities including all new technological means.

In their Kafka volume, Deleuze and Guattari enumerate the three characteristics of minor literature[4] as 'the deterritorialization of language, the connection of the individual to a political immediacy, and the collective assemblage of enunciation' (Deleuze and Guattari 1986, p. 18). In relation to Kafka, they state that

> Since articulated sound was a deterritorialized noise but one that will be reterritorialized in sense, it is now sound itself that will be deterritorialized irrevocably, absolutely. The sound or the word that traverses this new deterritorialisation no longer belongs to a language of sense, even though it derives from it, nor is it an organized music or song, even though it might appear to be. . . . Everywhere, organized music is traversed by a line of abolition – just as a language of sense is traversed by a line of escape – in order to liberate a living and expressive material that speaks for itself and has no need of being put into a form (Ibid., p. 21).

While Deleuze and Guattari are thinking primarily of the word in Kafka's idiosyncratic developments in language, this seems to be just as much the case with musical modernism where the individual parameters of sound open onto 'unexpected internal intensities – in short, an asignifying *intensive utilization*' of music (adapted from Deleuze and Guattari 1986, p. 22). Just as language for modernist author Louis-Ferdinand Céline can become 'nothing more than intensities', what Deleuze and Guattari refer to as 'a kind of "minor music"', Kafka's writing is 'always made up of deterritorialized sounds, a language that moves head over heels and away' in 'an escape for language, for music, for writing'. Again, it is making use of 'the polylingualism of one's own language, to make a minor or intensive use of it' (Ibid., pp. 26–7). In contrast with this, a major literature

> follows a vector that goes from content to expression. Since content is presented in a given form of the content, one must find, discover, or see the form of expression that goes with it. That which conceptualizes well expresses itself. But a minor, or revolutionary, literature begins by expressing itself and doesn't conceptualize until afterward. . . . Expression must break forms, encourage ruptures and new spoutings. When a form is broken, one must reconstruct the content that will necessarily be part of a rupture in the order of things' (Ibid., p. 28).

Lachenmann, molecularity and captured forces

While Deleuze is not an author who is cited by composer Helmut Lachenmann, his music is nevertheless a model of the molecularity theorized by Deleuze and Guattari and it may, after their work on Kafka, be termed a 'minor' music. Concerned in the late 1960s with freeing himself from a tonality which he thought of as obsolete in its 'mental models and forms of communication', by 1979, he had come to realize that the idea of a musical tabula rasa was unattainable, that it was impossible to escape tonality fully and that the composer's task was, by necessity, one of understanding the tonal determinations within musical material (Hockings 1995, p. 9). With the experience of the avant-garde from the early 1950s in mind, Lachenmann now accepts that tonality is implied not only in the tempered scale but also in the very idea of those sounds that are thought of as musical, in the pervasiveness of traditional playing techniques, conventional expressive gestures and musical linearity.

Beyond tonality, the new music has itself produced its own taxonomy of rhetorical figures, for example, in the gestures with which pieces conventionally begin or end, in 'dramatic percussion flourishes, trembling *ostinati*, formal *sforzati*, multiphonics or *clusters*' which form a collection of shared figures that are rooted in previous music (Kaltenecker 1993, p. 8). For Lachenmann, the music and ideas of the generation of Ligeti, Penderecki, Kagel, Schnebel and Berio, with its toleration of tonal elements that had been rejected by the serial composers, represent in the 1960s a 'veiled regression' followed in the 1970s by an 'open regression' to a reified concept of beauty. (Lachenmann 1980, pp. 20–1). This sees the return of 'pre-serial topoi, gestures, tonal relics and fragments in the widest sense, which had already proved their expressive qualities and as such had been "socialized"' (Lachenmann 1995, p. 95). Lachenmann instead follows the example of his former teacher Luigi Nono in attempting to empty the musical material of these historical, societal, traditional and conventional connotations to prepare it for renewed use.

In line with the Frankfurt School philosophers whose names and ideas appear explicitly in his articles (Lukács, Marcuse, Benjamin and Adorno), Lachenmann now articulates the impossibility of completely rooting out tonality as 'a dialectic of progression and regression' (Lachenmann 1995, p. 95). A composer can never recapture the virginity of musical material since every musical fragment or gesture, every sequence of notes contains within itself sedimented history which must be taken account of. While Nono, for example, is successful in his use of bel canto, filling this great historical category with new content, Lachenmann judges that Stockhausen's use of cowbells in *Gruppen* 'involuntarily affirm[s] a completely Mahlerian pastoral aura which is stronger than its underlying structure'. In saying so, Lachenmann recognizes, as a new starting point for composition, that the historical connotations within traditional material cannot be neglected or abandoned, and that it must be consciously integrated into a composer's use of the material. His own music is full of musical 'relics' and 'clichés', including scales, glissandi, arpeggios and ostinati which are integrated within his pieces only after he has attempted to dispose of their historical aura (Kaltenecker 1993, p. 9).

For Lachenmann, the concept of a naïve artist is a contradictory one and composers who merely add a little atonality to an essentially nineteenth-century palette fail to go beyond the expressive possibilities of the past. Consequently, his own compositions from the early 1980s entail processes of 'releasing, wrenching, tearing the specific sound elements in these structures from their existing, apparently self-evident context and allotting them to different, newly-created categories which the composer has to establish' (Lachenmann 1995, p. 100). When Hans Werner Henze accused him of composing a 'Musica Negativa', Lachemann responded that Henze had failed to engage properly with tradition, working instead with a 'complacent technique' (Steinitz 2000, p. 7). For Lachenmann, Henze's music 'merely *helps itself* to traditional materials (instead of developing them further)', and he wonders how it 'can justify such [an] unbroken rapport with what is already created' (Lachenmann 1997, pp. 189–90). Accusing Henze of unscrupulously exploiting traditional musical material rather than allowing it to reflect (Lachenmann 1997, p. 190), he opposes any form of contemporary composition that proceeds merely by 'using off-the-shelf products from the supermarket of tradition' (Lachenmann 1995, p. 93). For Lachenmann, 'expressive spontaneity' does not exist and it is a mistake to suggest that a composer can draw innocently from tradition. Composers subscribing to these views are mistaken in imagining that they can avoid the 'struggle of the fractured subject with itself' and consequently avoid engaging with traditional material (Ibid., p. 191).

While acknowledging that Lachenmann frames his critical approach to composition in the terminology of various Frankfurt School philosophers with their variable concepts of dialectic, of reification, of sedimented history within musical material, the rejection of socially accepted forms, the auratic quality of the work of art and so on, his work benefits also from being considered in Deleuzian terms, an alternative framework that is clearly not inimical to its spirit. There is a molecularity in the kind of musical material favoured by Lachenmann, and his rejection of the unreflective use of musical material seems to equate to what Deleuze and Guattari call the molar.

The 'aesthetic apparatus' composed of the instrumentarium, of playing techniques, expressive gestures, harmonic progressions, notational systems, musical institutions, markets and so on, equates to the Deleuze-Guattarian assemblage, and Lachenmann challenges composers to take account of the workings of all previous musical assemblages and the roles that individual component parts have played in each formation (Lachenmann 1980, p. 22). It is necessary that the composer clarifies the relationship between her or his 'own expressive will and the aesthetic apparatus . . . before composition begins' (Ibid., p. 24) in that each composer must avoid using molar material, finding new ways to molecularize it in the formation of new and distinctive musical assemblages.

Lachenmann is close to Deleuze in recognizing that what seem to be 'incompatible sounds and objects' are brought together as 'a musical sense-unit' as the composer works intuitively in search of something that is at first merely suspected (Lachenmann 1995, pp. 98–9). Dialectical structuralism is Lachenmann's way of referring to the process whereby composition results from 'a conscious-unconscious confrontation' with musical structures which are acknowledged but also broken and remade (Ibid., p. 100). His works emerge from the confrontation between the composer's creativity and a pre-organized 'network of possibilities', and while 'each event' is 'integrated into a new structural context', it nevertheless, 'seems always to remember the older context from which it was taken' (Lachenmann 2009, pp. 198–9).

What Lachenmann describes as a dialectical process, namely, the breaking up of previous musical structures and the production of 'different, newly-created categories' (Lachenmann 1995, p. 100), seems very similar to Deleuze-Guattarian deterritorialization and reterritorialization. The composer cannot appropriate traditional elements for composition without first emptying them of their conventional meanings, the associations, for example, surrounding the sound of a tam-tam must first be acknowledged and taken account of to render it capable of bearing new meanings. Even in the 1970s, when he begins to work again with elements from the Austro-Germanic tradition, manipulating associations with 'tonal gestures' from Mozart's clarinet concerto in *Accanto* (1975–76), citing elements of folk song in *Ein Kinderspiel* (1980), playing with traditional dance rhythms in the *Tanzsuite mit Deutschlandlied* (1979–80), working with the tendencies of musicians such as virtuosity or 'orchestral mannerisms (e.g. the unresolved romantic swell gesture in *Kontrakadenz*)' (1970–71), all of this is far from mere quotation and the material is transformed almost beyond recognition to the extent that, as Elke Hockings notes, 'it demands intensive deciphering' (Hockings 1995, p. 13).

Lachenmann distinguishes between music centred on 'affect' and music centred on 'aspect', a distinction between the traditionally expressive components of sound and the modernist notion of composition based purely on the self-reflection of musical materials. He prefers to speak of categories or 'aspects' rather than parameters, stating that 'the creative problem is not to discover a new sound or a new arrangement of sounds, but rather to make a new *aspect* of sound function as an element within a syntactical innovation' (Lachenmann 2009, pp. 197–8). While 'the conventional experience of sound . . . is always already affected, charged with conventions, and ultimately impure' the 'work of the composer is to create a context which can make it intact again, intact under a new aspect'. Relating the 'aspect' to the work of the serial generation of composers, Lachenmann locates the core of his own compositional processes in a concern with 'grading', 'desubjectivising', 'installing new continua' and with deliberating on/liberating ['dé-libération'] musical components charged with conventional resonances while activating new categories (Lachenmann 1993, p. 5).

Paolo de Assis identifies a closeness between what Lachenmann terms 'tonality' and what Deleuze and Guattari refer to as 'opinion'. In *What is Philosophy?* Deleuze and Guattari propose that 'opinion', by which they mean everything that is safely accepted and which seemingly protects us from chaos, is the enemy of art, and that it is art's function to oppose opinion and to pierce the fabric of chaos in order to cast a plane over it (Deleuze and Guattari 1994, pp. 202–4). Since there will always be imitators who wish to restore the clichés of opinion and to expel the previously 'incommunicable novelty' that has been rested from chaos, there is a continual need for new creators 'to carry out necessary and perhaps ever-greater destructions'. As Assis notes, both Deleuze-Guattarian 'opinion' and Lachenmann's 'tonality' are 'systems of domination and repression' which prohibit creativity and stimulate the engendering of empty and repetitive messages. Consequently, the Deleuzian struggle against opinion, as Lachenmann's reflection upon musical materials, constitutes a primary condition for the emergence of creativity (de Assis 2011, p. 11).

Both Deleuze and Lachenmann demonstrate the importance of investigating musical material at the molecular level of forces, and Lachenmann's position can be stated in Deleuzian terms as the constitution of every musical gesture by capturing and captured forces that produce the sign value of the heterogeneously assembled musical unit. As Assis notes 'what Lachenmann affirms as the first foundational activity of a composer (reflecting upon the material) is only meaningful if he or she is capable of identifying the forces behind signs and forms' (Ibid., p. 5). To this, it may be added that the composer must 'unveil false securities' and 'reveal new forces, signs and forms, which bring to light previously unnoticed qualities of the material'.

Aperghis and a Deleuzian logic of sense

The semiotic regime at play in the work of Georges Aperghis is no less rigorous than that of Lachenmann and relies on an equally fundamental rethinking of musical material, both found and newly created. While, as we saw in Chapter 2, semiotic signs from several media are mixed in Aperghis's music theatre works, Kurt D'Haeseleer notes that the images used in *Avis de tempête* 'form an autonomous system' with 'its own logic' (Houdart 2007, pp. 27–8) and Houdart observes similarly that, despite the impossibility of summarizing the libretto satisfactorily, it can nevertheless be read as an 'autonomous work' (Ibid., p. 85). The voice is central to Aperghis's work, even his purely instrumental works, and stimulates exploration of all aspects of what a voice can do in terms of speech, singing, murmuring, yelling and the entire range of expressive gestures (Ibid., p. 88). Like Lachenmann, Aperghis's semiotic vocabulary seems to be propelled by that Spinozan/Deleuzian question 'What can a body do?' (Deleuze 1992, pp. 217–34).

As Houdart recognizes, Aperghis's work is concerned fundamentally with vocality and the 'word' ['la parole'], and whatever signification is produced results, it seems, from engagement with this word in the form of recognizable words or sounds, instrumental gestures or pre-linguistic utterances. This engagement is not preceded by any pre-existing text since the quasi-linguistic units that are settled upon for the spectacle are devised in the course of the shared preparatory work. The sounds which emerge, the phonemes and words that are spoken or sung, are most often only 'minimally comprehensible' with fragments of recognizable expression or the remnants of aspects of musical material, as 'a kind of language reaches us, simultaneously near and far'. Aperghis acknowledges that he often attempts to produce 'a kind of false dialect' (Houdart 2007, p. 88), and he speaks of his *Sextet* (1992) for five female voices and cello in terms of 'the resurgence of a forgotten language'. As Houdart notes, perhaps with Deleuze in mind, the 'logic of sense' in these works is akin to that of poetry and dreams with their 'free associations, . . . derivations, floating states, visions, semi-dreams . . . It is a sensible logic, which questions what it is to feel, and as sensations are multiple and their combinations infinite, this logic always remains incomplete, open, undoubtedly to allow us all the better to hear, touch and breathe the uncertainties, complexities and paradoxes of the world' (Ibid., pp. 88–9).

In *Machinations* (2000), Aperghis works with the voices of four women who are seated at four tables beneath four video monitors. As he explains, 'their voices pronounce phonemes, forerunners of human speech, which gradually compose themselves into counterpoint and, according to the different mixtures, form "languages"' (Aperghis 2002, p. 2). He continues

> This formless matter sometimes organises itself as snatches of discourse that are themselves affected by human fragility, which rubs off on the speech: stammering, stuttering, asthma, etc. We thus have a concentrate here of both agglomerates of phonemes and various ways of pronouncing them like a concise, imaginary little history of the birth of languages and affects that are linked to them (Ibid., p. 2).

Along with this phonemic play, the four vocal performers produce a range of everyday objects including 'leaves, pebbles, bones, parts of hands, fingers, tree bark, hair, sand, seashells, seeds, feathers' which are placed on the table, picked up by video camera and projected onto the screens (Ibid., pp. 2–3). Aperghis describes the objects explicitly as 'like a concrete expression of the phonemes, as if what is uttered were naming these objects'. In addition to all of this, one further participant, a man who stands in front of a computer, intervenes in the spectacle, manipulating the sound of the women's voices and phrasing, emphasizing particular parameters as well as interfering with the images on their screens so that the phonemes, sound and visual objects become implicated in some kind of fugitive 'musical discourse' (Ibid., p. 3). François Regnault, who produced an 'assemblage' of literary texts in preparation for the work, notes that while these texts are linked coherently, this is for the most part submerged within the final work, appearing explicitly only in places. The fabric of the work is instead constituted by its 'phonemes, noise and the transformation of noises', with recognizable text becoming explicitly intelligible only at certain points (Aperghis and Regnault 2002, pp. 4–5).

This play of phonemes, their definition, selection and combination, is something that Aperghis has worked on since the 1980s. As he acknowledges, *Machinations* displays the practice in its most developed state since, by means of computer technology, he is able to generate combinations and associations of phonemes and consonants outwith all human language and capability. Fragments of the assembled text by Regnault appear only at particular points as 'precise markers' (Ibid., pp. 5–6).

Aperghis's phonemes are constructed in a fairly systematic way and while some are what he describes as 'predominantly vocalic (two vowels, one consonant)', others are 'predominantly consonantal', and he acknowledges here the influence of Deleuze's idea of 'generation by the middle rather than by the end or the beginning' (Ibid., p. 6). In the process, some consonants 'eat' vowels while other vowels are 'eaten' by consonants culminating in the production of melodies, Aperghis's aim being that the phonemes are 'heard as musical phrases' (Ibid., p. 7). He has filled several notebooks with 'phonemic associations' working out what he considers to be the most successful possibilities, and in terms of those phonemes which make the final score, he stresses that 'the melodies (pitches) come from the way of speaking, and exaggerations' that he favoured in rehearsal. Beyond the agency of the performer, the mediation of the computer brings about certain dissociations between phonemic content and aural expression so that, for example, the phonemic content 'rrr . . .', enunciated by a non-acting vocalist, is heard as 'anger' (Ibid., p. 8).

Addressing not only this phonematic play but also the play of images and that of gestures, Aperghis states that none of these 'serve as language' (Ibid., p. 9) and that 'the gestures no longer have a sense' since they have been 'freed', just as his phonemes begin to float when removed from traditionally semantic phrases (Ibid., p. 10).

As Regnault acknowledges, the work focuses on 'the significant rather than the signified', 'the characters' being 'born from the variations of the structure, and not from a "sense"' (Ibid., p. 12).

Aperghis refuses the easy assimilation of traditional linguistic materials and codes, instead rethinking and reinventing 'working practices, languages, relations between gestures and sounds' (cited in Rothstein 2003, p. 3), and as Rothstein puts it, 'the entire network of material on multiple levels (rhythmic, phonetic, melodic, gestural) has been exploded, shattered, and the residue is found, modified, everywhere' (Ibid., p. 5). His adoption of 'oulipian principles of organisation' contributes to the destabilizing of communication structures, and Rothstein notes a particularly strong link between Aperghis and Deleuze on the linguistic level where there is 'an expressivity-movement always bearing a foreign tongue within each language and non-linguistic categories within language as a whole (nomad, poetic lineages). One writes, then, on the same level as the real of an unformed matter, at the same time as that matter traverses and extends all of nonformal language' (Deleuze and Guattari 1988, p. 512). Similarly, of the musical level, Deleuze and Guattari write of 'that secret neuter language without constants and entirely in indirect discourse where the synthesizer and the instrument speak no less than the voice, and the voice plays no less than the instrument' (Ibid., p. 96).

The semiotic system in Aperghis's works is nomadic in nature for both the performer and the spectator (Rothstein 2003, p. 7), and the key principle governing the elements within the spectacle has to do with the misappropriation of 'objects, ideas [and] sounds' where he attempts 'to render the social intimate, the sound visual, the concert theatrical, the words music, the sentimental comic' (Aperghis, cited in Rothstein 2003, p. 10). As Rothstein observes

> even those [texts] which are presented in a comprehensible fashion and which are carriers of clear sense are only rarely exploited for their primary sense. More often they are used in a scenic context which sabotages all literal interpretation. . . . The misappropriation is therefore very often a function of destabilising juxtapositions or deterritorialisations, a sort of "aesthetic of disorder" (Rothstein 2003, p. 10).

Ultimately, 'it presents the image of a world which is disarticulated and in bits and pieces, in which one seeks in vain to discover an ordering hierarchy' (Aperghis, cited in Rothstein 2003, p. 10).

Levinas, the hybridization of sound and 'becoming-animal'

While Michaël Levinas was a founder member of the group *L'Itinéraire* in 1973, and he is often identified as part of the Spectral group of composers, he prefers to describe his work as having progressed in parallel with that of Tristan Murail, Gérard Grisey and Hugues Dufourt. Levinas differed early on from Grisey and Murail in his systemizing of paradoxical situations, privileging what Pierre Albert Castanet has called dirty sounds, that is unclassable hybrid sounds produced by electronic means and unconventional instrumental techniques (Castanet 1991, pp. 73–4).

As is clear from Levinas's music and writings, the notion of some kind of doubling within the production of instrumental sound has been a consistent part of his project from the early 1970s and has been accomplished in a number of ways. Having come to the conclusion around 1974 that it was not possible to base composition solely on the dimensions of musical sound, he turned instead to research into composition for instruments that would allow him to probe, with electronic assistance, previously unexplored aspects of 'living expression', conceptualized as prolongation of the body (Levinas 2002, p. 70).

He describes his compositional concerns from this time as the attempt to prolong the human body through, for example, the hybridization of the voice and instruments, an approach he was able to develop with electro-acoustic means (Ibid., pp. 70–2), and he has been concerned throughout his career with 'the sympathetic vibration of one instrument submitted to another' in which their timbral sources are amalgamated (Castanet 1991, p. 74). As Castanet notes, having chosen, in his early research into unexpected sonorities, to work primarily with the possibilities offered by the horn and the flute, the first of his experiments involves the placing of a horn on the skin of a drum, the drum skin and the metallic timbre vibrating in complete osmosis when the horn is sounded, producing a blurred, mixed sound. The mix of 'parasitic material' and electro-acoustic means is found throughout Levinas's works from 1977 onwards (Ibid., p. 76), the primary criterion being that the electronic adjustment of instrumental sound must generate a new instrumental mutation while not exhausting, falsifying or erasing the instrumental source (Levinas 2002, p. 34).

Working at IRCAM in Paris between 1988 and 1991, Levinas was able to make significant progress on hybridizing instrumental sounds through numerical synthesis (Ibid., pp. 89, 91). His aim was to hybridize 'different families of transitoires of attacks or modes of excitation of the sound body, for example crossing a percussion attack with a trombone attack; crossing the explosion of a human laugh with an attack of ['choquées'] clashing cymbals; crossing the friction or rubbing ['frottement'] of a violin bow with the plucking of a harp string' (Ibid., p. 91).

As a first step, he attempts to explain how in formulating sonic hybrids, the composer's intuition is often in advance of scientific rationality and how the human ear can present viable possibilities, such as the result of 'crossing a low tuba sound with the attack of the skin of a bass drum', before any theoretical explanation can be offered for its working (Ibid., p. 91). A second phase entails working out exactly which instrumental sounds can be combined with one another to good effect, a stage which again involves having confidence in the composer's intuition and which results in the formulation of 'families of sounds susceptible musically to hybridisation among themselves'. He calls this 'the new mixity ['mixité']' (Ibid., pp. 91–3). Levinas tells us that *Préfixes* (1991) was conceived and composed in terms of the new mixity of sound hybridizations and that the work led him to lay out the instrumental families more systematically, arranging them in order of 'spectral coherence' (Ibid., p. 96). Ultimately, he describes his compositional trajectory as chimerical and utopian, and taken up with ideas of how to transform particular instrumental sounds, how to metamorphose them through putting them in vibration with external sound bodies, attempting, for example, to imagine how 'to make an instrument laugh' (Ibid., p. 180).

In their explorations of Kafka's work, Deleuze and Guattari discuss the central place of the 'becoming-animal' (Deleuze and Guattari 1986, p. 87), a concept that is further developed in *A Thousand Plateaus*. To note just a few examples, the concept of 'becoming-animal' is one that links Deleuze and Guattari not only with Messiaen, the bird-lover par excellence for whom so many of his compositions are birdsong become music (or music become birdsong), but also his pupils Gérard Grisey and Michaël Levinas. It is facilitated perfectly by Levinas's sonic hybridizations in, for example, the *Ouverture pour une fête étrange* (1979) for two orchestras and electronic device ['dispositif'] in which the sound is amplified to the point that it becomes 'an almost animal living mob' (Levinas 2002, p. 71). Of the musical spectacle *La Conférence des oiseuax* (1985), he acknowledges that his treatment of the French language is modified to evoke an 'animal cry' (Ibid., p. 251), and 'the animal world' is drawn upon as a sonic filter. In the rawness of the hybrid sounds, in this and earlier works, he detects a 'physical, animal, vocal energy, of the order of the cry' (Ibid., p. 252). Levinas again identifies 'the animal dimension of the instrumental world' as key for the opera *La Métamorphose* (2010) based on Kafka's short story. Impressed by the paintings of Hieronymus Bosch, and by their 'instrumental allegories that extend the animals' snouts, horns, serpents, bells, in which vocality and monstrosity are combined' (Levinas 2012, p. 18), he states that *La Métamorphose* 'develops a completely different set of themes from *La Conférence des oiseaux*' while authorizing 'comparable hybridisations between these three sound worlds: vocal, instrumental and animal'. Gregor's lament, for example, is said to be 'neither totally human nor perfectly animal', and his voice is subdivided and multiplied (Ibid., p. 19).

Conclusion

As with Lachenmann and Aperghis, the novel sounds produced in Levinas's experiments have a semiotic dimension that brings them into the territory of Deleuze-Guattarian molecularity. The notion of the molecular, which has been an underlying theme throughout this book, irrigates musical modernity, from the manipulation of musical motifs and cells in Beethoven, Brahms, Schoenberg and others; in the pointillism that begins with Webern and that marks the music of Boulez and Stockhausen around 1951–52; in the pulverizing of musical material demanded by Varèse and the expectation that composers must refashion musical material. We have encountered Lachenmann's molecularizing of sound, but we are equally in the land of the molecular with Stockhausen's exploration of the inner life of a sound in *Stimmung* and the later experiments of the spectral composers, particularly Grisey's 'instrumental synthesis' with its generation of musical material from the destructuring of a musical sound into its harmonic and inharmonic components.

As with all of the chapters of this book, we have only explored some of the many possibilities for music and musicology presented by the semiotics of Deleuze and Guattari. Deleuze's volumes on cinema, taken together with his work on regimes of signs in *A Thousand Plateaus*, presents the possibility of a semiotics that is fit to consider the workings of signs that no longer look for validation to verbal language operating, as they do, below the level of the conventional sign and in the realm of the molecular. Deleuze's semiotics is one of forces that produce signs that are not intended to become part of a common currency or a lingua franca, and which are destined to remain as parts of an always novel musical idiolect. It is a semiotics that is fit for the singular nature of the modernist art work, exemplified in literary terms by the work of Lewis Carroll, Mallarmé or Joyce as much as in music.

The appropriation in Deleuze and Guattari of Hjelmslev's theory of expression and content is significant once again in drawing attention to the previously undervalued 'substrate' from which signs emerge as musical part-signs or sign-particles and as dissolved forces re-assemble in novel and significant ways. The semiotic enterprise is now one of identifying not only territorialized or deterritorialized semiotic components but, more importantly, their interfaces, the abstract relations they trace and the diagrams they produce.

In the work of Lachenmann, Aperghis and Levinas, we have taken only three recent examples of composers whose work is equal to the theoretical challenge articulated philosophically by Deleuze and Guattari. In all three, not only is sound rethought, but the sound material, at the most molecular levels currently manageable, is re-envisaged and its components are variably emptied, detached, split, pulverized, connected, related, spliced and hybridized, thus producing not only interesting sounds but completely novel sonic conjunctions and relations, replete with new semiotic potential and fresh for renewed exploration.

Conclusion

The concepts that have been introduced in each chapter are interconnected and mutually explanatory, each one hopefully contributing to our understanding of all of the others and working together towards a conception of music that may be considered in some sense Deleuzian. It should by now be clear that music after Deleuze is a difference-based music that eschews identity whether this be from the perspective of the composer, the performer or the listener. The preeminent musical values from a Deleuzian perspective are not those of the same, the similar or the identical, and there is no primacy of original statement or form of a musical unit over subsequent enunciations. Multiplicity is a key principle whether this be in relation to the possibilities thrown up by compositional or improvised material, the wealth of interpretative choices open to performers or the possibilities for innovative approaches to listening. Repetition, no longer subject to identity, is given new force and musical works are understood productively in terms of the concepts of the virtual and the actual, the virtual operating at multiple levels including that of the musical motive, theme, line, form, work or repertoire.

While Deleuzian difference with its prioritizing of multiplicity seems to be a distinctly modernist concern and its workings have been explored at length in relation to Schoenberg, Webern, Stravinsky, Boulez, Stockhausen, Lang and others, it is clear that Deleuzian difference is just as applicable to music that pre-dates the moment of modernity including aspects of the work of Bach, Beethoven and Brahms as well as the practice of heterophony in its multiple manifestations in various ethnic musics from around the world. Ultimately, Deleuzian difference offers a new point of approach for the exploration of musical repertoires and a coherent ontology of the musical work.

Following Deleuze and Guattari, musical works are not to be conceived as narrowly defined or hermetically sealed areas of activity but should rather be considered in terms of dynamic assemblages of multiple and heterogeneous forces, rhizomatic lines of flight that are deterritorialized and reterritorialized from various milieus. The challenge for the musicologist or composer is to consider the molecular forces at work in each assemblage, musical work or body of works while ensuring that molar categories do not pass lazily from one assemblage to another. In this view, new music in all of its manifestations forms bodies without organs, bodies with initially indeterminate functions where specific capacities are formulated and defined only in the course of their working out. The musical body without organs is one in which the familiar aspects and functions (organs) of recognizable systems (bodies) such as tonality, modality or serialism are no longer apparent, as we are confronted with new possibilities in situations where such functions (organs) are not already predetermined.

As was argued in Chapter 5, this rhizomatic approach leads to a theory of content and expression where artworks are approached as bundles of capturing and captured forces and the possibility of a semiotic theory capable of engaging with the molecular nature of much innovative music. A Deleuzian conception of music is one in which all of music's elements become-molecular, not only our concepts of sound, pitch, duration, rhythm, melody, harmony, line, form and so on, but the very concept of music itself. In such music, previously stable and secure musical units are dismantled and recast in new ways, engaging ever differently with multiple elements beyond the sub-components of sound. For Deleuze, all of this entails the tracing of a new diagram in which new relations between the elements are produced.

The dimension of pitch space was explored in Chapter 3 where it was shown across a range of repertoires that music can once again be studied productively in line with the expanded concepts of smooth and striated space which Deleuze and Guattari developed from the work of Boulez. Music in so many ways is thought in terms of continua, and beyond the taxonomies of pitch spaces that were identified in Wyschnegradsky and Boulez, it was argued that the question of pitch spaces and their divisions goes well beyond the purely musical. The concepts of State philosophy and Nomad thought introduced by Deleuze and Guattari suggest that, as with music of identity and difference, pitch spaces at times reveal elements of confrontations between musical forces, politics and world views. This is suggested in the undoubted dominance in Western theory and practice of equal temperament over all alternative tuning systems, of tonality over all other systems of working with the twelve chromatic pitches, of the 12-tone chromatic scale over all microtonal possibilities and of Western scientific systems of pitch calibration over more informal and ethnically specific methods of tuning. The cases that were explored are only examples and there is no reason to believe that many others cannot also be found. It is also the case that pitch space, as it is defined in this study, is only one, rather reductive aspect of sound phenomena and that a number of other aspects of sound can equally be considered in terms of continuity and discontinuity, to chart the dominant and dominated forces at works in particular music over time.

While Chapter 4 presents something of the richness of Deleuze's thinking of time, once again as something fundamentally multiple in its aspects, it was suggested that it is exactly this multiplicity that makes his concepts so interesting for the study of music. It was argued that the temporal multiplicity of Deleuze's theory resonates already with aspects of the music of Wagner and Brahms, but even more so in relation to a number of composers from around 1900 onwards whose work is intimately caught up with innovative aspects of human understanding and perception of time. While certain parallels are clearly evident linking Deleuze's temporalities with those of Boulez and Messiaen, it is not claimed that the temporal theory or practice of any composer maps onto or can be illuminated or explained completely through the agency of any one philosophical theory of time. In presenting something of the temporal practice of Wagner, Brahms, Debussy, Messiaen, Boulez, Stockhausen, Carter and Grisey, an attempt has been made merely to display the temporal multiplicity that is opened up in musical modernism and beyond. It is precisely this multiplicity that we find in Deleuze, with temporal poles that map out a zone for appreciation of the various temporal possibilities thrown up by a range of music.

Given the focus of this study on Deleuzian concepts and their interest for the musical domain, it is important to reiterate that, for

Deleuze and Guattari, the two domains are unquestionably distinct, as is their mode of operation. Where conceptual thought pertains to the philosophical domain, the job of the aesthetic dimension is 'to push the limits of representation' through the creation of affects and percepts (Criton 2005; Deleuze and Guattari 1994, pp. 163–99). Consequently, while Deleuze attempts to think space and time philosophically, and there is frequent discussion of musical space and time, it is never implied that these philosophical and musical enterprises are at all the same. Each domain confronts such questions in its own way, philosophically through conceptual thought and musically through the production of sonic percepts and affects.

Despite the fact that Deleuze's work has been used profitably by a significant number of scholars in studies of a wide range of music, the treatment of music that is found in the writings of Deleuze (and Guattari) is unmistakably modernist in preference and outlook. His concepts are also drawn upon by composers, musicologists and music analysts and theorists in a variety of situations. While proper discussion or any attempt at compiling a comprehensive listing of the composers and musicologists who cite Deleuze as an important figure for their work would necessitate a chapter in itself, we have been able to note something of the music of Dusapin and Aperghis with its rhizomes, the *Differenz/Wiederholung* compositions of Bernhard Lang with their fixation on aspects of difference and repetition, Pascale Criton's microtonal explorations, and the writings of Ivanka Stoïanova, who, it seems, first connected Deleuze's work with developments in new music, before the philosopher had himself taken this step. Discussion has nonetheless been limited, and we have not covered, for example, anything of the work of Brian Ferneyhough, who notes the importance of Deleuze's *Logic of Sensation* (1981; 2003), the notion of capturing forces and the concept of the figure, stating that the Deleuze-Guattarian refrain, described as a 'habitat', 'is perhaps [the] controlled deterritorialization of subjective space which [he was] aiming at most consciously in [his] writing' (Ferneyhough 1995, p. 507).

The concepts that have been selected for consideration are partial, and there is no doubt that alternative, equally valid and useful selections would have been made by different authors. In the course of the text, a number of key Deleuzian concepts are given a generous amount of attention, others receive some attention while others again are mentioned only in passing or are absent altogether. Concepts which could either have been included or explored more profitably include the 'logic of sensation', the 'sensible', the 'affect' the 'figure', 'sheets of time' and the 'event'. With all of this in mind, it is hoped that the reader will now be in a position to approach Deleuze's own texts, following up some of the pathways that are suggested here in the knowledge that this is indeed a very rich philosophy with great potential for the study of music.

Notes

Chapter 1

1 Gandillac was the supervisor of Deleuze's doctoral thesis, which was later published as *Difference and Repetition*. Gandillac's notion of the virtual is not identical to what we find in Deleuze. See Campbell 2010, pp. 190–2.
2 I am grateful to Cambridge University Press for allowing me to use material in this chapter that appeared previously in my book *Boulez, Music and Philosophy*, Cambridge University Press, 2010.
3 Deleuze explicitly applies his thinking of difference and repetition to Boulez's music and thought in the essay 'Boulez, Proust and Time' (2006, pp. 292–9).
4 For a comprehensive discussion, see Campbell 2010, pp. 154–218.
5 The discussion of Gaelic psalm singing draws on Purser (1992), Collinson and Duesenberry (2007–13) and MacBean (1887).
6 This section draws on Kernfield (2007–13).
7 Heile notes that Auslander has more recently made the suggestion that 'in fact, audiences cannot distinguish between improvised and non-improvised music since there is no absolute difference between the two. Instead, "the perception of improvisation arises from the social relationship between performers and audience rather than the formal or ontological characteristics of the music"' (Heile 2013).
8 Spitzer traces the 'Beethoven-Hegelian tradition of music theory' as extending from Hoffmann, A. B. Marx, and Halm through Schoenberg and Schenker, Adorno, Ratz and Dahlhaus, up to present-day theorists such as Schmalfeldt and Caplin (Spitzer 2006, p. 241; Schmalfeldt 1995, pp. 37–71).
9 Deleuze and Guattari do in fact note that 'Beethoven produced the most astonishing polyphonic richness with relatively scanty themes of three or four notes' (Deleuze and Guattari 1988, p. 270).
10 For Haimo, the essence of the definition formulated by Schoenberg in the treatise *Coherence, Counterpoint, Instrumentation, Instruction in Form* provides a dependable 'constant' throughout (Haimo 1997, p. 350).

Chapter 2

1. Stoïanova suggests that even in those passages that feature 'clear repetition', these are 'in reality "false trails" like those of Borges. These apparently repeated elements are immediately mutated into rhizomatic diffusions' (Stoïanova 1993, p. 194).
2. Jacques Amblard places Dusapin at the end of a line of composers which includes Monteverdi, Mussorgsky, Wolf, Janácek and Varèse, and all of whom shared a keen interest in the melodic possibilities inherent within human speech (Amblard 2002, pp. 12–13).
3. A conversation between Félix Guattari, Georges Aperghis and Antoine Gindt took place on 22 December 1991 (Guattari, Aperghis and Gindt 2000, pp. 9–12).
4. Only some details from Houdart's account are presented here in order to give the reader a sense of the work.
5. There is a double CD of remixes of *DW 1.2* titled 'trio x 3'. New Jazz Meeting Baden-Baden 2002, hatOLOGY 2-607, Basel, 2003 and a single CD of remixes titled 'Steve Lacy at the New Jazz Meeting Baden-Baden 2002', hatOLOGY 631, Basel, 2006.

Chapter 3

1. I am grateful to Cambridge University Press for allowing me to use material in this chapter that appeared previously in my book *Boulez, Music and Philosophy*, Cambridge University Press, 2010.
2. For much more comprehensive surveys of the panoply of musical spaces, see Harley 1994 and Ojala 2009.
3. E-mail from Pascale Criton to the author, 25 May 2008. Criton brought to Deleuze an interest in continuity and discontinuity in music. She provided a number of musical inputs for Deleuze and his students introducing to the seminar recordings of Debussy's 'La Cathédrale engloutie', Messiaen's *Chronochromie*, African chants noted down by ethnomusicologist Gilbert Rouget and the temporal processes of the spectral composer Gérard Grisey (Criton 2005; Dosse 2007, pp. 524–6).
4. A fuller account of the development of the ideas of smooth and striated space in Boulez can be found in Campbell 2010, pp. 221–8.
5. For Deleuze and Guattari, 'the two spaces in fact exist only in mixture: smooth space is constantly being translated, transversed into a striated space; striated space is constantly being reversed, returned to a smooth space' (1988, 474). The smooth and the striated are also discussed at length in '1227: Treatise on Nomadology – The War Machine' (Ibid., pp. 351–423).

6   D# is exactly one comma lower than Eb. In all, there are nine commas in a whole tone, five commas in a major semitone, and a total of 55 commas in a full octave. 'A major scale, for example, has five whole tones and two major (diatonic) semitones . . . . Five whole tones contains 5 x 9 = 45 commas, and two major semitones contains 2 x 5 = 10 commas, so an octave consists of 45 + 10 = 55 commas' (Duffin 2007, p. 53).
7   'An 11-limit system is . . . one that includes ratios of 2, 3, 5, 7 and 11 but no higher' (Gilmore 1998, p. 63).
8   Rowell acknowledges that he examines early Tamil pitch collections 'from the point of view of a Western musicologist, against the background of Western concepts of scale and mode, translating the musical details into Western concepts and categories' (Rowell 2000, p. 140).
9   Beyond Ellis, the technological means available at the beginning of the twenty-first century provide access to much smaller frequency divisions, but such denominations are generally beyond the perception of listeners. A number of studies have been undertaken in psychoacoustics into 'frequency discrimination' understood as 'our ability to detect differences in the frequencies of sounds which are presented successively', a phenomenon that is also referred to as 'frequency difference thresholds (df), frequency difference limen (DLF) or just noticeable differences in frequency (or frequency jnd)' (Mannell 1994). I am grateful to Suk-Jun Kim for this information.

Chapter 4

1   I am grateful to Cambridge University Press for allowing me to use material in this chapter that appeared previously in my book *Boulez, Music and Philosophy*, Cambridge University Press, 2010.
2   In *The Logic of Sense*, the spelling 'Aion' is used, whereas in *A Thousand Plateaus*, it has become 'Aeon'.
3   Boulez states that Deleuze's interest in his article on Wagner, 'Time Re-explored', was the starting point for the philosopher's reflections on musical time (Menger 1990, p. 9), and he recalls that Deleuze requested to be included in the 1978 IRCAM seminar on time. Having found Deleuze's contribution to be genuinely insightful, Boulez had it published.
4   http://www.le-terrier.net/deleuze/19ircam-78.htm (accessed 24 June 2008). At the IRCAM seminar *Le Temps musical*, Barthes, Deleuze and Foucault were invited to participate in a debate. A massed gathering of over 2000 people assembled for a discussion chaired by

Boulez in which, of the three philosophers 'only Deleuze entered into the public debate with any enthusiasm' (Macey 1993, pp. 398–9).

5 While Goldschmidt's study purports to reassemble notions of time from the writings of several important Stoic philosophers, he nevertheless acknowledges the lack of clarity in Stoic ideas of time (Goldschmidt 1953, pp. 37–40). For John Sellars, there is no evidence that the Stoics acknowledged these two distinct notions of time as part of a unified theory or that these times were referred to as aiôn and chronos (Sellars 2007, p. 194). Ultimately, while Deleuze's concepts of Chronos and Aion are based on 'a speculative reading of the ancient Stoics' that cannot be said to draw on an authentically ancient Stoic position, this does not present any serious philosophical problem for Deleuze's theory of time (Sellars 2007, p. 204).

6 The three Passive Syntheses of time are not mentioned in *A Thousand Plateaus*.

7 Bergson's early understanding of duration underwent a number of modifications in his various writings from 1889, 1896, 1907 and 1911 (Emery 1998, pp. 488–500). It is important to note that Bergson's *Time and Free Will* (1889), and *Matter and Memory* (1896), were published in advance of Husserl's *On the phenomenology of the consciousness of internal time (1893–1917)*.

8 Clayton does not use this phrase.

9 The term 'module' may be understood as whatever durational value or tempo is accepted as standard and from which related durations or tempi can be derived, while 'partition' seems to denote the division of the temporal continuum within striated time. This is achieved in practice through the placing of either clearly perceptible durations or tempi.

10 See Carter's article 'The Rhythmic Basis of American Music' (1955) (Carter 1997, pp. 59–62).

11 Carter explores the subject of musical time in a number of essays including 'Sound, Silence and Time' (1957), 'A Further Step" (1958), 'The Time Dimension in Music' (1965), 'Time Lecture' (1965/94) and 'Music and the Time Screen' (1976).

12 Bernard attributes this insight to Carter's reading of Souvtchinsky, for whom there may be unlimited varieties of musical time between the chronometric and the chronoametric (Bernard 1995, pp. 647–8).

13 As John Link notes, 'Carter's interest in long-range polyrhythms dates back to at least the early 1960s' (Link 1994, p. 3). Carter's polyrhythmic practice is considered in detail in Link 1994 and Coulembier 2013.

14 See Meyer and Shreffler 2008, p. 137.

Chapter 5

1. Deleuze draws also on Peirce's distinction of 'firstness, 'secondness' and 'thirdness' where firstness pertains to 'something that only refers to itself', secondness to 'something that refers to itself only through something else' and thirdness to 'something that refers to itself only by comparing one thing to another' (Deleuze 2005b, p. 29).
2. Peter Osborne suggests that Deleuze pays insufficient attention to Peirce's third term, the 'interpretant', and that he is wrong in thinking that icons, indexes and symbols are 'distinguished by signifier-signified relations' since all signification for Peirce is triadic rather than binary, requiring the interpretant over and above the signifier and the signified (Osborne 2000, p. 49). While it is undoubtedly the case that signification is triadic for Peirce, this point does not really affect the validity of understanding Peirce's terms in terms of territoriality and deterritorialization.
3. In *What is Philosophy?* (1994), Deleuze and Guattari set out 'percepts' and 'affects' as the material specific to the arts (1994, pp. 163–99).
4. The notion of a 'minor literature' is introduced by Deleuze and Guattari in their book on Kafka which has the subtitle 'Toward a Minor Literature' (1986). The concept of the 'minor' is further developed in *A Thousand Plateaus*.

Bibliography

Adorno, T. W. (1998), *Beethoven: The Philosophy of Music*. Ed. R. Tiedemann, trans. E. Jephcott. Oxford: Polity Press.
Agawu, K. (2009), *Music as Discourse*. Oxford: Oxford University Press.
Amblard, J. (2002), *Pascal Dusapin: l'intonation ou le secret*. Paris: Musica Falsa.
Aperghis, G. (1993), 'Some reflections on musical theatre'. *Contemporary Music Review* 8(1), 113–14.
— (2002), 'Machinations', in CD booklet, Accord 472 916-2, pp. 2–3, Paris.
Aperghis, G. and Regnault, F. (2002), 'The making of Machinations', in CD booklet, Accord 472 916-2, pp. 4–13, Paris.
Aperghis, G. et al. (2005), 'Storms', in CD booklet, trans. J. Drake. Cypres: CYP5621, pp. 15–18, Brussels.
Assis, P. de. (2011), 'The conditions of creation and the haecceity of music material', *Filigrane, Deleuze et la musique*, published online 23 January 2012, http://revues.mshparisnord.org/filigrane/index.php?id=422.
Bachelard, G. (2001), *La Dialectique de la durée*. Paris: Quadrige, PUF.
Baroni, M. (1983), 'The concept of musical grammar', trans. S. Maguire with the assistance of W. Drabkin. *Music Analysis* 2(2), 175–208.
Bayer, F. (1981), *De Schönberg à Cage: Essai sur la notion d'espace sonore dans la musique contemporaine*. Paris: Klincksieck.
Benson, D. (2008), *Music: A Mathematical Offering*, http://www.homepages.abdn.ac.uk/mth192/pages/html/maths-music.html, accessed 6 April 2012.
Bergson, H. (1910), *Time and Free Will*. Trans. F. L. Pogson. London: George Allen & Unwin.
— (2004), *Matter and Memory*. Trans. N. M. Paul and W. Scott Palmer. Mineola, New York: Dover.
Berio, L. (1989), 'Eco in ascolto'. *Contemporary Music Review* 5(1), 1–8.
Bernard, J. W. (1988), 'The evolution of Elliott Carter's rhythmic practice'. *Perspectives of New Music* 26(2), 164–203.
— (1995), 'Elliott Carter and the modern meaning of time'. *The Musical Quarterly* 79(4), 644–82.
Bogue, R. (1989), *Deleuze and Guattari*. London and New York: Routledge.

— (2003), *Deleuze on Music, Painting and the Arts*. New York and London: Routledge.
— (2004), 'Violence in three shades of metal: death, doom and black', in I. Buchanan and M. Swiboda (eds), *Deleuze and Music*. Edinburgh: Edinburgh University Press, pp. 95–117.
Boulez, P. (1971), *Boulez on Music Today*. Trans. S. Bradshaw and R. R. Bennett. London: Faber & Faber.
— (1986), *Orientations: Collected Writings*. Ed. J.-J. Nattiez, trans. M. Cooper. London: Faber & Faber.
— (1989), *Le Pays fertile: Paul Klee*. Texte préparé et présenté par P. Thévenin. Paris: Gallimard.
— (1991), *Stocktakings from an Apprenticeship*. Collected and presented by P. Thévenin, trans. S. Walsh. Oxford: Clarendon Press.
— (2005a), *Regards sur autrui (Points de repère II)*. Textes réunis et présentés par J.-J. Nattiez and S. Galaise. Paris: Christian Bourgois.
— (2005b), *Leçons de musique (Points de repère III)*. Textes réunis et établis par J-J. Nattiez. Paris: Christian Bourgois.
Brecht, B. (1964), *Brecht on Theatre*. Ed. and trans. J. Willett. New York: Hill and Wang.
Burnham, S. (1995), *Beethoven Hero*. Princeton: Princeton University Press.
Busch, R. (1985), 'On the horizontal and vertical presentation of musical ideas and on musical space (1)'. *Tempo* 154, 2–10.
Campbell, E. (2000), '*Boulez and Expression: A DeleuzoGuattarian Approach*'. Ph.D. diss. University of Edinburgh.
— (2010), *Boulez, Music and Philosophy*. Cambridge: Cambridge University Press.
Carter, E. (1997), *Collected Essays and Lectures, 1937-1995*. Ed. J. W. Bernard. Rochester, NY: University of Rochester Press.
Castanet, P.-A. (1991), 'Michaël Levinas: la musique et son double'. *La Revue Musicale*, L'Itinéraire (421-422-423-424), 73–91.
Cimini, A. (2010), 'Gilles Deleuze and the musical Spinoza', in B. Hulse and N. Nesbitt (eds), *Sounding the Virtual*. Surrey: Ashgate, pp. 129–44.
Clayton, M. R. L. (1996). 'Free rhythm: ethnomusicology and the study of music without metre'. *Bulletin of the School of Oriental and African Studies* 59(2), 323–32.
Cohen-Levinas, D. (1998), 'Deleuze musicien', *Rue Descartes, Gilles Deleuze, Immanence et vie*, 20. Paris: PUF, 137–47.
Collinson, F. and Duesenberry, P. (2007–13). 'Scotland', 'Gaelic psalms', in *New Grove Online*. Oxford University Press, accessed 25 January 2013.
Cooke, P. (2007–13), 'Heterophony', in *New Grove Online*. Oxford University Press, accessed 25 January 2013.

Coulembier, K. (2013), Multi-temporality: Analyzing simultaneous time layers in selected compositions by Elliott Carter and Claus-Steffen Mahnkopf. PhD diss. University of Leuven.
Criton, P. (2005), 'L'invitation', in Dir. A. Bernhold et R. Pinhas, *Deleuze épars, approches et portraits.* Hermann.
— (2011a), 'Nothing is established forever', in E. Alliez and A. Goffey (eds), *The Guattari Effect.* London: Continuum, 235–50.
— (2011b), 'Bords à bords: vers une pensée-musique', *Filigrane, Deleuze et la musique*, published online 20 January 2012 http://www.revues.mshparisnord.org/filigrane/index.php?id=415, accessed 8 March 2012.
Curry, B. (2012). 'Time, subjectivity and contested signs: developing Monelle's application of Peirce's 1903 typology to music', in E. Sheinberg (ed.), *Music Semiotics: A Network of Significations.* Surrey: Ashgate, pp. 149–61.
Cuvillier, A. (1972), *Nouveau précis de philosophie: La connaissance* (8th edn). Paris: Armand Colin.
Dahlhaus, C. (1989), *Nineteenth-Century Music.* Trans. J. B. Robinson. Berkeley: University of California Press.
— (1991), *Ludwig van Beethoven: Approaches to His Music.* Trans. M. Whittall. Oxford: Clarendon Press.
Deleuze, G. (1983), *Nietzsche and Philosophy.* Trans. H. Tomlinson. London: Athlone.
— (1986). 'Boulez, Proust et le temps: "occuper sans compter"', in C. Samuel (ed.), *Éclats/Boulez.* Paris: Editions du Centre Pompidou, pp. 98–100.
— (1988), *Spinoza: Practical Philosophy.* Trans. R. Hurley. San Francisco: City Lights Books.
— (1990), *The Logic of Sense.* Trans. M. Lester with C. Stivale, ed. C. V. Boundas. New York: Columbia University Press.
— (1991), *Bergsonism.* Trans. H. Tomlinson and B. Habberjam. New York: Zone.
— (1992), *Expressionism in Philosophy: Spinoza.* Trans. M. Joughin. New York: Zone.
— (1993), *The Fold: Leibniz and the Baroque.* Trans. T. Conley. London: Athlone.
— (1994), *Difference and Repetition.* Trans. P. Patton. London: Athlone.
— (1995), *Negotiations.* Trans. M. Joughin. New York: Columbia University Press.
— (2004), *Desert Islands and Other Texts: 1953–1974.* Ed. D. Lapoujade, trans. M. Taormina. Los Angeles: Semiotext(e).
— (2005a), *Cinema 1: The Movement-Image.* Trans. H. Tomlinson and B. Habberjam. London: Continuum.
— (2005b), *Cinema 2: The Time-Image.* Trans. H. Tomlinson and R. Galeta. London: Continuum.

— (2006), *Two Regimes of Madness: Texts and Interviews 1975–1995*. Ed. D. Lapoujade, trans. A. Hodges and M. Taormina. Boston: MIT Press, Semiotext(e).
Deleuze, G. and Guattari, F. (1986), *Kafka: Toward a Minor Literature*. Trans. D. Polan. Minneapolis: University of Minnesota Press.
— (1988), *A Thousand Plateaus: Capitalism and Schizophrenia*. Trans. B. Massumi. London: Athlone.
— (1994), *What is Philosophy?* Trans. G. Burchell and H. Tomlinson. London: Verso.
Doeser, L. (1995), *The Life and Works of Klee*. Bristol: Parragon.
Dosse, F. (1997), *History of Structuralism*, 2 vols. Trans. D. Glassman. Minneapolis: University of Minnesota Press.
— (2007), *Gilles Deleuze et Félix Guattari: Biographie croisée*. Paris: La Découverte.
— (2010), *Gilles Deleuze and Félix Guattari: Intersecting Lives*. Trans. D. Glassman. New York: Columbia University Press.
Duffin, R. W. (2007), *How Equal Temperament Ruined Harmony (and Why You Should Care)*. New York and London: W.W. Norton.
Dusapin, P. (2006), 'Telling a tale of Faustus . . .', in DVD booklet for *Faustus, The Last Night*. Naïve, M0 782177, pp. 15–19.
— (2009), *Une musique en train de se faire*. Paris: Editions du Seuil.
Eco, U. (1976), *A Theory of Semiotics*. Bloomington: Indiana University Press.
— (1984), *Semiotics and the Philosophy of Language*. London: Macmillan.
— (1989), *The Open Work*. Trans. A. Cancogni. Cambridge, MA: Harvard University Press.
Emery, E. (1998), *Temps et Musique*. Lausanne: L'Age d'Homme.
Ferneyhough. B. (1995), *Collected Writings*. Ed. J. Boros and R. Toop. Amsterdam: Harwood Academic Publishers.
Fleury, M. (1996), *L'impressionisme et la musique*. Paris: Fayard.
Foucault, M. (1977), 'Theatrum Philosophicum', in D. F. Bouchard (ed.), trans. D. F. Bouchard and S. Simon, *Language, Counter-Memory, Practice*. Ithaca, NY: Cornell University Press, pp. 165–96.
Frisch, W. (1982), 'Brahms, developing variation, and the Schoenberg critical tradition'. *19th Century Music* 5(3), 215–32.
— (1984), *Brahms and the Principle of Developing Variation*. Berkeley: University of California Press.
Gallope, M. (2010), 'The sound of repeating life: ethics and metaphysics in Deleuze's philosophy of music', in B. Hulse and N. Nesbitt (eds), *Sounding the Virtual*. Surrey: Ashgate, pp. 77–102.
Gallope, M., Kane, B., Rings, S., Hepokoski, J., Lochhead, J., Puri, M. J. and Currie, J. R. (2012), 'Vladimir Jankélévitch's philosophy of music'. *Journal of the American Musicological Society* 65(1), 215–56.

Gilbert. J. (2004), 'Becoming-music: the rhizomatic moment of improvisation', in I. Buchanan and M. Swiboda (eds), *Deleuze and Music*. Edinburgh: Edinburgh University Press, pp. 118–39.

Gilmore, B. (1998), *Harry Partch: A Biography*. New Haven and London: Yale University Press.

Goebbels, H. (2007), 'Composing and directing for theatre', European Graduate School lecture. http://www.youtube.com/watch?v=qplpz23JZ6U, accessed 2 January 2013.

Goldschmidt, V. (1953), *Le Système stoïcien et l'idée de temps*. Paris: Vrin.

Grant. M. J. (2003), 'Experimental music semiotics'. *International Review of the Aesthetics and Sociology of Music* 34(2), 173–91.

Griffiths, P. (1995), *Modern Music and After: Directions Since 1945*. Oxford: Oxford University Press.

Grisey, G. (1987), 'Tempus ex machina: a composer's reflections on musical time'. *Contemporary Music Review* 2(1), 239–75.

— (2008), *Écrits ou l'invention de la musique spectrale*. Ed. G. Lelong. avec la collaboration d'A-M. Réby. Paris: Musica Falsa.

Guattari, F, Aperghis, G. and Gindt, A. (2000), 'L'hétérogenèse dans la création musicale'. *Chimères* 38, 9–12.

Haimo, E. (1997), 'Developing variation and Schoenberg's serial music'. *Music Analysis* 16(3), 349–65.

Hall, M. (1984), *Harrison Birtwistle*. London: Robson Books

Harley, M. A. (1994), '*Space and Spatialization in Contemporary Music: History and Analysis, Ideas and Implementations*'. Ph.D. diss., McGill University. http://www.moonrisepress.com/SpaceDissertationTitleLists.pdf, accessed 16 April 2012.

Hatten, R. S. (1994), *Musical Meaning in Beethoven: Markedness, Correlation, and Interpretation*. Bloomington and Indianapolis: Indiana University Press.

Heile, B. (2006), *The Music of Mauricio Kagel*. Surrey: Ashgate.

— (2011), '"You had to be there": reflections on performance, "liveness", mediality and spectatorship'. Programme book for the International Conference on Music Since 1900/Lancaster University Music Analysis Conference. University of Lancaster, England, p. 89.

— (2013), 'Play it again, Duke: jazz performance, improvisation, and the construction of spontaneity'. Forthcoming article.

Helmholtz, H. (1954), *On the Sensations of Tone*. Trans. A. J. Ellis. New York: Dover Publications.

Hemment, D. (2004), 'Affect and individuation in popular electronic music', in I. Buchanan and M. Swiboda (eds), *Deleuze and Music*. Edinburgh: Edinburgh University Press, pp. 76–94.

Hindemith, P. (1942). *Craft of Musical Composition, 1. Theory*. Mainz and London: Schott.

Hockings, E. (1995), 'Helmut Lachenmann's concept of rejection'. *Tempo* 193, 4–14.
Horsley, I. (2007–13), 'Improvisation, §II: Western art music. History to 1600', in *New Grove Online*. Oxford University Press, accessed 25 January 2013.
Houdart, C. (2007), *Avis de tempête: Georges Aperghis: Journal d'une oeuvre*. Paris: Éditions Intervalles.
Hulse, B. and Nesbitt, N. (eds) (2010), *Sounding the Virtual: Gilles Deleuze and the Theory and Philosophy of Music*. Surrey: Ashgate.
Hulse, B. (2010), 'Thinking musical difference: music theory as minor science', in B. Hulse and N. Nesbitt (eds), *Sounding the Virtual*. Surrey: Ashgate, pp. 23–50.
Iverson, J. J. (2009), *'Historical Memory and György Ligeti's Sound-Mass Music 1958–1968'*. Ph.D. diss. The University of Texas at Austin. http://repositories.lib.utexas.edu/handle/2152/6905, accessed 3 May 2012.
Jagodzinski, J. (2000), 'The oral/e Eye', in CD booklet, Kairos 0012112KAI, pp. 5–7, Vienna.
Jankélévitch, V. (1989), *Debussy et le mystère de l'instant* (2nd edn). Paris: Plon.
Jedrzejewski, F. (2005), 'Avant-propos' to Une philosophie dialectique de l'art musical. Paris: L'Harmattan.
Kager, R. (2003), 'Persistent loops at the Baden-Baden new jazz meeting 2002', in CD sleevenote, hatOLOGY 2-607, Basel.
— (2006), 'An overwhelming passion for sonic exploration', in CD sleevenote, hatOLOGY 631, Basel.
Kaltenecker, M. (1993), 'H.L.', in *Helmut Lachenmann*, programme book for Le Festival d'automne à Paris, pp. 8–10. http://www.festival-automne.com/Publish/archive_pdf/FAP_1993_MU_07_PRGS.pdf, accessed 9 January 2013.
Kartomi, M. J. (2007–13), 'Gamelan', in *New Grove Online*. Oxford University Press, accessed 14 May 2012.
Kawabata, T. (2003), 'Time to "think different", says Pierre Boulez', *The Japan Times*, 30 April 2003, http://www.japantimes.co.jp/text/fm20030430a2.html, accessed 13 June 2012.
Kernfield, Barry. (2007–13), 'Improvisation, §III: Jazz', in *New Grove Online*. Oxford University Press, accessed 25 January 2013.
Kielian-Gilbert, M. (2010), 'Music and the difference in becoming', in B. Hulse and N. Nesbitt (eds), *Sounding the Virtual*. Surrey: Ashgate, pp. 199–225.
Kimbell, D. (1991), *Italian Opera*. Cambridge: Cambridge University Press.
Klee, P. (1953), *Pedagogical Sketchbook*. Trans. and intro. S. Moholy-Nagy. London: Faber & Faber.

— (1961), *The Thinking Eye*. Ed. J. Spiller, trans. R. Manheim with assistance from C. Weidler and J. Wittenborn. London: Lund Humphries.
Kramer, J. D. (1978), 'Moment form in twentieth-century music'. *The Musical Quarterly* 64(2), 177–94.
Lachenmann, H. (1980), 'The "beautiful" in music today'. *Tempo* 135, 20–4.
— (1993), 'L' Aspect et l'affect', in *Helmut Lachenmann*, programme book for Le Festival d'automne à Paris, pp. 11–14. http://www.festival- automne.com/Publish/archive_pdf/FAP_1993_MU_07_PRGS.pdf, accessed 9 January 2013.
— (1995), 'On structuralism'. *Contemporary Music Review* 12(1), 93–102.
— (1997), 'Open letter to Hans Werner Henze'. *Perspectives of New Music* 35(2), 189–200.
— (2009), *Écrits et Entretiens*. Choisis et préfacés par M. Kaltenecker. Genève: Contrechamps.
Lang, B. (1998), Programme note for *Difference/Repetition 1*, http://www.members.chello.at/bernhard.lang/, accessed 12 December 2012.
— (2000), Literary texts for DW 2, CD booklet, Kairos 0012112KAI, pp. 8–13, Vienna.
— (2002), 'Loop aestetics Darmstadt 2002'. http://members.chello.at/bernhard.lang/publikationen/loop_aestet.pdf, accessed 12 June 2012.
— (2004), Programme notes for DW 8, DW 15 and DW 3, in CD booklet, col legno WWE 1CD 20090, pp. 7–12, Vienna.
Langer, S. (1953), *Feeling and Form*. London: Routledge and Kegan Paul Limited.
Lesure, F. and Nichols, R. (eds). (1987), *Debussy Letters*. London: Faber & Faber.
Levinas, M. (2002), *Le Compositeur trouvère: écrits et entretiens (1982-2002)*. Textes réunis et annotés par P. A. Castanet et D. Cohen-Levinas. Paris: L'Harmattan.
— (2012), ' . . . Things like that happen – rarely, but they do happen'. Interview with Michaël Levinas, carried out by Jean-Luc Plouvier, in CD booklet, AECD 1220, pp. 18–25. Brussels.
Levy, K. (1988), 'Is tonality a natural law?'. *Proceedings of the American Philosophical Society* 132(3), 299–303.
Link, J. F. (1994), Long-range polyrhythms in Elliott Carter's recent music. PhD diss. The City University of New York.
MacBean, L. (1887), Introduction to *Gaelic Psalmody including the Ancient Tunes and Precentors' Recitatives*. Edinburgh: MacLachlan and Stewart.
Macey, D. (1993), *The Lives of Michel Foucault*. London: Vintage.

Maconie, R. (1976), *The Works of Karlheinz Stockhausen*. London: Oxford University Press.
Malm, W. P. (1977), *Music Cultures of the Pacific, the Near East and Asia* (2nd edn). New Jersey: Prentice-Hall.
Mannell, R. H. (1994), 'The perceptual and auditory implications of parametric scaling in synthetic speech'. Ph.D. diss. Macquarrie University. http://clas.mq.edu.au/perception/psychoacoustics/chapter2.html#sect_2_2_1_1, accessed 10 February 2013.
Marcel, G. (2005), *Music and Philosophy*. Trans. S. Maddux and R. E. Wood. Milwaukee: Marquette University Press.
Massumi, B. (1988), 'Pleasures of philosophy', Foreword to *A Thousand Plateaus: Capitalism and Schizophrenia*. London: Athlone, pp. ix–xv.
— (1992), *A User's Guide to Capitalism and Schizophrenia: Deviations from Deleuze and Guattari*. Cambridge, MA: MIT Press: Swerve Edition.
Matossian, N. (1990), *Xenakis*. London: Kahn & Averill.
Menger, P-M. (1990), 'From the Domaine Musical to IRCAM: Pierre Boulez in conversation with Pierre-Michel Menger', Trans. J. W. Bernard. *Perspectives of New Music* 28(1), 6–18.
Messiaen, O. (1994), Traité de rythme, de couleur, et d'ornithologie, vol. 1. Paris: Alphonse Leduc.
Meyer, F. and Shreffler, A. C. (2008), *Elliott Carter: A Centennial Portrait in Letters and Documents*. Woodbridge, Suffolk: The Boydell Press.
Monelle. R. (1991), 'Music and the Peircean trichotomies'. *International Review of the Aesthetics and Sociology of Music* 22(1), 99–108.
— (1992), *Linguistics and Semiotics in Music*. Chur: Harwood Academic Publishers.
Nattiez, J.-J. (1990), *Music and Discourse: Toward a Semiology of Music*. Trans. C. Abbate. Princeton: Princeton University Press.
Nesbitt, N. (2004), 'Deleuze, Adorno and the composition of musical multiplicity', in I. Buchanan and M. Swiboda (eds), *Deleuze and Music*. Edinburgh: Edinburgh University Press, pp. 54–75.
— (2010), 'Critique and clinique: from sounding bodies to the musical event', in B. Hulse and N. Nesbitt (eds), *Sounding the Virtual*. Surrey: Ashgate, pp. 159–79.
Nettl, B. (2007–13), 'Improvisation, §I: Concepts and practices', in *New Grove Online*. Oxford University Press, accessed 25 January 2013.
Neuwirth, O. (2006), 'Afterthoughts on *Lost Highway* "Waiting for Godot" of passion and proximity – an experimental arrangement of futility', in CD booklet, Kairos 0012542KAI, pp. 37–41, Vienna.
Ojala, J. (2009), *Space in Musical Semiotics: An Abductive Theory of the Musical Composition Process*. Approaches to Musical Semiotics 12. Semiotic Society of Finland. http://www.doria.fi/bitstream/handle/10024/45039/spaceinm.p df?seq uence=1, accessed 15 April 2012.

Osborne, P. (2000), *Philosophy in Cultural Theory*. London and New York: Routledge.
Pasler, J. (1982), 'Debussy, "Jeux": playing with time and form'. *19th-Century Music* 6(1), 60–75.
— (2008), 'Resituating the spectral revolution: French antecedents', in *Writing through Music: Essays on Music, Culture and Politics*. New York: Oxford University Press, pp. 82–98.
Patton, P. (1994), 'Anti-Platonism and art', in C. V. Boundas and D. Olkowski (eds), *Gilles Deleuze and the Theater of Philosophy*. New York and London: Routledge, pp. 141–56.
Peirce, C. S. (1998), *The Essential Peirce: Selected Philosophical Writings. Volume 2 (1893-1913)*. Ed. Peirce Edition Project. Bloomington and Indianapolis: Indiana University Press.
Pietsch Lima, A. (2006), 'De l'individuation en musique (Simondon/Deleuze & Guattari)', http://www.entretemps.asso.fr/philo/Pietsch-Lima.htm, accessed 16 December 2012.
Powers, H. S. and Widdess, R. (2007–13), 'India, §III, 1: Theory and practice of classical music: tonal systems', in *The New Grove Online*, accessed 14 May 2012.
Purser, J. (1992), *Scotland's Music: A History of the Traditional and Classical Music of Scotland from Earliest Times to the Present Day*. Edinburgh: Mainstream.
Quaglia, B. (2010). 'Transformation and becoming other in the music and poetics of Luciano Berio', in B. Hulse and N. Nesbitt (eds), *Sounding the Virtual*. Surrey: Ashgate, pp. 227–48.
Rahn, J. (1978), 'Javanese Pélog tunings reconsidered'. *Yearbook of the International Folk Music Council* 10, 69–82.
Rings, S. (2008), 'Mystères limpides: time and transformation in Debussy's Des pas sur la neige'. *19th-Century Music* 32(2), 178–208.
Rosen, C. (1976), *Schoenberg*. Glasgow: Fontana/Collins.
Rothstein, E. (2003), 'Le théâtre musical d'Aperghis: un sommaire provisoire', in *Musique et Dramaturgie: esthétique de la représentation au xxe siècle*, sous la direction de L. Feneyrou. Paris: Publications de la Sorbonne, pp. 465–86.
— (2003), 'Le théâtre musical d'Aperghis: un sommaire provisoire', http://www.aperghis.com/txt.html, 1–12, accessed 10 November 2010.
Rowell, L. (1992), *Music and Musical Thought in Early India*. New Delhi: Munshiram Manoharlal Publishers Pvt. Ltd.
— (2000), 'Scale and mode in the music of the early Tamils of south India'. *Music Theory Spectrum* 22(2), 135–56.
Samuel, C. (1994), *Olivier Messiaen: Music and Color: Conversations with Claude Samuel*. Trans. E. T Glasow. Portland, OR: Amadeus Press.

Schiff, D. (1983), *The Music of Elliott Carter* (1st Edition). London: Eulenburg.
Schloezer, B. de. (1928), 'A la recherche de la réalité musicale'. *La Revue Musicale* 9(3), 214–28.
— (1947), *Introduction à J.-S. Bach. Essai d'esthétique musicale*. Paris: Gallimard (Bibliothèque des idées).
Schmalfeldt, J. (1995), 'Form as the process of becoming: the Beethoven-Hegelian tradition and the "Tempest" sonata. *Beethoven Forum* 4, 37–71.
Schoenberg, A. (1975), *Style and Idea*. Ed. L. Stein, trans. L. Black. London: Faber & Faber.
Scruton, R. (1997), *The Aesthetics of Music*. Oxford: Clarendon Press.
Sellars, J. (2007), 'Aiôn and chronos: Deleuze and the Stoic theory of time', in R. Mackay (ed.), *COLLAPSE* III, pp. 177–205.
Semetsky, I. (2010), 'Semiotics', in A. Parr (ed.), *The Deleuze Dictionary* (rev. edn). Edinburgh: Edinburgh University Press, pp. 243–4.
Shaviro, S. (2007), 'Deleuze's encounter with Whitehead', draft chapter. http://shaviro.com/Othertexts/DeleuzeWhitehead.pdf, accessed 29 June 2012.
— (2009), *Without Criteria: Kant, Whitehead, Deleuze, and Aesthetics*. Cambridge, MA: MIT Press.
Sisman, E. (2007–13), 'Variations', in *New Grove Online*. Oxford University Press, accessed 25 January 2013.
Smith, D. W. (2007), *Husserl*. London and New York: Routledge.
Smith. P. H. (2001), 'Brahms and the shifting barline: metrical displacement and formal process in the trios with wind instruments', in D. Brodbeck (ed.), *Brahms Studies* 3. Lincoln: University of Nebraska Press, pp. 191–229.
Souvtchinsky, P. (1990), *(Re) Lire Souvtchinski*. Textes choisis par E. Hubertclaude. La Bresse.
— (2004), *Un siècle de musique russe (1830-1930)*. Réalisée et présentée par Frank Langlois. Arles: Actes Sud/Association Pierre Souvtchinsky.
Spitzer, M. (2006), *Music as Philosophy: Adorno and Beethoven's Late Style*. Bloomington and Indianapolis: Indiana University Press.
Steinitz, Richard. (2000), 'Helmut Lachenmann', in programme book for the Huddersfield Contemporary Music Festival, p. 7.
Stockhausen, K. (1958), 'Structure and experiential time', *die Reihe* 2, trans. L. Black, 64–74.
— (1959), '. . . how time passes . . .', *die Reihe* 3, trans. C. Cardew, 10–40.
— (1989), *Stockhausen on Music: Lectures and Interviews*. Comp. Ed. R. Maconie. London: Marion Boyars.

Stoïanova, I. (1974), 'La troisième sonate de Boulez et le projet mallarméen du livre'. *Musique en jeu* 16, 9–28.
— (1978), *Geste – texte – musique*. Paris: Union Générale d'Éditions.
— (1993), 'Pascal Dusapin: febrile music'. *Contemporary Music Review* 8(1), 183–96.
Tarasti, E. (1979), *Myth and Music*. Approaches to Semiotics 51. Berlin: Mouton de Gruyter.
— (1994), *A Theory of Musical Semiotics*. Bloomington: Indiana University Press.
— (1996), 'Music history revisited (by a semiotician), in E. Tarasti (ed.), P. Forsell and R. Littlefield (ass. eds), *Musical Semiotics in Growth*. Bloomington: Indiana University Press, pp. 5–36.
— (2000), *Existential Semiotics*. Bloomington and Indianapolis: Indiana University Press.
Taruskin, R. (1996), *Stravinsky and the Russian Traditions: A Biography of the Works Through Mavra*. 2 vols. Oxford: Oxford University Press.
Tusa, J. (2003), Transcript of the John Tusa Interview with Heiner Goebbels. http://www.bbc.co.uk/radio3/johntusainterview/goebbels_transcript.shtml, accessed 9 January 2013.
Varga, B. A. (2009), *György Kurtág: Three Interviews and Ligeti Homages*. Compiled and ed. B. A. Varga. Rochester, NY: University of Rochester Press.
Van den Toorn, P. C. (1983), *The Music of Igor Stravinsky*. New Haven and London: Yale University Press.
Varèse, E. (1998), 'The liberation of sound', in E. Schwartz and B. Childs (eds), *Contemporary Composers on Contemporary Music* (Expanded Edn). Cambridge, MA: Da Capo Press, pp. 196–208.
Vetter, R. (1989), 'A retrospect on a century of gamelan tone measurements'. *Ethnomusicology* 33(2), 217–27.
Webern, A. (1963), *The Path to the New Music*. Ed. W. Reich, trans. L. Black. Bryn Mawr, PA: Theodore Presser Co.
Whitehead, A. N. (1978), *Process and Reality* (Corrected Edn). Eds D. R. Griffin and D. W. Sherburne. New York: The Free Press.
— (1967), *Adventures of Ideas*. New York: The Free Press.
Whittall, A. (2007–13), 'Form', in *New Grove Online*. Oxford University Press, accessed 25 January 2013.
Williams, J. (2003), *Gilles Deleuze's Difference and Repetition: A Critical Introduction and Guide*. Edinburgh: Edinburgh University Press.
— (2008), *Gilles Deleuze's Logic of Sense. A Critical Introduction and Guide*. Edinburgh: University of Edinburgh.
— (2011), *Gilles Deleuze's Philosophy of Time: A Critical Introduction and Guide*. Edinburgh: Edinburgh University Press.
Wyschnegradsky, I. (1927), 'Musique et pansonorité'. *La Revue Musicale* 9, 143–52.

— (1996), *La Loi de la pansonorité*. Texte établi et annoté par F.
Jedrzejewski avec la collaboration de P. Criton. Genève: Contrechamps.
— (2005), *Une philosophie dialectique de l'art musical*. Edité et annoté
par F. Jedrzejewski. Paris: L'Harmattan.
Zukofsky, P. (1997/2004). 'Á la recherche du [cinq] temps perdu'. http://
www.musicalobservations.com/publications/brahms.html, accessed
21 August 2012.

Index

abstract machine 54, 134
acoustics 77–8, 80, 87
   harmonic series 81, 86
actual *see* virtual
Adams, John 78
Adorno, Theodor 27, 29, 31, 150
affects 39, 146, 155, 166 *see also* percepts
aion 100, 103–7, 110, 129 *see also* chronos
Aperghis, Georges 53–60, 64, 137, 154–8, 160–1, 166
   ATEM (Atelier Théâtre et Musique) 54
   Avis de tempête 55–9, 154
   Machinations 155–7
   Sextet 155
Aquinas, St Thomas 115
arborescence 36–7, 47–8, 75 *see also* rhizome
Aristotle 8, 52
Aristoxenus 85
Armstrong, Louis 26
Arnold, Martin 61
Artaud, Antonin 10
assemblage 34–6, 38–42, 46–8, 52–61, 64–5, 70, 121, 146, 151–4, 156, 164
   collective assemblage of enunciation 131, 141, 148
athematicism 11–16, 27–31 *see also* thematicism
atonality 15, 70, 150
Auslander, Philip 26

Bach, J. S. 3, 31, 77, 163
Bachelard, Gaston 108, 130
Baroni, Mario 139, 141
Barthes, Roland 141
Bartók, Béla 11
Baudelaire, Charles 55
Baudrillard, Jean 141
becoming-animal 51, 147–8, 159–60
Beethoven, Ludwig van 3, 6, 11, 23, 27–32, 160, 163
   Eroica Variations, Op. 35 30
   Grosse Fuge, Op. 133 30–1
   Piano Sonata in D major, Op. 10 no. 3 28–9
   Piano Sonata in D minor, Op. 31 no. 2 29–30
   String Quartet in Bb major, Op. 130 30–1
   String Quartet in C# minor Op. 131 30–1
   String Quartet in A minor, Op. 132 30–1
   Symphony No. 3 (the Eroica) 30
   Symphony No. 5 3
   C minor Piano Variations, WoO 80 29
Benjamin, Walter 150
Berg, Alban 11, 69
Bergson, Henri 7–10, 67, 70–1, 91, 106–8, 112–16, 122, 129–31 *see also* virtual

INDEX

Berio, Luciano   17, 45–6, 53, 64, 150
  Sequenzas   45
  Chemins   45–6
Berliner, Paul   26
Bernstein, Leonard   78
Birtwistle, Harrison   22, 34
Blake, William   49–50
body without organs   35, 40–1, 143–4, 164
Bosanquet, Robert   84
Bosch, Hieronymus   160
Boulez, Pierre   11, 36, 38, 40, 77, 79, 100–2, 160, 165
  accumulative development   11, 19–20
  athematicism (virtual theme)   11–16
  difference   11–22, 163
  heterophony (virtual line)   11, 20–2
  open form (virtual form)   17–18
  smooth and striated space   67, 71–6, 78, 96–7, 164
  smooth and striated time (pulsed and unpulsed)   99–100, 103–5, 112, 116–20, 125–6, 129, 131
  cummings ist der dichter   21
  Domaines   18
  Éclat   18, 101
  ...explosante-fixe...   20
  Figures - Doubles - Prismes   21
  Le Marteau sans maître   119
  Le Visage nuptial   21
  Pli selon pli (Don)   18, 21
  Répons   73, 102
  Rituel   18, 20–1
  Sonatine for flute and piano   15–17, 119
  Structures Book 2   18
  Third Sonata for piano   17–18

Bourdieu, Pierre   141
Brahms, Johannes   11, 23, 31–3, 77, 111–12, 160, 163, 165
  String Quartet in G-minor, Op. 25   32
Brecht, Bertolt   53, 59
Brelet, Gisèle   117, 122, 130
Brown, Earle
  Folio   43
Burroughs, William   63
  cut-up method   37, 49, 57–8, 61
Bussotti, Sylvano
  pièces de chair II – Part XIV, piano piece for David Tudor 4   43

Cage, John   38, 68–9, 73, 120
  Concert for Piano and Orchestra   43
  indeterminacy   17, 38
Can   46–7
Canetti, Elias   59–60
Carrillo, Julián   72, 85–6
Carroll, Lewis   161
Carter, Elliot
  musical time   99–100, 102, 120, 122–5, 129, 131, 165
  Concerto for Orchestra   123–4
  Double Concerto for Harpsichord and Piano   123
  Esprit rude/Esprit doux I   125
  Esprit rude/Esprit doux II   125
  A Mirror on which to Dwell   101
  Sonata for Cello and Piano   122–3
  String Quartet No. 1   123
  String Quartet No. 2   123
  String Quartet No. 3   124

INDEX

Symphony of Three
  Orchestras   124
Triple Duo   124–5
Variations for
  Orchestra   123
Céline, Louis-Ferdinand   148
chromaticism   33, 69, 71, 77, 79,
  85, 87, 94, 97, 113, 138, 165
  generalized chromaticism
    37–8
chronos   100, 103–6, 110, 129
  see also aion
Claggett, Charles   84
clouds (sound)   95–6
clusters   56, 92–6, 150
Coltrane, John   26–7, 46
  'Blue Train'   26–7
  Giant Steps   46
  Out of this World   46
compossible   22, 132 see also
  incompossible
content   65, 137–47, 149–50, 156,
  161, 164 see also expression
continuity/continuum   67–8,
  70–3, 76, 79, 81, 91–7, 102,
  107–8, 126–7, 135, 165 see also
  discontinuity
Courtès, Joseph   140–1
Cowell, Henry   122
Criton, Pascale   1–2, 71, 128,
  146–7, 166
Cuvillier, Armand   116

Dahlhaus, Carl   27–32
Davis, Miles   46–7
  Bitches Brew   46
  On the Corner   46
Debussy, Claude   11
  musical time   99, 108, 112–15,
    119, 129, 165
  Ballade de Villon   113
  Colloque sentimental   113
  Des pas sur la neige   113–14
  En blanc et noir   113
  Études   113

Jardins sous la pluie   113
Jeux   113–14
Parfums de la nuit   113
Pour le piano   113
Prélude à l'après-midi d'un
  faune   112
The Snow is dancing   113
Sonata for flute, viola and
  harp   113
Violin Sonata   113
Derrida, Jacques   141
desiring machine   45
deterritorialization   38–42, 48,
  54–5, 80, 117, 134, 142, 148–9,
  152, 157, 161, 164, 166 see
  also reterritorialization
D'Haeseleer, Kurt   56–7, 154
diagonal (transversal)   36, 40–1,
  74–6, 146
diagram   134, 143, 145–7, 161,
  164
dialectic   7–8, 27, 31, 65, 70, 94,
  150–2
difference   3–35, 47, 60–3, 75,
  97, 163, 165–6 see also
  repetition
discontinuity   42, 67–8, 70–1,
  76, 79, 91–2, 94, 96, 108, 111,
  126–7, 165 see also continuity
disjunctive synthesis   132
DJ culture   48, 60–3
Dufourt, Hugues   158
Dusapin, Pascal   48–52, 64, 166
  Á quia   52
  Études   52
  Faustus, The Last Night
    49–52, 64
  Niobé ou Le Rocher de
    Sipyle   49
  Perelà uomo di fumo   52

Eco, Umberto   133, 136, 138, 141
electronic music   38, 47–8, 53,
  55–8, 60, 62–3, 73, 76, 79, 93,
  158–60

Ellington, Duke   26
  Take the A Train   26
Ellis, Alexander   84, 89–90
expression   65, 137–47, 149, 154, 156, 158, 161, 164 *see also* content

Feldman, Morton   120
Ferneyhough, Brian   166
Fokker, Adriaan   84
fold, the   22, 75, 79
force   2, 10, 46, 52–3, 59, 64–5, 80, 97, 101–3, 105, 137, 144–7, 153–4, 161, 163–6
form, musical   6, 11–20, 25–9, 31, 33–4
  open form   17–18
Foucault, Michel   141
Franklin, Benjamin   57

gaelic psalm singing   11, 20, 23–4
gamelan (Balinese/Javanese)   20, 25, 80, 88–90, 112, 115, 119
Gandillac, Maurice de   5
Garlandia, Johannes de   110
glissandi   85, 92–6, 150
Godard, Jean-Luc   49
Goebbels, Heiner   59–60, 64
  Eraritjaritjaka   59–60
Goethe, Johann Wolfgang von   14, 50
Goeyvaerts, Karel   120
Goldschmidt, Victor   100, 103
graphic score works   38, 42–3, 64
Greimas, Algirdas Julien   140–1
Grisey, Gérard   158, 160–1
  musical time   99–100, 102, 112, 114, 120, 125–9, 131, 165
    Le Temps et l'écume   128
    Tempus ex machina   128
    Vortex Temporum   128
Grosz, Elizabeth   40–1

Hába, Alois   72, 85–6, 88, 97
haecceity   121
Hanslick, Eduard   137
Harrison, Lou   84
Haubenstock-Ramati, Roman   43
Haydn, Joseph   6, 32
Hegel, G. W. F.   7–8, 23, 27, 31, 65, 70
Heidegger, Martin   122, 130, 142
Helmholtz, Hermann von   77, 87
Henze, Hans Werner   151
heterophony   11, 20, 117, 132, 163
  Boulez   20–2
  Gaelic psalm singing   11, 20, 23–4
Hindemith, Paul   77
Hjelmslev, Louis   133, 137–41, 143–5, 161
Hoffmann, E. T. A.   4, 27
Hugo, Victor   55
Hume, David   7
Husserl, Edmund   108–10, 122, 124, 129–31
Huygens, Christiaan   84

identity-thinking
  Deleuze's critique of   7–11, 23, 163, 165
  in music   3–6, 18–19, 21, 25, 29, 33–4
image of thought (new)   7–8, 35–7, 39–40, 65, 68, 75, 103, 105
improvisation   54, 59–63
  and composition   24–7, 62, 163
  jazz   11, 23, 26–7, 38, 46–7, 60–3, 110
impulsion texts   42–3, 64
incompossible   22 *see also* compossible
Indian music   25, 72, 80, 88, 90–2, 119
IRCAM   55, 101, 159
Ives, Charles   122

INDEX

Jakobson, Roman 140
Jankélévitch, Vladimir 112–14
   eternal presents 113–14
Japanese music and culture 119–20
   gagaku 20, 115, 119
   haiku verse 121
   noh theatre 121
Jazz *see* improvisation
Jeck, Phil 61
Jones, Elvin 46
Joyce, James 10, 37, 124, 161
   Finnegans Wake 9

Kafka, Franz 55, 148–9, 159–60
Kagel, Mauricio 34, 43, 150
   instrumental theatre 43
      Morceau de concours 34
      Sonant 43–4
      Staatstheater 44
Kant, Immanuel 7
Klee, Paul 10, 21–2
Koechlin, Charles 108, 122, 130
Kristeva, Julia 141
Kùrtag, György 4–5
   Stele 5

Lachenmann, Helmut 137, 149–54, 160–1
   affect and aspect 152–3
   dialectical structuralism 152
      Accanto 152
      Ein Kinderspiel 152
      Kontrakadenz 152
      Tanzsuite mit Deutschlandlied 152
Lacy, Steve 62
Laloy, Louis 113
Lang, Bernhard 60–4
   Differenz/Wiederholung 61–3, 166
Langer, Susanne 105, 122, 130
language 37, 51, 54–5, 58–9, 68, 117, 128, 137–8, 140, 143, 145, 148–9, 154–8, 160–1

Latour, Bruno 46
Leibniz, Gottfried Wilhelm 8, 22
Levinas, Michaël 137, 158–61
   hybridization/new mixity 148, 158–61
   La Conférence des oiseaux 160
   La Métamorphose 160
   Ouverture pour une fête étrange 160
   Préfixes 159
Lévi-Strauss, Claude 141
libretto 44, 49, 55, 59, 64, 154, 156–8
Ligeti, György 93–4, 99–100, 102, 150
   Apparitions 93–4
   Atmosphères 93–4
   Chamber Concerto 101
   Lontano 93
Liszt Franz 113
Logothetis, Anestis 43
Loidl Christian 61, 63
Lorca, Federico, García 121
Lotman, Yuri 141
Lucretius 7
Lukács, György 150
Lynch, David 60
Lyotard, Jean-François 132

Macero, Ted 47
Maeterlinck, Maurice 112
Mahnkopf, Claus-Steffen 131
Mallarmé, Stéphane 10, 18, 22, 75, 112, 161
   Livre 9, 17
   'Un Coup de dés' 17
Marcel, Gabriel 107
Marcuse, Herbert 150
Marlowe, Christopher 49–50
Marx, A. B. 6
Marxism (base-superstructure) 65
Melville, Herman 55
   Bartleby 49–50
   Moby Dick 55–6

Messiaen, Olivier   22, 160
    musical time   99, 102, 112, 115–17, 119, 125, 129, 131, 165
        structured time and duration   116
    Technique de mon langage musical   115
    Traité de rythme, de couleur, et d'ornithologie   115
        Cantéjodayâ   115
        Chronochromie   22, 115, 117
        Couleurs de la cité céleste   115
        Livre d'orgue   115
        Mode de valeurs et d'intensités   101
        Sept Haïkaï   115
        Turangalîla-Symphonie   115
        Visions de l'Amen   115
microtonality   70, 72, 78, 80, 84–92, 95–7, 165–6
milieus   41–2, 52–5, 59, 64, 146, 164
minor literature   148–9
minor music   78, 148–9
mode and modality (in music)   33, 46, 51–2, 69–70, 77, 80–1, 85, 89–92, 96, 101, 110, 164
modernism/modernity   2, 9–11, 22–3, 33, 37, 69, 77, 79, 99, 104–5, 111, 133, 148, 153, 160–1, 163, 165–6
molar   31, 117, 135, 137, 146–7, 151–2, 164 *see also* molecular
molecular   31, 34–5, 45, 48, 54, 84, 117, 135, 137, 141–2, 146–53, 160–1, 164 *see also* molar
moment form *see* Stockhausen
Monelle, Raymond   133, 136, 138, 140–1
Mozart, Wolfgang Amadeus   6, 152

Murail, Tristan   158
music theatre   42, 44, 52–60, 64, 154 *see also* opera
musique concrète   73

Nancarrow, Conlon   122
Nattiez, Jean-Jacques   133, 136, 138
neoromanticism   78
Neuwirth, Olga   60, 64
    Lost Highway   60
Nietzsche, Friedrich   7–8, 10, 97, 115
    eternal return   9–10
noise   44, 48, 58, 60, 63, 148, 156
nomad thought   75–6, 78, 80, 83, 86, 88–92, 96–7, 102, 157, 164
    see also state philosophy
Nono, Luigi   150

opera, contemporary   44, 49–60, 64 *see also* libretto; music theatre

Parker, Charlie   26
Partch, Harry   72, 86–8, 97
    The Wayward   88
passive syntheses of time (Deleuze)   105–7, 110, 129
Peirce, Charles Sanders   133–7, 141–2, 145
Penderecki, Krzysztof   94–5, 150
    Polymorphia   94
    Threnody to the Victims of Hiroshima   94–5
percepts   105, 146, 166 *see also* affects
phenomenology   5, 63, 105, 108–9, 125, 127, 130–1
pitch space
    smooth and striated space   67–97, 102, 164–5
plane of immanence (or consistency)   35, 38–40, 103, 120, 143–4

plane of organization 38–40
Plato and Platonism 7–8, 23, 115
post-structuralism 133, 136–7, 141
Pousseur, Henri 17
Proust, Marcel 10, 102, 105, 108, 124
Pythagoreans, the 84

Rancière, Jacques 65
reformation, the 24
refrain 41–2, 117, 166 see also ritornello
Regnault, François 156–7
reification 31, 150–1
repetition 9–14, 16–19, 27, 33–4, 49, 51, 60–4, 163, 166 see also difference; Nietzsche, eternal return
reterritorialization 38–42, 46, 48, 55, 134, 142, 148, 152, 164 see also deterritorialization
rhizome 34–8, 42–50, 52, 54, 56, 61, 64–5, 75, 164, 166 see also arborescence
rhythm 16, 19, 24–5, 27, 46, 51, 99–100, 110–11, 115–19, 122–7, 131, 136, 140–1, 143, 152, 157, 164
ritornello 41 see also refrain
Roux, Sébastien 55, 57–8

Saunier, Johanne 57
Saussure, Ferdinand de 133, 138–9, 141
Schaeffer, Pierre 73
Schloezer, Boris de 5, 107–8
Schnebel, Dieter 43, 150
Schoenberg, Arnold 11, 23, 27, 68–9, 77, 160, 163
　　and repetition (and variation) 12–14, 31–3, 61
　　Chamber Symphony, Op. 9 16
　　Die Jakobsleiter 32

Erwartung, Op. 17 12
Five Piano Pieces, Op. 23 12–13
Variations for Orchestra, Op. 31 14
scores of programmed actions 42–3, 64
Scriabin, Alexander 86
semiology 133–4, 143
semiotics of music 36, 65, 133–61, 164
serialism (series) 12, 14–15, 27, 33, 38, 69, 72, 93, 96, 102, 120, 150, 153, 164
Shakespeare, William 49, 55
Taming of the Shrew 50
signs 133–61 see also semiology; semiotics
　　cinematic sign types (Deleuze) 135
　　regimes of signs 36, 65, 142–3, 154, 161
　　signifier and signified 134, 136, 138–40, 143–4, 146, 157
sound recording technology 46–8, 64
Souvtchinsky, Pierre
　　and time (chronometric and chrono-ametric) 108, 122, 130
Spinoza, Baruch de 7, 45, 64, 154
St Augustine 49–50
state philosophy and nomad thought 75–6, 80, 83, 86, 88–92, 96–7, 164
Stockhausen, Karlheinz 16–17, 102, 160, 163
　　moment form 100, 114, 121
　　musical time 99–100, 112, 120–1, 126, 131, 165
　　Aus den sieben Tagen 43
　　Carré 121
　　Gruppen 120, 150

Klavierstück XI 17, 120
Kontakte 121
Stimmung 161
Zeitmasse 101, 120
Stoïanova, Ivanka 18, 42–4, 49, 64, 166
Stoic philosophy 100, 103
Stravinsky, Igor 11, 19, 99, 108, 163
  Les Noces 19
  The Rite of Spring 99
  Symphonies of Wind Instruments 19
Strayhorn, Billy 26
structuralism 108, 133, 136–7, 141–2, 144
Szendy, Peter 55–7

Tarasti, Eero 133, 139–42
thematicism 5–6, 11–16, 18–20, 23, 26–34 *see also* athematicism
time, musical 99–132, 165–6
  see Boulez
  pulsed and unpulsed time 100–5, 110–11, 130–1
Tolstoy, Leo
  War and Peace 5
tonality 33, 37, 69–70, 76–80, 88, 97, 149–50, 152, 164–5
tuning systems 72, 81–92, 97, 138–9, 165
  early Indian 90–2
  equal temperament 72–3, 78, 80, 82–3, 87–8, 97, 165
  gamelan 88–90

just intonation 83, 86–7
mean tone temperaments 83
Pythagorean tuning 81
twelve-tone system (dodecaphony) 12–14, 69
Tyner, McCoy 46

Valéry, Paul 5
Varèse, Edgard 11, 72, 160
  Amériques 72
variation, musical 3, 5–6, 12–15, 18, 20–1, 23, 25–7, 29–33, 38, 100, 123
video installation 56–7, 60, 155
Vincentino, Nicola 84
virtual 31, 33–4, 129–30, 136, 163 *see also* actual; Boulez
  in Bergson 9–10
  in Deleuze 7–11, 51, 163
  in Schloezer 5

Wagner, Richard 53, 77, 100–2, 108, 111–12, 165
Webern, Anton von 11, 13–16, 50, 69–70, 160, 163
  Six Bagatelles, Op. 9 13
  Variations for piano, Op. 27 14
Whitehead, Alfred North 79, 109, 115, 122, 124, 129–31
Whittall, Arnold 6
Wyschnegradsky, Ivan 70–2, 79, 85–6, 96, 130, 164

Xenakis, Iannis 93
  Pithoprakta 93

www.ingramcontent.com/pod-product-compliance
Lightning Source LLC
Chambersburg PA
CBHW050139240426
43673CB00043B/1733